Labour Transfer
and Economic
Development

Labour Transfer and Economic Development
Theoretical Perspectives and Case Studies from Iran

Hassan Hakimian
Lecturer in Agricultural Development
Department of Agricultural Economics
Wye College, University of London

HC
475
.H35
1990

Indiana
Purdue
Library
Fort Wayne

New York • London • Toronto • Sydney • Tokyo • Singapore

First published 1990 by
Harvester Wheatsheaf
66 Wood Lane End, Hemel Hempstead
Hertfordshire HP2 4RG
A division of
Simon & Schuster International Group

Distributed in North and South America by
Lynne Rienner Publishers, Inc.,
1800 30th Street, Suite 314,
Boulder, CO 80301, U.S.A.

© Hassan Hakimian, 1990

All rights reserved. No part of this publication may be
reproduced, stored in a retrieval system, or transmitted,
in any form or by any means, electronic, mechanical,
photocopying, recording or otherwise, without prior
permission, in writing, from the publisher.

Typeset in 10/12pt Times
by Witwell Limited

Printed and bound in Great Britain by
BPCC Wheatons Ltd, Exeter

British Library Cataloguing in Publication Data

Hakimian, Hassan, *1955–*
 Labour transfer and economic development : theoretical
 perspectives and case studies from Iran.
 1. Iran. Economic development. Effect of migration of
 personnel. Iran. Personnel. Migration. Effects on economic
 development
 I. Title
 331.12'7'0955

ISBN 0–7450–0554–3

1 2 3 4 5   94 93 92 91 90

To my mother and in memory of my father

Contents

Preface	xi
1 Introduction	**1**
Note	5
2 The political economy of labour transfer	**7**
Introduction	7
The classical economists	8
Marx and surplus population	15
Development theory and labour transfer	19
A critical appraisal	31
Studies from Iran	41
Notes	42
3 Labour transfer in historical perspective: Persian workers in Southern Russia, 1880-1914	**45**
Introduction	45
The scale of migration	46
The salient features of migration	50
Forces behind migration	55
The social and political significance of migration	62
Summary and conclusion	64
Notes	65

4 Agrarian change I: an outline of Iran's land reform — 67
Introduction — 67
Landholding and tenurial relations before the land reform — 68
General features of the programme — 71
General results — 74
Some reflections on the causes of the land reform — 79
Summary and conclusion — 81
Notes — 82

5 Agrarian change II: labour and the land reform — 83
Introduction — 83
Factors affecting the supply of labour — 84
Factors affecting the demand for labour — 89
Agrarian reform and the labour constraint — 100
Summary and conclusion — 103
Notes — 104

6 The onset of the oil boom in the 1970s — 107
Introduction — 107
New circumstances, old ideas — 108
The oil boom and changing 'effort-intensity' of income in the labour and agricultural produce markets — 110
The rural non-farm sector — 116
Agriculture and the oil boom — 119
Summary and conclusion — 123
Notes — 124

7 Labour transfer and the rural economy — 128
Introduction — 128
The decline of farm population — 129
Labour transfer: dimensions and characteristics — 138
The impact on the rural economy — 139
Summary and conclusion — 144
Notes — 146

8 Labour transfer from the urban perspective — 148
Introduction — 148
Urban population: growth and composition — 148
The urban labour supply — 151
Labour absorption — 156
Summary and conclusion — 159
Notes — 159

9 Conclusion	**161**
Appendix A: Estimating labour flows to urban areas, 1966–76	168
Appendix B: Urban supplies of labour, 1966–76	171
Appendix C: Statistical data	177
Bibliography	**187**
Index	**201**

Preface

This book attempts to draw together two contrasting aspects of interest in the field of economic development: the much debated labour transfer theories and the widely neglected Middle East (including Iran) as an area of scholarly research.

Until recently, the study of the Middle Eastern societies and economies had remained a largely unexplored territory. The onset of the oil boom (better known in the West as the oil crisis) changed the situation to some extent; but even then, much of the newly generated interest revolves around selected areas such as the impact of the incoming oil revenues, and new international trade and investment opportunities for the countries concerned. Rare, indeed, are studies which focus on the region in terms of its human resources. Iran – one of the most populous, resource-rich and advanced countries of the region – is no exception to this rule.

Yet, few topics have been as instrumental in founding, shaping and advancing thinking in development economics as those concerned with the question of labour transfer. A great many of the early ideas in that field may be traced back to labour transfer debates – as testified by the fact that the celebrated development economist, Sir Arthur Lewis, was awarded the Nobel Prize in 1979 in explicit (though not exclusive) recognition of his seminal contribution 'Economic development with unlimited supplies of labour' (Lewis, 1954).

The happy marriage of the two aforementioned areas is not the only aim of this book. It has a more important objective: one which is rooted in intellectual and policy interest in the subject of labour transfer in developing countries from a long-term perspective. By tracing the antecedents of the labour transfer tradition in the writings of classical political economists – from Adam Smith through to Marx – I also seek to place the postwar debates within the framework of what I call 'the longwaves and short swings' in thinking on the subject. Despite its current unpopularity, particularly among mainstream development economists, I maintain that the subject is here to stay – for at least as long as the strategic question of the productive distribution of population and labour remains at the heart of economic development and structural change. It is to this end that the book is ultimately dedicated and its eventual contribution may be judged.

As is inevitably the case with works of this volume, many individuals have offered their generous help in the various stages of its preparation. First and foremost, my thanks are due to Robin Murray, who diligently supervised my doctorate at the Institute of Development Studies (University of Sussex), where the work originated. The combination of his critical mind and tolerance made the exercise a highly educating experience for me. To Terry Byres and Chris Colclough I owe the rare privilege of turning my oral examination into a purposeful and enlightening debate. Terry's subsequent support has been the single most important encouragement behind the decision to publish this book.

I should also like to thank: J. L. Bridge, M. Godfrey, A. Jazayeri, M. Karshenas, M. Messkoub, F. Radfar, A. Seyf, W. Spring, G. Standing and H. Stonefrost, all of whom have been very helpful in various ways and capacities. The staff of the IDS, LSE and SOAS libraries also deserve my special thanks as do the staff of computing centres at the University of Sussex and at Staffordshire Polytechnic, where, before joining Wye College, preparation of the manuscript continued between 1987 and 1989.

I wish also to thank the following publishers for kindly allowing me to include two chapters in this book which have already appeared elsewhere: Cambridge University Press, publishers of Chapter 3 in *The International Journal of Middle East Studies* (vol. 17, no. 2, 1985); and Frank Cass, publishers of *The Journal of Peasant Studies* (vol. 15, no. 4, 1988), where a version of Chapter 6 has appeared.

The final word goes to Mitra, who may not find her trace too apparent here. Yet, no words can do her justice for what has for me been the most valuable source of inspiration in the journey which has culminated in the present work.

H. H.
November 1989

1
Introduction

> When by the improvement and cultivation of land . . . the labour of half the society becomes sufficient to provide food for the whole, the other half . . . can be employed . . . in satisfying the other wants and fancies of mankind.
> Adam Smith, *The Wealth of Nations*

A study of labour transfer from agriculture to other sectors of the economy has aroused considerable interest among several generations of economists, stretching from classical political economists to contemporary development theorists. This interest is rooted partly in the historical experience of development in mature industrial nations, and partly in theoretical and analytical attention given to the role of industrialisation in the course of economic development. In both forms, such interest has been predicated upon the recognition of the widely acclaimed downward secular trend in the quantitative importance of agriculture in general, and its labour force in particular.[1]

Among the classicists, Adam Smith's position was unique in that it placed labour transfer within an overall framework of growth and accumulation in the long term. As with other classicists, Smith believed that the dynamics of population change were regulated by the laws of the market. Accordingly, the 'production of men' was constrained by the quantity of food and other necessities of life: increasing in times of prosperity and decreasing in times of hardship. But, contrasting Malthus and Ricardo, who were concerned with the 'evils' of overpopulation, Smith viewed labour transfer as an organic element in the rise of the new industrial order in England. This placed labour transfer in the realm of the division of labour and the growing commercial relations between the town and country, and

1

2 Labour transfer and economic development

appeared as a natural consequence of the expansion of market relations.

Marx's approach resembled Smith's in that it incorporated labour transfer into a wider theory or conception of the development of capitalism, but differed from it and other classical economists' in several important respects: the emphasis was placed on the relationship between labour and the means of production (rather than the means of subsistence); different forms of surplus population were highlighted; and although his analysis centred on the 'classic' case in England, the historical character and the social conditioning of the mechanism governing this process were stressed.

In the contemporary period, too, the subject has featured prominently in the postwar literature on development, which has proliferated in the past three decades. It is common knowledge that in its nascent days in the postwar era development theory was boosted significantly by debates around the subject of labour transfer in less developed countries (LDCs). A great many ideas indeed originated in these debates. Sir Arthur Lewis's pioneering article 'Economic development with unlimited supplies of labour' is a prominent example of such contribution, which sparked off and kept alive a foray of discussions and controversies since the 1950s. Hailed by some as the single most influential piece of work in development theory (Findlay, 1982:2), the work's importance is matched by the unique position that its author continues to occupy in the profession as one of the few development economists to have been awarded the Nobel Prize (in 1979).

More specifically, however, thinking on the subject has evolved through two distinct phases in this period. The first, boosted by Lewis's contribution, covered mainly the 1950s and to some extent the 1960s. Here, labour transfer rose to the status of a formal theory or explanation of continued underdevelopment and economic backwardness in 'overpopulated' countries of the Third World. The problem, as it appeared then, was the withdrawal of 'surplus labour' from the countryside for urban expansion without reducing agricultural output. The Smithian optimism of this period focused attention on the existence, identification and measurement of 'removable labour', discounting such important aspects of the process as its determinants and social characteristics.

In the second phase, nearing the 1970s, the importance of the need to understand the mechanisms of labour transfer was coupled with a shift in focus of the underlying problem. With surging open unemployment in many urban areas of LDCs, attention shifted away from the transfer of labour to its almost exact opposite: finding ways of controlling population growth, generating additional employment in towns, and even to policies designed to keep labour on the land. But, as the pendulum swung from 'rural underemployment' to 'open urban unemployment', the economists' faith in the efficacy of the market mechanism was reaffirmed by ascribing the decision to migrate to the maximisation behaviour of individuals responding to marginal changes in the key economic variables. The earlier period's determination to quantify 'removable labour' has since been paralleled by the more recent efforts to construct elaborate 'migration functions' and to measure migration elasticities.

This book departs from the mainstream tradition in development by highlighting the structural context in which labour transfer can take place. By focusing on studies from three periods of Iran's experience of economic development, it aims to study the character of labour transfer as well as the overall framework in which it came about. It seeks to assess the significance of such a process, and to look at its wider implications in the social and political context of the time.

The theoretical framework of the book is, therefore, based on two interrelated premises: that structural change and socioeconomic transformations are the main determinants of the form, nature and mechanisms of labour transfer; and that an understanding of the wider framework of development is pertinent to an understanding of the dynamics of labour transfer.

This approach is derived from the recognition of the important historical fact that the quantitative diminution in the significance of agriculture, and with it farm population, is generally accompanied by a far-reaching process of change and restructuring which alters the character of the social relations of production in the countryside. The rise of a capitalist farming class in Britain and its contrasting counterpart in France, the consolidation of an independent peasantry, are only two such examples of important agrarian transformations in historical perspective. A similar study of labour transfer in Latin America, Asia and Africa points to an equally diverse, contradictory and drawn-out history of agrarian change, in which rural transformation appears to act as the *sine qua non* for modern industrial progress.

By choosing three studies of important periods in Iran's labour transfer history, the book aims to demonstrate the varied nature of the labour transfer process throughout different phases of the development experience in one country and to disclose its historical specificity. My hope is that this should then posit both Marx's 'classic' case – emphasising labour extrusion and proletarianisation – and the economists' induced mechanism – stressing incentives and choice – as limiting, or special, historical possibilities. The complexity of the labour transfer process arises from the varied nature of structural change and dislocations which accompany it.

The first study is a historical one and discusses the international labour transfer from Iran to her northern neighbour (Russia) at the beginning of

4 Labour transfer and economic development

this century. The second and the third studies cover the two decades of the 1960s and the 1970s, examining domestic labour transfer in a period which witnessed a process of change and industrial transformation unprecedented in the country's history.

The historical study traces the origins of a wage-labouring class in Iran to the structural transformations which swept her powerful northern neighbour. This places the question of the migration of Persian workers to the contiguous Russian provinces in the context of the integration of the more backward northern provinces of Iran into the economic orbit of the more advanced economy of southern Russia. This framework is then used to explain the salient features of migration and to reflect on its major determinants.

The ensuing studies, which constitute the bulk of the book, take up labour transfer between 1960 and 1979 – commencing with the introduction of a wide-ranging package of social reforms, with a land reform as its master plan, and culminating in the overthrow of the monarchy in the mass uprising of 1979. In these two decades, Iran experienced rapid urban growth accompanied by massive rural-to-urban population and labour flows. Yet the nature of the structural changes in these two decades – unceremoniously dubbed 'the Shah's era' – differed radically before and after the oil boom in the early 1970s. A correct understanding of this point has serious implications for understanding the dynamics, form and mechanism of labour transfer in either phase: a point which has been widely overlooked.

The first phase, or the more familiar 'watershed era', began with the introduction of a land reform programme in 1962 and continued until the early 1970s. This stage was characterised by a continuous restructuring process, which included the redefinition of property rights in the rural areas. In the light of this characteristic, it will be argued that the 'unlimited' supplies of labour in this period were to a large extent the result of structural changes in which institutional mechanisms predominated.

The second phase began with the oil boom in the early 1970s. This was characterised by an explosion of economic activity in the urban areas, on a scale which altered beyond recognition the context in which labour transfer was taking place. Firstly, institutional forces largely (though not totally) gave way to the operation of the market. Secondly, contrary to the earlier phase (when agricultural wages had stagnated), this phase saw an increase in temporary forms of migration coupled with a significant upturn in agricultural wages. As mentioned above, a general failure to distinguish the specificities of these two phases accounts for the serious misjudgements on the nature of labour transfer in the 1970s – widely portrayed as an epoch of massive 'destruction' and 'decay' in the Iranian countryside.

Introduction 5

The selection of the three periods reflects partly practical considerations of access to data, and partly the relative importance, in my judgement, of each period in Iran's modern period economic development. Their choice, therefore, reflects my objective of examining labour transfer during some of the most dynamic phases of growth and structural change in the country. Rather than being a comprehensive treatise on Iran's history of labour transfer, therefore, the book is best regarded as a selective approach to the subject, which will hopefully inspire much-needed research in future relating to these as well as other periods not dealt with in this volume.

The format of the book is as follows. Chapter 2 is a critical review and an appraisal of the different theories of labour transfer from the classical economists through to Marx and the contemporary development theorists. This chapter sets up the framework and asks the questions that will constitute the main lines of enquiry in the three studies. Chapter 3 takes up the first of these with a study of Persian migration to southern Russia at the turn of the century. Chapters 4 and 5 deal with the second, which concerns labour transfer during the 1960s or the decade of the land reform. The former provides a general overview of the programme and examines its results, whereas the latter focuses on its implications for labour transfer. Chapter 6 presents the third and final of these case studies, relating to the 1970s or the oil boom years. Chapters 7 and 8 pursue the migration and the labour transfer of these two latter decades in more detail. The former focuses on the rural context, seeking to establish the relative significance of labour transfer, its characteristics, and its effects on the rural economy. The latter re-examines labour transfer from the perspective of the urban areas, in an attempt to assess its relative contribution and effects on the receiving sectors and areas. Finally, Chapter 9 summarises the results and offers the main conclusions of the book.

Note

1. Over the past century or so, the share of agriculture in the domestic output of major industrialised nations decreased from 40 per cent to less than 10 per cent (Kuznets, 1971:309). The distribution of the workforce has followed a similar pattern. In Britain, agriculture's share of the labour force declined from 35 per cent in 1801 to 5 per cent in 1951; while in France, in less than a century between 1866 and 1951, the share had fallen to 20 per cent from 43 per cent. The decline was even more marked in the USA, where in just over a century (1840-1950), those engaged in agricultural occupations were reduced from 68 per cent of the total workforce to only 12 per cent (Kuznets, 1966:106-7). For Europe as a whole, agricultural labour fell to one-third of

6 Labour transfer and economic development

the total workforce in 1960 from one-half in 1900. There was a similar diminution in the USSR in the heydey of her industrialisation between 1928 and 1958, when a total share of 71 per cent was reduced to 40 per cent only (Sutcliffe, 1971:30).

2
The political economy of labour transfer

Introduction

This chapter has two objectives: to trace the significance attached to labour transfer in the course of economic development in the various schools of thought since Adam Smith, and to compare alternative conceptualisations of its determinants and characteristics.

The proponents of the classical school are shown to share a common perception of population change based on the relationship between labour and the means of subsistence, while significantly differing on the importance attributed to labour transfer. In Malthus and Ricardo, concern with the 'production' of population and labour takes precedence over its transfer, whereas Adam Smith provides an integrated view of labour transfer as a natural consequence of the expansion of the market.

This is followed by Marx's discussion of labour transfer in the context of primitive accumulation or the establishment of modern landed property in the countryside. This highlights his emphasis on the relationship between labour and the means of production and employment (rather than the means of subsistence), and focuses on the role of capital accumulation in the creation of a relative surplus population on the land and the formation of an industrial reserve army in the towns.

The ensuing section reviews and critically appraises postwar development literature on the subject. It is shown that in the two distinct phases which have seen the 'rise' and 'fall' of labour surplus models, development theory has either abstracted from an explicit discussion of the determinants of labour transfer, or ascribed it to the rational decision-making behaviour of individual economic agents. This explains the overt optimism of the first period and the absence of adequate considerations

8 *Labour transfer and economic development*

in the second for the social and structural context in which labour transfer typically takes place.

Finally, two broad models of labour transfer are presented: the 'dissolution/separation' and the 'involution/preservation' models. These centre on the nature of the changing relationship between labour and the means of production through the transfer process. In both cases, it is argued, the form and the dynamics of labour transfer arise from the structural context of economic development and closely reflect its characteristics.

The classical economists

Adam Smith

A study of labour supplies did not constitute a central theme of classical political economy. Nevertheless, economists of this school shared a common perception of population change in which the quantity of food and other means of subsistence regulated the 'production of men': increasing it at times of prosperity and decreasing it at times of hardship. In this way, therefore, they envisaged the supply of labour in the long run to be unlimited in the sense that it could be continually recruited to an expanding industrial sector at a constant wage around the subsistence level.

In the mainstream (that is, non-Marxian) tradition of the school, this perception was best seen in a formulation of the long run interaction between fertility and trends in real wages. According to Adam Smith's vision of self-regulatory and unhampered markets, such interaction was subject to the same principle which governed the operation of the 'invisible hand' in bringing about the progressive extension of the division of labour, exchange, and the expansion of the market in general: 'The demand for men, like that for any other commodity, necessarily regulates the production of men; quickens it when it goes on too slowly, and stops it when it advances too fast' (Smith, 1776:183). Accordingly, at times of relative prosperity, when, in his words: '[the demand for labour] is continually increasing, the reward of labour must necessarily encourage in such a manner the marriage and multiplication of labourers, as may enable them to supply that continually increasing demand by a continually increasing population' (1776:183).

Otherwise, as in the depressing conditions of Bengal, where 'the funds destined for the maintenance of the labouring poor are fast decaying', hunger and mortality would cut the number of hands available, thus removing the imbalance between population and the nation's wealth (1776:173). It was this conception of the dynamics of population change – according to the operation of the law of supply and demand – that led

The political economy of labour transfer 9

Smith to consider 'the increase of the number of inhabitants' of a country to be its 'most decisive mark of prosperity' (1776:173). While all major classical economists shared this broad formulation of population change, not all were equally concerned with the subject of labour transfer in economic development. In fact, Adam Smith was unique in advancing a theory of labour transfer which was similarly based on the operation of the market: if the quantity of food and necessities determines the 'production of men', so must its volume affect their 'distribution'. This arises from the peculiarity of land, which, 'almost in any situation, produces a greater quantity of food than what is sufficient to maintain all the labour necessary for bringing it to market' (1776:250). It thus becomes not only possible, but also desirable, that the increased powers of labour on the land should be channelled into other lines of production:

> But when by the improvement and cultivation of land the labour of one family can provide food for two, the labour of half the society becomes sufficient to provide food for the whole. The other half, therefore, or at least the greater part of them, can be employed in providing other things, or in satisfying the other wants and fancies of mankind. (1776:268)

Implicit in Smith's theoretical structure of labour transfer – as in this passage – are three key issues. Firstly, the rising productivity of labour. In Smith this was inextricably related to technological progress and, associated with that, the division of labour. Although for him the scope for technical change in manufacturing unambiguously surpassed that in agriculture (Spengler, 1959:404; Hollander, 1973:102, 209–10), he nevertheless took account of the rising importance of a number of technical advances in English agriculture. Included in these were such capital improvements as 'making and maintaining the necessary drains and enclosures' undertaken by landlords, but also the introduction of new crops such as fodder crops, and most importantly, 'potatoes and maize', which he described as 'the two most important improvements which the agriculture of Europe ... has received from the great extension of its commerce and navigation' (cited in Hollander, 1973:229). The net result of such improvements was that increased production of food was now made possible with the same amount of land or labour. Moreover, the process which led to improvements in the productive powers of labour on the land was accompanied by important changes in the organisation of production. Although Smith was not explicit on the *source* of labour transfer, he left little doubt as to whom he had in mind when he referred to 'the diminution of the number of cottagers and other small occupiers of land; [as] an event which has in every part of Europe been the immediate forerunner of improvement and better cultivation' (Smith, 1776:331–2).

10 Labour transfer and economic development

Similarly, although the greater part of Smith's attention in dealing with specialisation was geared towards the manufacturing sector in general, and the division of labour within the plant in particular (Hollander, 1973:104), his treatment of the separation of employments and the wider social division of labour was carried out by analogy to this. The whole of society appeared to him as a gigantic manufactory, where the work is divided up between thousands of separate but mutually complementary enterprises. Each individual, although motivated by self-interest, is useful to all the other members of society, and depends in turn on them for their mutual assistance: 'the most dissimilar geniuses are of use to one another' (1776:121). A complete harmony of interests is thus thought by Smith to characterise the relationship between society's individual members and their respective specialisations (Rubin, 1979).

Secondly, in Smith's conception of labour transfer is the notion of 'food surplus' and its trade with the towns. As mentioned above, this is a recurrent theme in his discussion of the development of agriculture, and occupies a central place in his perception of population change, labour supplies to towns, and the greater 'prosperity of nations'.

There are two ways in which 'food surplus' is linked to Smith's ideas of the division of labour: the individual and the social levels. On the former, he makes the plain observation that: 'The desire of food is limited in every man by the narrow capacity of the human stomach. . . . Those, therefore, who have the command of more food than they themselves can consume, are always willing to exchange the surplus' (1776:269). It is this idea that he then projects onto the social plain in the context of his discussion of the growth of trade between town and country, or in his terminology, 'that great commerce of every civilised society'. In chapter 1, Book 3 of *The Wealth of Nations,* Smith shows how 'the natural progress of opulence' is consequent upon the mobilisation of a quantity of food surplus, the trading of which results in 'mutual and reciprocal gains' for the town and the country alike:

> The country supplies the town with the means of subsistence and the materials of manufacture. The town repays this supply by sending back a part of the manufactured produce to the inhabitants of the country . . . .
> The division of labour is in this, as in all other cases, advantageous to all the different persons employed in the various occupations into which it is subdivided. (1776:479)

Thus the country/town trade, which itself arises from the greater productivity of labour on the land, widens the market, in turn making possible the greater separation and specialisation of tasks. This sets into motion a process of self-sustained growth and expansion which feeds upon further divisions of labour and exchange.

This trajectory of unhindered growth enabled Smith to sidestep any potential obstacles to the circulation of 'surplus product'. The possibility that peasants may withhold their surplus from the towns – by consuming rather than exchanging it – preoccupied many development debates in the postwar era. Yet, for Smith, any such tendency seemed to be tangential to the logic of reciprocity and the harmony of interests which governed transactions not only between individuals but also between the town and country.

The third and final point in Smith's theoretical conception of labour transfer pertained to its mobility, or the free circulation of men 'from employment to employment and from place to place'. Attacking the Poor Laws and the settlement laws (which restricted relief rights to the parish where labourers resided), Smith lamented labour immobility in England, 'where it is often more difficult for a poor man to pass the artificial boundaries of a parish than an arm of the sea or a ridge of high mountains' (1776:222, 245).

Despite Smith's vociferous attacks on these institutional impediments, his long-term vision of capitalism was highly optimistic. As Adolph Lowe has aptly remarked, such optimism was rooted in his treatment of technical progress, since 'in Smith, mechanisation is seen as complement to labour' (1954:136). This enabled Smith to rule out unemployment as a long-term feature of the new ascending order in England: workers could easily transfer from declining trades to expanding ones. Similarly, his treatment of the geographical mobility of labour was highly optimistic – going as far as overlooking his own earlier remark in a different context that, 'a man is of all sorts of luggage the most difficult to be transported' (Smith, 1776:178; Hollander, 1973:261–2).

Thus, although some pessimistic elements were also present in his analysis (see Hollander, 1973:182–7 for instance on the falling rate of profit), in his long-term vision capitalism remained free from any major impediments. Constraints such as diminishing returns, population 'check', falling rate of profit, lack of effective demand, etc., have no doubt featured prominently in the writings of major economic thinkers from Malthus, Ricardo and Marx through to Keynes, Schumpeter and the postwar development theorists (Singer, 1975). Yet, Smith's allusions to the progressive powers of technical change enabled him to by-pass any such major 'checks' and 'traps' that might impede the forward march of the new economic order. In this framework, labour transfer, too, followed the natural logic of market expansion and reflected its characteristics.

12 Labour transfer and economic development

Malthus

Malthus shared Smith's concern for food supplies; but rather than stressing the quantity of *surplus,* he was preoccupied with the *total* quantity of food. This in turn emanated from a second and more important concern in Malthus: the general conditions governing the 'production' of labour rather than its transfer. For it was in his hands that the aforementioned interplay of forces regulating the relation between labour and its means of subsistence was elevated to a general theory of population. Warning that, 'the power of population is indefinitely greater than the power in the earth to produce subsistence for man,' he went on to argue that:

> Population, when unchecked, increases in a geometrical ratio. Subsistence increases only in an arithmetical ratio. A slight acquaintance with numbers will shew [sic] the immensity of the first power in comparison of the second . . . . This implies a strong and constantly operating check on population from the difficulty of subsistence . . . . This natural inequality of the two powers of population, and of production in the earth, and that great law of our nature which constantly keep their effects equal, form the great difficulty that to me appears insurmountable in the way to the perfectibility of society. (1798:13–16)

Thus, if in Smith it was the rising productivity of labour which propelled labour transfer and economic growth, in Malthus it was the opposite, i.e. the want of such productive powers, that increased population pressure on the land and arrested future growth potentials. He used the logic of this 'iron law' to attack the Poor Laws. Unlike Smith who had criticised these laws for their crippling effects on the mobility of labour, Malthus assailed them for their harmful impact on population growth. In a passage, which appeared in the second edition of his *Essay on the Principle of Population* but was omitted from the later editions, he went as far as to state categorically that:

> A man who is born into a world already possessed, if he cannot get subsistence from his parents on whom he has a just demand, and if the society do not want his labour, has no claim of *right* to the smallest portion of food, and in fact, has no business to be where he is. At nature's mighty feast there is no vacant cover for him. She tells him to be gone, and will quickly execute her own orders, if he do not work upon the compassion of some of her guests. If these guests get up and make room for him, other intruders immediately appear demanding the same favour. (Cited in Meek, 1971:8; emphasis original)

His subsequent relentless campaign against the Poor Laws in essence reflected this political nature of his theory of population. As Professor

Meek has observed, in Malthus, 'not only had the poor no right to relief, but they must also be punished for their poverty' (1971:9). It is no wonder that this controversial aspect of Malthus's theory of population has continued to prevail alongside his critics' discussions either of the logical or empirical validity of his thesis.

Ricardo

In Ricardo, too, similar concerns with the 'evils' of overpopulation overshadowed any discussions of labour transfer. He accepted fully the essence of Malthus's iron law of population. Attacking the Poor Laws for essentially the same reasons, he paid homage to the 'able hand of Mr Malthus' for lifting the mystery over 'the pernicious tendency of these laws'; going on to stress that: 'No scheme for the amendment of the poor laws merits the least attention which has not their abolition for its ultimate object' (1821:61–2).

But Ricardo went further. Firstly, he used the Malthusian law of *population* to formulate a theory of *labour* supply in the long run. This was based on a mechanism of adjustment between the 'natural price' of labour and its 'market price' (wages). The former is 'that price which is necessary to enable the labourers, one with another, to subsist and to perpetuate their race, without either increase or diminution.' Far from being a physiological minimum, this depends 'on the habits and customs of the people', and refers to the different quantities of 'food, necessaries, and conveniences of life' in different societies and in different points in time, which is required for the upkeep of labourers and their families. Market price, on the other hand, refers to the actual price that labourers receive for their services 'from the natural operation of the proportion of the supply to the demand' (1821:52–5). Ricardo maintained that in the long run market price would gravitate towards the natural price of labour as the operation of the Malthusian law of population would ensure that the number of labourers would expand at times of prosperity and diminish under hardship by an amount sufficient to check any real divergence between the two.

Secondly, he qualified this law by introducing a distinction between its operation in countries with an abundance of fertile lands and those where all fertile land is under cultivation (1821:56). Taking exception to Malthus's utterly pessimistic outlook that saw 'no escape from the weight of this law ... even for a single century' (Malthus, 1798:16), Ricardo argued that in countries where fertile land was bountiful, pressure on food supplies could be alleviated by extending the area under cultivation. Elsewhere, however, it remained true that the brute logic of the

14 *Labour transfer and economic development*

population law would continue to exert itself fully, making a reduction in the number of people highly desirable:

> It is a truth which admits not a doubt that the comforts and well-being of the poor cannot be permanently secured without some regard on their part, or some effort on the part of the legislature, to regulate the increase of their numbers, and to render less frequent among them early and improvident marriages. (1821:61)

Finally, Ricardo diverged sharply from Malthus on the important question of rent. Much as they had agreed on the damaging effects of overpopulation, their views on the landed gentry and the implications of rent for long-term growth and distribution could hardly have been more dissimilar. Whereas the 'error of Mr Malthus' lay in 'supposing rent to be a clear gain and a new creation of riches' (1821:272), Ricardo considered the interests of this class to be diametrically opposite to those of capitalists. Such antagonism surfaced also in these two groups' concurrent attitude towards the question of the price of grain: the capitalists favoured a lowering of these (hence of labour costs) via free importation from abroad; while the landlords bitterly resisted such a policy.

Ricardo utilised a simple 'corn' model of growth and distribution, whereby the long-run tendency of the rate of profit in industry was governed by the operation of the law of diminishing returns in agriculture. As more land of inferior quality is brought under cultivation, rents – the difference between corn product of labour on average and marginal lands – would rise, hence squeezing out profits.[1] With the lowering of the rate of profit – the source of all accumulation – the rate of growth of the economy in general will continue to slow down, ultimately resulting in 'the stationary state', where accumulation ceases because 'profits are so low as not to afford them [the farmer and the manufacturer] an adequate compensation for their trouble, and the risk which they must necessarily encounter in employing their capital productively' (1821:73).

In summary, despite a common conception of the mechanism of population change, the classical economists were divided on the relative significance of population growth and labour transfer. Adam Smith, who emphasised the rising productivity of labour on the land, was unique in offering an integrated vision of labour transfer as an intrinsic element in the rise of the new industrial order in England. This placed labour transfer firmly in the realm of the growing commercial relations between the town and country, and presented it as a natural consequence of the expansion of the market. In Malthus and Ricardo, by contrast, a discussion of labour transfer was overshadowed by preoccupation with the harmful effects of population growth. This dichotomy, as we shall see, was to re-emerge later in the context of postwar development debates on surplus labour and labour transfer.

Marx and surplus population[2]

Marx's approach resembled Smith's in two respects. Firstly, he too stressed the rising productivity of labour on the land. This was the point which both Marx and Engels laboriously pointed out in their discussion of 'forced emigration' from Ireland: 'It is not the want of productive power which creates a surplus population; it is the increase of productive power which demands a diminution of population and drives away the surplus by famine or emigration.' And to turn Malthus on his head: 'It is not population that presses on productive power; it is productive power that presses on population' (Marx and Engels, 1971:57).

Secondly, Marx too incorporated labour transfer into a wider theory or conception of the development of capitalism. As this section will demonstrate, in his framework labour transfer acted as a key link between changing agrarian relations and the expansion of modern industry in towns.

Nevertheless, his approach differed from Smith's and other classicists' in several important respects. First and foremost, whereas his predecessors had largely focused on a 'theory of population', Marx's attention was primarily directed towards determinants of labour supply under capitalism. Secondly, and related to this, he identified two types of surplus population: *absolute* and *relative.* This distinction reflected a third point of variance between him and the classical economists: the former concept referred to population pressure against the means of *subsistence,* the latter against the means of *production.* Given Marx's preoccupation with labour supplies, his emphasis was firmly on the latter of these two relationships. Fourthly, he identified three sources or *forms* of surplus population: latent, floating and stagnant. The latent labour pool comprised all of those who could potentially move to capitalist enterprises (such as those in rural areas and 'housewives'). The floating reserve consisted of the jobless urban proletariat; and the stagnant reserve was made up of those endemically unemployed or underemployed (such as artisans and craftsmen). A fifth and final point of divergence between Marx and classicists was that although Marx's analysis centred on the 'classic' case in England, he stressed the historical character and the social conditioning of the mechanisms which governed labour transfer.

In his rough drafts in the *Grundrisse,* Marx criticised Malthus on the grounds that 'he stupidly relates a specific quantity of people to a specific

16 Labour transfer and economic development

quantity of necessaries'. While commending Ricardo for having demonstrated that 'the quantity of grain available is completely irrelevant to the worker if he has no *employment',* he went on to add, 'it is therefore the means of employment and not of subsistence which put him in the category of surplus population' (Marx, 1973:607; emphasis original).[3] He departed thus radically from his predecessors' framework as exemplified by Adam Smith that, 'countries are populous . . . in proportion to the number of people whom their produce can . . . feed' (1776:268). Instead of restricting such 'abstract numbers' to the limits imposed by 'the necessaries of life', he turned his attention to the study of a 'historically determined relation' which is rooted in the changing character of the social relations of production:

> As soon as capitalist production takes possession of agriculture, and in proportion to the extent to which it does so, the demand for an agricultural labouring population falls absolutely . . . without this repulsion being, as in non-agricultural industries, compensated by a greater attraction. Part of the labouring population is therefore constantly on the point of passing over into an urban or manufacturing proletariat, and on the look-out for circumstances favourable to this transformation. (1867:601)

Aware of the complexities surrounding the formation and transfer of labour from one pole of capital accumulation to another, he went on to add: 'This source of relative surplus population is thus constantly flowing. But the constant flow towards the towns presupposes, in the country itself, a constant *latent* surplus population, the extent of which becomes evident only when its channels of outlet open to exceptional width' (1867:601–2; emphasis added).

A study of these 'channels' directed Marx to a study, firstly, of the development of modern landed property in the countryside (the so-called primitive accumulation), and secondly, to an examination of the laws governing the self-expansion of capital in modern industry.

On primitive accumulation, Marx observes that the immediate producer in agriculture, the labourer, can only dispose of his own person after he has ceased to be attached to the soil. This, in turn, presupposes the dissolution of all relations 'in which the *workers themselves,* the *living labour capacities* themselves, still belong *directly among the objective conditions of production,* and are appropriated as such' (1973:498; emphasis original).

Although taking different forms in different societies, the separation of the peasantry from their lands transforms the social means of subsistence and of production into capital, and turns the immediate producers into wage-labourers: 'The so-called primitive accumulation, therefore, is nothing else than the historical process of divorcing the producer from the means of production' (1867:668).

In England, where expropriation took its 'classic' form, it was the forcible expulsion of labour from land which produced the primary impetus to the generation of surplus population in its *floating* form. Here, 'the spoliation of the church's property, the fraudulent alienation of the State domains, the robbery of the common lands, the usurpation of feudal and clan property' – in all 'reckless terrorism' – played the main part in transferring land into modern private property and setting 'free' the necessary supply of proletariat.

The enclosure movement – or the 'parliamentary form of robbery' – in particular, had ravaging effects on the English peasantry.The usurpation of communal and semi-communal lands and their conversion into private plots deprived a great many peasants of their traditional sources of subsistence. This released sizable portions of the agricultural population from the land, increased their compulsion to labour, and pushed down their wages to levels 'not enough for the absolute necessaries of life'. By the nineteenth century, the movement had been so effective that 'the very memory of the connection between the agricultural labourer and the communal property had . . . vanished' (1867:680-1).

But not all labour release mechanisms take the form of direct or institutional expropriation. Firstly, the expansion of capitalist relations in agriculture pauperises important sections of the peasantry in rural areas. The commodification of the means of subsistence and their transformation into material elements of variable capital tends to reduce the socially-necessary labour time required for their production. This happens because the revolution in the conditions of landed property is historically accompanied by extensive reorganisations of production as seen in the adoption of improved methods of culture, greater co-operation, and concentration of the means of production, which greatly reduce the demand for labour. While enriching some peasants by turning them into successful commercial farmers, this deprives a great many others of their most essential sources of livelihood. This is the process which ' "clears" . . . the land of its excess mouths, tears the children of the earth from the breast on which they were raised', and turns 'the cottiers, serfs, bondsmen, tenants for life, cottagers, etc.' into day labourers (1973:276).

Secondly, the separation of agriculture and industry leads to a process of destruction/transformation of the rural crafts. While the primary function of this process is to extend and deepen the home market, its effects on rural artisans are particularly harsh. It is among this social group that the *stagnant* form of surplus population takes shape, furnishing capital with another 'inexhaustible' reservoir of disposable labour. Engels had in mind a bleak picture of their future prospects in Germany when making the observation that, 'no factory worker would have changed places with the slowly but surely starving rural hand weaver' (Marx and Engels, 1969:300).

The combined effect of primitive accumulation and the subsequent expansion of capitalism in agriculture is to expand wage relations in the countryside, while at the same time diminishing *absolutely* the numbers employed in agricultural production:

> It is in the nature of capitalist production to continually reduce the agricultural population as compared with the non-agricultural, because in industry (in the strict sense) the increase of constant capital in relation to variable capital goes hand in hand with an absolute increase, though relative decrease, in variable capital; on the other hand, in agriculture the variable capital required for the exploitation of a certain plot of land decreases absolutely; it can thus only increase to the extent that new land is taken into cultivation, but this again requires as a prerequisite a still greater growth of the non-agricultural population. (1959:637)

In modern industry, on the other hand, the increase in the organic composition of capital leads to the generation of a relative surplus population in its floating form – that is, a population 'of greater extent than suffices for the average needs of the self-expansion of capital' (1867:590). This happens because, despite an *absolute* increase in the size of variable capital, its *relative* share (compared to constant capital) diminishes progressively in the course of accumulation and centralisation. Given that the demand for labour is determined by this (i.e. variable) constituent of capital alone, a fall in the latter would give rise to a mass of 'relatively redundant labourers' at the industrial pole of accumulation, thus constituting 'a disposable industrial reserve army, that belongs to capital quite as absolutely as if the latter had bred it at its own cost' (1867:592). This point was emphatically reiterated by him in part 2 of *The Theories of Surplus Value*: 'The constant artificial production of a surplus population, which disappears only in times of feverish prosperity, is one of the necessary conditions of production of modern industry' (1969:560).

Once created, the reserve army takes on three important functions in the process of capitalist development. Firstly, it comes to constitute the labour reservoir on which capitalism relies for its 'unexpected contingencies'. When expanding, capital continues to recruit large numbers from among these 'partially or entirely pauperised people' – only to reject them later as soon as depression sets in. In this respect, surplus population makes it possible for capital to draw its required labour through changing phases of the economic cycle 'without injury to the scale of production in other spheres' (1867:592).

Secondly, the ready availability of a mass of labourers in reserve exerts a regulatory role in the determination of capitalist wages. These are determined not by the absolute number of workers (as Malthus had envisaged), but by the division of the working class into an active and a reserve army: 'by the extent to which it is now absorbed, now set free' (1867:596). This division itself clearly changes in accordance with the changing tempo of capital accumulation: 'The industrial reserve army, during the phases of stagnation and average prosperity, weighs down the active labour-army; during the periods of overproduction and paroxysm, it holds its pretensions in check. Relative surplus population is therefore the pivot upon which the law of demand and supply of labour works' (1867:598).

Thirdly, and reflecting the previous point, such divisions act to discipline the employed section of the working class. The ready formation of a 'light infantry' of workers – deployed at times of advance and sacrificed under retreat – increases pressure on workers outside the reserve to yield to the demands and conditions imposed by capital:

> The overwork of the employed part of the working class swells the ranks of the reserve, whilst conversely the greater pressure that the latter by its competition exerts on the former, forces these to submit to overwork and to subjugation under the dictates of capital. The condemnation of one part of the working class to enforced idleness by the overwork of the other part, and the converse, becomes a means of enriching the individual capitalists. (1867:595-6)

To sum up, in Marx's formulation of the development of industrial capitalism, the critical factor is the creation of a permanent industrial labour force which has little or no alternative to selling its labour to obtain the necessities of life. The process which brings this about occurs in turn with the weakening and eventual destruction of a relatively self-sufficient agrarian economy. Such destruction may be achieved through direct political mechanisms (such as taxation and land enclosures), or through the action of market forces in concentrating and commercialising production. Labour transfer from the land contributes towards the creation of a stable supply of labour in towns which serves capital's accumulation needs through its contradictory phases of expansion and contraction.

Development theory and labour transfer

As with the classical period, postwar thinking on labour transfer evolved through two distinct and contradictory phases. First came a vigorous revival of interest in the subject in the 1950s and 1960s. In this phase, which showed signs of Smithian optimism, the existence of rural surplus labour was brought to light and the necessity for its removal was

20 *Labour transfer and economic development*

emphasised. In the subsequent period, by contrast, the strategy of labour transfer was brought into question in the face of rapid population growth and rising urban unemployment in the late 1960s. In this phase, Malthusian apprehensions about the undesirable effects of labour transfer shifted the emphasis from redistributing labour to controlling its production, diverted attention from removing labour to keeping it on the land, and emphasised rural development at the expense of industrial expansion. The course of the three decades which connected these two 'swings' in development theory witnessed some of the most active and fertile debates in the history of its evolution. We study each of these in turn.

The rise of labour surplus models

Early postwar interest in surplus labour and labour transfer was rooted in a wider concern with the sources of economic growth in under-developed countries (UDCs). Influenced by the Harrod–Domar type of growth models, a generation of development economists sought to explain the process which led different societies first to their 'take-off', and subsequently to a path of self-sustained growth. Thus emerged a strand of thought, which despite its apparent diversity, was united on two grounds: (1) the process of economic growth in UDCs had been arrested or held down by an interlocking set of vicious circles; and (2) it would require not piecemeal efforts but a 'critical minimum effort', a 'big push', or a crash development programme in order to break out of this situation.[4] Strongly influenced by the postwar climate of reconstruction in Europe, minds were focused on the sources of domestic savings and capital formation as a way out of poverty and economic backwardness (Sunkel, 1977; Singer, 1975).

Nurkse was among the first to cast overpopulation and surplus labour explicitly in terms of the problems associated with capital formation in UDCs. He utilised the concept of 'disguised unemployment' to describe a situation where 'in technical terms, the marginal product of labour over a wide range is zero', implying that, 'even with unchanged techniques of production, a large part of the population engaged in agriculture could be removed without reducing agricultural output' (1953:32–3).[5] The saving potential concealed in such rural underemployment would thus become apparent when transferred workers were set to work on capital projects (such as in irrigation, drainage, roads, railways, and so on): aggregate output would expand without creating undue pressures on food supplies.

Lewis, who shared his contemporaries' central interest in the relationship between savings, capital formation and growth, cast his theory in the classical spirit of dynamic accumulation. In an article which was to become a classic of modern development theory (1954), he argued that labour/land and labour/capital ratios were so high in developing countries that, given the existing techniques of production, part of their labour force in traditional occupations was redundant. This, he argued, could favour the modern capitalist sectors in these countries by providing them with 'unlimited supplies of labour', the recruitment of which at constant real wages could expand the industrial base without lowering subsistence output.

Analytically, the Lewis model comprised two sectors: a low productivity, subsistence sector, and a high productivity, capitalist sector. The former, characterised by 'disguised unemployment' of labour with 'negligible, zero or even negative' marginal productivity[6] consisted not only of agriculture, as is often thought, but included also petty retail trading, domestic service, and a whole range of other casual jobs done by dock workers, porters, jobbing gardeners, and so on (1954:402). Here, individuals maintain customary rights to receiving means of subsistence in quantities determined by the 'code of ethical behaviour' (as in domestic service) or by the average productivity of labour (as on family farms).

In contrast, in the capitalist sector, where profit maximisation motives prevail, workers are employed only up to the point where the wage rate equals the marginal productivity of labour. The minimum to these wages is set by what people can earn outside that sector (i.e. what they would be able to consume if they retained their traditional occupations). Although this sets the floor, actual wages in the capitalist sector have to be higher – usually by some 30 per cent – partly to allow for the higher cost of living in towns, and partly to induce subsistence workers to leave their traditional activities. Set in this framework, the transfer of labour from the low-paid to the high-paid sector is deemed possible, without lowering the subsistence supplies. The capitalist sector is thus said to enjoy 'unlimited supplies' of labour in the sense that it can expand indefinitely without an increase in wages being necessary to attract a growing number of workers.

The key to the process of expansion is the use made of the capitalist surplus. This, Lewis maintained, would be reinvested in the same sector, resulting in its further expansion, in turn boosting demand for labour from the subsistence sector. Thus a process of self-generating growth and reinvestment will be unleashed until the emergence of a 'turning point', when wages begin to rise and surplus labour in the subsistence sector disappears.[7]

The enormous influence of this simple model in shaping development thinking and policy in the coming years was rooted in the very nature of

22 Labour transfer and economic development

its contribution: the identification of a relatively 'cost-free' path to industrial growth. Abstracted from this model were both the wider theoretical determinants of labour transfer as well as the more practical considerations of population growth and the absorptive capacity of the capitalist sector. Yet, these abstractions were considered to be justifiable in the spirit of identifying potential sources of growth in UDCs. Such a spirit was widely shared by subsequent reformulations of the model, most notably in its Fei–Ranis version.

In this model, labour surplus was pinned down as a source of economic backwardness. Overpopulation was located at the 'heart of the development problem', with the main task confronting policy-makers identified as 'the reallocation of population between the two sectors [of the economy] in order to promote a gradual expansion of industrial employment and output' (Fei and Ranis, 1964:7). Their attempt to inject more 'rigour' into the model, however, took it into the neo-classical terrain and brought about new complications.

Firstly, Fei and Ranis's redefinition of Lewis's 'subsistence' and 'capitalist' sectors to 'food' and 'non-food' sectors moved their analysis closer to a study of rural-to-urban migration (Bienefeld and Godfrey, 1978:10; Godfrey, 1986). Secondly, their explicit concern with policy issues moved them away from the analytically wider and potentially more flexible framework of the Lewis model. This was seen in their greater emphasis on the operation of market forces, but more specifically in their allowance for the possibilities of accumulation in both sectors. In the event, this increased their reliance on special institutional assumptions governing the production and distribution of the 'investible surplus'.

In their dual economy framework, too, agriculture is characterised by the existence of surplus labour – described as parasitic, redundant, or disguised unemployed[8] – whereas in the industrial sector, workers are employed only up to the point where wages equal their marginal productivity. Moreover, the minimum at which labour can be had is now set by the 'constant institutional wage' (CIW) in the food sector. This, Fei and Ranis argued, is determined by 'the entire noneconomic nexus of mores and relationships', but in practice it is 'related more or less to the average productivity of the agricultural labour' (1964:21–2).

Labour transfer fulfils two functions: (1) it cushions the impact on industrial wages of changes in the demand for these workers, and (2) it releases the much-needed 'hidden rural savings' (the difference between total agricultural output and the consumption demand of the remaining agricultural labourers) for the development of the industrial sector.

More specifically, Fei and Ranis envisage three stages in this process. In stage 1, as already described above, the marginal product of labour is zero: total agricultural output remains constant as unproductive workers are transferred to the capitalist sector at constant wages. In stage 2, the marginal product of labour rises to a positive level, called the 'shortage point'. Further transfers of labourers, who now make a positive contribution to production, would lower the volume of agricultural output and push up the price of subsistence commodities. Finally, stage 3 is attained with complete commercialisation of labour in both sectors: workers receive wages equal to the marginal productivity of labour. The entire economy is operating along capitalist lines and the allocation of labour is deemed to have achieved efficiency in both food and non-food sectors.[9]

Before giving way to concerns with the deteriorating prospects of urban employment, the Lewis model and its variants provided development thinking and policy with a major source of inspiration. On the theoretical side, attention focused on identifying the sources of 'removable' surplus, while on the empirical side, considerable effort was spent on quantifying its size. Before long, however, this sparked off various analytical debates on a number of issues ranging from the meaning of 'surplus labour' to the conceptualisation of economic sectors, the behaviour of sectoral earnings, and the possibility of a 'turning point' (Reynolds, 1969; see also Worrell, 1980; Leeson, 1979).

Given its central feature in the model, the very concept of surplus labour became the subject of a fierce debate, which before long eroded some of its earlier apparent simplicity. Although Lewis had been careful from the start not to coin this notion in terms of the zero marginal productivity of labour, the central place accorded to it in other writings nevertheless dictated the terms of the debate for a considerable length of time.[10] Inevitably, the question arose as to why, assuming that work has some disutility, any labour at all should be applied beyond the point where its marginal productivity reaches zero. Tackling the problem, Sen (1960) found that much of the earlier discussions of disguised unemployment had been marred by confusion on the use of an appropriate unit of measurement for labour. He distinguished between the number of *agricultural workers* and the number of *hours of labour* applied. This enabled him to envisage a situation where the marginal product of *labour* becomes zero (whereby no more units of labour will be applied), but extra *workers* may be taken on to perform their progressively diminishing share of effort in a given and constant total number of labour units: 'It is not that too much labour is being spent in the production process, but that too many labourers are spending it' (1960:3–5). Sen's later lucid demonstration that a work equilibrium at zero marginal product of labour is neither necessary nor sufficient for the existence of disguised unemployment, came perhaps too late to settle some of the earlier debates, and to redirect more fruitfully the course of their progress (1975:32–5).

24 Labour transfer and economic development

Meanwhile, a multiplicity of terms were used to denote ostensibly disguised unemployment but, on a closer examination, they were found to refer to very different situations (Robinson, 1969). Seasonal unemployment, a common feature of agriculture in UDCs, is a good case in point. As explained later by Myint, labour may be so abundant in the agricultural sector that not all workers can be productively employed for an arbitrarily set 'normal' working day, month or year. The entire labour force may thus be idle *part of the time* (1980:71–2). Although real, this type of seasonal unemployment, is not 'removable' in the strict sense – that is, without some regard for the reorganisation of tasks and labour time in the post-transfer period. This weakened particularly those versions which had optimistically sought to identify disguised unemployment in the presence of individually idle workers.[11]

The *ceteris paribus* nature of assumptions about the process of removing surplus labour raised similar problems for the analysis, identification, and measurement of 'disguised unemployment'. It is hard to imagine labour withdrawals in the absence of any reorganisation, as such transfers would typically take place side by side with 'other changes'. This point had been recognised, and indeed emphasised, by both Smith and Marx, who envisaged major changes in the organisation of agricultural production prior to labour transfer.[12] Nurkse in contrast had excluded the possibility of drastic reorganisation of work such as occasioned by 'technological advance, more equipment, mechanisation, better seeds, improvements in drainage, irrigation,' but had allowed for minor ones such as 'consolidation of scattered strips and plots of land' (1953:33). Where later writers came to draw the line became largely a matter of personal choice.

Complications arise, in particular, if one allows for different types of withdrawal. For instance, labour may be transferred locally (to another job), or geographically (across the village frontiers). It may be withdrawn temporarily (for the off-peak period), or permanently (leaving land for good). Finally, such withdrawal may take place indiscriminately (as a consequence of famines and fatal epidemics),[13] or 'selectively' (in response to economic motives). In any one of these situations, not only will the amount and the form of transferred labour be different, the consequences for the local division of labour and the structure of production on the land are also likely to differ a great deal.

In particular, if one allows for changes in the intensity of effort by remaining workers – as might be expected in the absence of transferred workers – then the model's specificity is drastically reduced and its implications potentially trivialised. This problem was recognised by Jacob Viner, who expressed reservations about the application of this theme to agriculture:

> I find it impossible to conceive of a farm of any kind on which, other factors of production being held constant in quantity, and even in form as well, it would not be possible, by known methods, to obtain some addition to the crop by using additional labour in more careful selection and planting of the seed, more intensive weeding, cultivation, thinning, and mulching, more painstaking harvesting, gleaning, and cleaning of the crop. (1976:147-8)

It was considerations such as these that led, albeit gradually, to a more widespread recognition that, 'the existence of disguised unemployment is largely a matter of definition and the assumptions about the institutional forces involved' (Kao *et al.*, 1964:141). What had earlier optimistically appeared as a reasonably straightforward transfer of 'redundant' workers, now appeared to embrace a wide range of policy courses from 'a "crash" malaria-eradication programme to a local public works programme in rural areas' (Robinson, 1969:381). This helped not only to erode the positivist confidence which had surrounded the concept of 'disguised unemployment', but more importantly, to a sustained scaling down of the expectations raised by the model. Similar situations were arising from other lines of debate and inquiry.

Discussions of sectoral wage behaviour, in particular, raised new problems for the Lewis and Fei-Ranis models, and in the latter case particularly, made more transparent the fragility of the special institutional assumptions which governed their envisaged labour transfer process (Godfrey, 1986).

Both models – later dubbed austerity models (Reynolds, 1969:93) – relied broadly on the assumption that real wages in both food and non-food sectors would remain constant during a 'successful' process of labour transfer. Reflecting the importance of such an assumption, Jorgenson went as far as stipulating that, 'the classical approach stands or falls on this [constancy of agricultural wages] hypothesis' (1966:54). Initially, Lewis showed some awareness of the possibility of a rise in per capita peasant consumption as workers are moved from agriculture, and of its adverse effects on industrial wages. Later, however, he modified this as being unlikely, partly on the grounds of the existing gap between earnings in the two sectors, and partly on the grounds of the possibility of increases in the labour force through population growth and greater participation of women. Moreover, Lewis introduced a new distinction – within the 'surplus' sector – between the wages of landless farm workers and the earnings of small farmers, with 'the crucial test of whether labour is in surplus supply' now determined by 'what happens to the wages of landless agricultural labourers' (1972:87-8).

The problem with these modifications was not so much that they altered his original 'subsistence' and 'capitalist' sectors (only in the latter was labour to be hired), but that they loosened the connection between the two. But as Leeson has observed: 'If the wage link is weakened too drastically . . . there might not be much of the model left' (1979:200–201). Indeed, in the absence of a rigorous link between the two sectors of the economy, there will always be a ready supply of labour at the prevailing wage rate, regardless of variations in subsistence income. The danger thus facing this model is that of degenerating into a 'trivial generality', whereby it might be argued that labour transfer from any sector or subsector with lower labour productivity to any other sector with a higher level of productivity would expand net output. This may be deemed possible within any organisational unit which involves some division of labour: within and between households, plants, industries, wider economic sectors, etc. – in developed economies as much as in underdeveloped countries.

For Fei and Ranis, meanwhile, constancy of wages appeared to be an integral, if not somewhat self-evident, aspect of the labour transfer process: 'the dualistic underdeveloped economy will follow a path of *natural austerity* as income increases are channelised *automatically* toward entrepreneurial saving classes' (1964:116; emphasis added).

This, however, presupposes that average income in the food sector should remain constant as workers leave this sector. But, even allowing for the possibility that the departing workers are absolutely redundant, this is arithmetically impossible as the same quantity of total output will be produced and (in the absence of countervailing forces) distributed among a progressively smaller number of people.

In the likely event that per capita peasant consumption does rise, the industrial sector will be adversely affected in two ways. Firstly, labour supplies may now be secured only at a greater minimum level of income; and secondly, if the two sectors trade, soaring food prices will push up urban wages, thus reducing profits. As a result, the entire 'success' of the model is put into question as the possibility of generating the maximum amount of surplus to be reinvested in the high-growth industrial sector is imperilled.

Perhaps none of these complications would arise if one shared Nurkse's forthright optimism that, 'there is no question of asking the peasants who remain on the land to eat less than before, only of preventing them from eating more' (1953:38). Similar problems may be avoided in a simple world where, like Fei and Ranis, it is possible to think of the transferred workers, 'as initially consuming only agricultural goods and carrying their CIW [constant institutional wage] bundle of food along with them as they move from sitting idly on the land to engaging in rural road construction projects' (1964:207).

In reality, though, 'preventing peasants from eating more' is far more complicated than either of these two passages seems to admit. Firstly, the production and the distribution of agricultural surplus depends on the specific social and institutional setting in which the labour transfer is envisaged. For instance, in an agrarian system which is dominated by a myriad of small peasant plots, it may be more difficult to rely on 'unlimited' quantities of labour at a constant wage as the surplus extracted by the exit of rural workers may lead to a rise in peasant incomes and consumption. The maximum-growth path of economic development is thus jeopardised as urban wages rise and capitalist profits decline.

Ironically, a perfectly elastic supply curve for labour may be more compatible with the framework of a centrally commanded system, in which the 'iron hand of the state' regulates the peasants' standard of living. As the low productivity workers leave, the consumption of the remaining farm population is prevented from rising so as to provide the largest surplus available for reinvestment in the modern sector.

Secondly, the price at which subsistence labour may be procured by the capitalist sector is also determined by the nature of the relationship between direct producers and their means of production. With easy access to land and other means of production, much higher wages are required before workers' participation in the labour market can be secured. On the contrary, separation from the means of production increases compulsion to labour in return for wages. This point was widely observed by early colonial thinkers[14] and explains why successive colonial administrations (particularly in Africa) resorted to a number of practices ranging from enticement to coercion to secure their required supply of indigenous labour (see pp. 37-8).

The Fei and Ranis attempt to get round this issue resulted in more problems for their model. Whereas Lewis had abstracted from history (which explains the more versatile nature of his model), they appealed to economic history to illuminate their case. But this made only more apparent the type of institutional setting which they implied for 'successful' economic development.

Their reliance on the existence of a landlord-cum-entrepreneur in the food sector – along the lines of nineteenth century Japan – posits, at an early stage of development for UDCs, 'a rather unusual organisation of agriculture, in which landlords hire wage-labourers' (Reynolds, 1969:93). In this context, the landlord is given an all too powerful role to play: 'He should be eager to save. He should sell his surplus to industry, and should transfer his savings to industrial entrepreneurs. He should be eager to innovate, and thereby to improve the technology in agriculture' (Dixit, 1973:342).

However, as Weeks has observed, this shifts the model closer to 'a marginalist translation of the Marxian model of capitalist development through "primitive accumulation" ' (1971:475). In this 'landlord-dominated economy', too, an exploiting class appears centre-stage of the labour transfer process. Yet, whereas for Marx this process is historically drawn-out and contradictory in nature, in the Fei–Ranis world it collapses into a technical process of sectoral allocation of labour, devoid of any social and political sequels.

Surplus labour in retreat

Just as postwar interest in labour transfer had been invigorated by revived interest in the role of the modern industrial sector, the beginning of its demise in the late 1960s and early 1970s was also prompted by a loss of faith in this sector's ability to act as a primary engine of economic growth. Although the theoretical perspectives which lay behind this turnabout in thinking were disparate and varied in nature,[15] they nevertheless shared concerns about growing evidence on open urban unemployment, which by ILO admission had become 'chronic and intractable in nearly every developing country' (ILO, 1972:xi; see also Turnham, 1970, and Frank, 1968, for empirical evidence on this period).

Two considerations in particular accounted for this redefinition of priorities away from the industrial sector and towards the primary sector, both of which raised new questions about the successful implementation of surplus labour models. These were population growth and the nature of modern sector technology. The first of these affected the number of subsistence workers (the size of the labour 'pool'); the second related to the demand for them in the modern sector. Combined, they hinged on the overall capacity of the industrial sector to absorb transferred workers, and hence the possibility of a final turning point. As the envisaged 'golden age' was to come with the depletion of the subsistence labour reservoir, attention was now focused on the realism of the model's assumptions regarding these two parameters.

Writing in the optimistic climate of the mid-1950s, Lewis himself had explicitly played down the potential damage of population growth to his model. Similarly, the famous UN report 'Measures for economic development', to which he had made a significant contribution, assumed a rate of population growth in Third World countries of no more than 1 per cent (UN, 1951). On the absorptive capacity of the modern sector, too, Lewis found little cause for concern. He readily dismissed Marx for 'his curious model in which the short-run effect of accumulation is to reduce unemployment, raise wages and thus provoke a crisis, while the long-run effect is to increase the reserve army of unemployed.' Of all the classical economists, Lewis found comfort in Adam Smith who 'saw clearly that capital accumulation would eventually create a shortage of labour, and raise wages above the subsistence level' (1954:435). On both these accounts, therefore, Lewis thought his model was fully capable of sorting itself out. Yet, the reality of the situation, approaching the 1970s, was beginning to suggest otherwise.

Firstly, with the sharply revised population growth estimates emerging from the UN (2.5–3% per annum) it was clear that, on the supply side, far more people were joining the search for a modern sector job than had been anticipated.[16] Secondly, with the highly capital-intensive nature of (the often imported) modern sector technology coming to light, it was becoming apparent that on the demand side, too, far fewer jobs were being created than had been foreseen (or hoped for).

With migration continuing unabated in the face of the evident incapacity of the industrial sector to create the required jobs, the overwhelming picture emerging from UDCs at this time was various forms of urban (rather than rural) overpopulation. The wisdom of the past labour transfer policies was gradually being brought into question as it was increasingly realised that 'the social and political implications of open urban unemployment [were] more far-reaching than those of rural idleness' (Bruton, 1973:19). Thus in a typical reversal of direction, if a decade before the desirability of labour withdrawal from the countryside and its positive impact on industrial growth had been stressed, now apprehensions about population growth took over, the deleterious effects of labour transfer were emphasised, and new perspectives on urban bias, open unemployment, marginality, and the informal sector were finding their way into development debates.[17] In brief, what was only a decade before identified as an 'opportunity' had now turned into a 'constraint' (Godfrey, 1986).

It was in this climate that the discussions of the 'decision to migrate' moved centre-stage of development debates. If labour transfer was to be cut, curtailed or controlled, then a close understanding of its primary determinants was essential. The inadequacy of the subject's earlier treatment had become particularly transparent ever since the curious co-existence of massive urban unemployment and continued rural-to-urban migration had been established as the development puzzle of the decade. If, indeed, migrants were induced by the prospects of higher urban wages – as had been sustained hitherto – the question was asked as to why they were not dissuaded by the increasing difficulties of finding an urban job.

Tackling this in the context of the African economies, Todaro resorted to the rationality of individual migrants to explain the forces behind migration. He elaborated a formal model of migration decision-making in which individuals respond to an evaluation of the private costs and benefits of a likely move to urban areas. This evaluation is based on two sets of considerations: the magnitude of rural/urban income differentials and the likelihood of securing a higher-paid urban job. If they expect a period of unemployment, before they succeed in obtaining urban employment, this will be duly reflected in a lower *expected* (rather than *actual*) earnings in towns. But, 'as long as the "present value" of the net stream of expected urban income over the migrant's planning horizon exceeds that of the expected rural incomes, the decision to migrate is justifiable' (Todaro, 1985:260; also Todaro, 1969; Harris and Todaro, 1970). Viewed from this perspective, therefore, migration appears as a succession of movements along an 'equilibrium path' by individuals, who aim to maximise their lifetime or permanent income.

The interest which has since been generated by this 'probabilistic' approach is best explained by the strength of its paradoxical conclusion: government policies designed to ameliorate urban employment opportunities may in fact exacerbate the tide of rural-to-urban population flow; more appropriate policies would have to take account of improvements in rural incomes or indeed a cut in (or a slower growth of) urban wages (Bruton, 1973:19–20 explores both these possibilities; for a critique, see Jolly, 1973, and Stewart, 1973).

This powerful message signalled the beginning of the end for an important era in mainstream development thinking. If, previously, modern industry had been assigned the role of the primary engine for growth in dual economies, now 'rural development' and appropriate government policy towards agriculture became the focal point of analysis and policy formulation. If the problem then appeared to be how to transfer removable labour from the countryside for urban expansion without reducing agricultural output, now it seemed to be how to find additional employment for a rapidly rising rural population and to raise agricultural output more than in proportion to the increase in rural population. Finally, if the labour transfer strategy had previously argued the case for a more productive 'distribution' of population, focus now shifted back to conditions governing its 'production'. The analogy with the classical period was complete: Smithian optimism was a spent force, the Malthusian calls for restraining population growth had triumphed.

But as the pendulum swung from 'rural underemployment' to 'open urban unemployment', the economists' faith in the efficacy of the market mechanism was nevertheless reasserted. Todaro's 'breakthrough' located the primary impetus to migration in the maximisation behaviour of rational individuals who respond to marginal changes in the key economic variables. The old orthodoxy of quantifying 'removable labour' was replaced with a new drive to construct realistic 'migration functions' and to measure migration elasticities.

A critical appraisal

The course of the three decades that have seen the rise and fall of the labour surplus models has marked an important period in the evolution of development theory. In the first phase, the persistence of rural surplus labour in the traditional sector of overpopulated Third World countries was elevated to the status of a quasi-formal explanation of their continued economic backwardness. The dualist theories of this period viewed labour transfer as a strategy designed to narrow intersectoral productivity differentials, to mobilise 'hidden rural savings', and to stimulate industrial growth. In sharp contrast, in the second phase, which embraces the present conjuncture in development thinking, interest in the subject has been reversed as concerns about the deleterious effects of rural-to-urban migration have come to dominate the discussions. Firstly, the theme of overpopulation has replaced that of surplus labour. Secondly, focus has shifted decisively towards keeping population on the land (and controlling its pressure) rather than transferring it to other sectors. As a consequence, in more recent years a new wisdom in development has come to view migration 'as an economic liability in the urban setting', and has had as its 'unstated but important demographic goal' the discouragement of migration to urban areas (Shrestha, 1987:338; see also Oberai, 1981; Rhoda, 1983).

Yet, throughout these two ostensibly contradictory phases of growth, development theory has either abstracted from an explicit discussion of the determinants of labour transfer or sought its impetus in the rational choice-making of individual migrants. Hence the consistent absence, in this tradition, of the social, institutional and historical considerations which typically characterise the migration process.

Lewis, whose principal objective was to explain the reasons for the rising share of savings in national income, relied on a more flexible analytical framework in which the tapping of 'unlimited' supplies of subsistence labour provided the basis for the self-expansion of the modern capitalist sector. The mechanism governing this process as well as the social prerequisites for its successful implementation were left largely unexplored.

In the marginalist formulation provided by Fei and Ranis, explicit concern with policy making prevailed but their technicist approach to development was based on rigid institutional assumptions about the production and distribution of the surplus product in the food sector.

Similarly, Todaro, who did offer an alternative explanation of the reasons for migration, missed the most interesting aspects of this process by reducing it to a technical relationship between expected income differentials and the individual's propensity to migrate. This, as we shall

32 Labour transfer and economic development

demonstrate, stripped it of its inherently contradictory character, historical specificity and richness of forms.

Several important points have emerged from the discussion of these models and their precursors which warrant further elaboration. This is done below.

Formation of surplus labour and production relations leading to its transfer

For labour to be transferred, it has first to be generated (i.e. it has to become surplus); and second, appropriate social conditions must be brought about, both on the land and elsewhere, to make such removal possible.

Both Smith and Marx were aware of this and emphasised the dynamic context in which the transfer of labour was effected. As seen before, Adam Smith located the origin of this process in the rising productivity of labour on the land and sought its impetus in the dynamics of market expansion.

For Marx the same process was rooted in the proletarianisation of important sections of the rural population, partly through the forcible extrusion of labour from the common lands (enclosures), and partly through the development of capitalism in agriculture (commercialisation, consolidation of holdings and changes in methods of production). In either case, the separation of the direct producers from their means of production provided the main mechanism for the release of labour from the countryside and its future deployment in urban industry.

In more recent years, however, Marx's position has been questioned from two different perspectives. Firstly, 'neo-Malthusian' economic historians have expressed doubt about the significance of enclosures by stressing population growth, rather than expropriations, as the primary force behind the rise of a rural proletariat in England (Chambers, 1953; Ashton, 1961; Mingay, 1963; Landes, 1969). While Marxists have generally maintained the importance of enclosures (Saville, 1969; Lazonick, 1974), they have nevertheless continued to treat demography either as subservient to socioeconomic transformations or placed it 'beyond the pale of legitimate scrutiny and investigation' (Seccombe, 1983:22).[18]

Secondly, and more importantly, feminists too have sought to shift and supplement Marx's focus on 'production' with a decisive emphasis on 'reproduction'. One strand within this school has criticised Marx for concentrating on wage-labour at the expense of domestic labour, while another has called for the broadening of the concept of the mode of production to include a study of the production of labour power (Delphy, 1984; Hartman, 1979). Although far from being either conclusive or successful, these criticisms have nevertheless had two major impacts on contemporary Marxist thinking: by shedding light on its traditionally 'sex-blind' character, they have helped to bring gender relations into the fore of its discussions; and by exposing its abstraction from demography, they have brought home the necessity for the formulation of a materialist theory of population. It is not surprising, therefore, that recent Marxist attempts to overcome these gaps reflect a synthesis of both these influences (Seccombe, 1983).

Yet sharply contrasting both Smith and Marx, development economists have taken a static view of the formation of surplus labour. For them, overpopulation appears in the form of a technical datum (in the sense of labour or population ratios to land or capital). Manifestations of this phenomenon are seen in the lower productivity of labour in the traditional sector, or an imbalance between the supply of and the demand for such labour. An inquiry into the causes of this imbalance is generally conceived to lie outside the domain of their discipline.

As elaborated above, this static view abstracts from important changes which must take place before labour may be considered to be either 'surplus' or 'removable'. Seasonal labour, for instance, indicates surplus labour time, but one which is not *strictly* removable. Similarly, surplus labour time (in the social sense) may exist even in the absence of individually idle or redundant workers. In both these cases, a certain reallocation of social labour time will affect both the extent and form of transferable labour. Unless these changes are correctly delineated, discussions of surplus labour will lack an adequate understanding of the circumstances in which this process takes place historically.

Conditions accompanying labour transfer

In a similar manner, an understanding of the social relations of production envisaged to accompany labour transfer remains central to an understanding of the entire process. Our discussion in the previous sections has shown that at least two of the key variables with which the relative success of the model is closely associated are strongly conditioned by the nature of these social relations.

In the subsistence sector, the production and distribution of 'surplus product' is determined not only by the number of people remaining on the land and the quantity of output produced, but more importantly, by a number of other socioeconomic factors. These may range from the nature of relations between the property-owning and the propertyless classes to the organisation of tasks within the remaining domestic households.

As seen earlier, the dualist models of the period applied the Malthusian theory of *population* change in the long run to arrive at a horizontal supply curve for *labour* at some conventional minimum level of income (Collier and Lall, 1986:3). But to expect that subsistence sector incomes will maintain their traditional levels throughout the transfer process, requires the operation of an intermediary mechanism (such as the state or a landowning class), which extracts the surplus so as to prevent incomes from rising. Even though empirically or historically plausible, this assumption is external to the model and does not follow its internal logic.

Likewise, the behaviour of wages in towns or in the modern sector is socially determined. To assume that these will stay constant or will rise in line with the predictions of the model is again dependent upon specific social assumptions (such as the role played by the state in overseeing the general behaviour of wages). Any deviations from this maximum growth path can only weaken the predictive sequences of the model.

If the link between subsistence earnings and capitalist wages is broken or substantially loosened, the supply of labour can no longer be considered 'unlimited' as income variations in both sectors will influence in their own right the quantity of labour which is 'transferable'. Alternatively, to assume that either of the above two socially determined economic variables will behave in accordance with the assumptions of the model is far from satisfactory. This is tantamount not only to positing the expected outcome before the actual realisation of a complicated process, but also to reducing it to the level of a technical process, the results of which are deemed controllable by design.

The mechanisms and forms of labour transfer

Neither the Lewis nor the Fei–Ranis models had much to say about the causes of migration. Apart from some allusions to the higher level of wages in towns, which made such a move sufficiently attractive for subsistence workers, little else was offered to explain the mechanism whereby this process might be realised. A great deal of the subsequent effort to bridge the gap, however, has focused on the statistical explanations of migration. With the formulation of Todaro's micro approach, in particular, focus has shifted towards ways of constructing an explicit 'migration function', in which the decision to migrate may be 'explained' through the behaviour of a number of quantifiable variables.

To start with, an array of empirical studies has sought to verify the relevance or adequacy of the model in relation to the migration experience of a number of Third World countries. This has in general given rise to a great deal of econometric work in which the authors have attempted to improve the model by introducing more elaborate time-lagged variables, using more disaggregated data, or incorporating other suitable variables designed to raise its explanatory power (Barnum and Sabot, 1976, Barnum, 1977, on Tanzania; Schultz, 1971, on Colombia; Greenwood, 1969 and 1971, on Egypt and India respectively; Levy and Wadycki, 1972, on Venezuela; Speare, 1976, on Taiwan; Lucas, 1985, on Botswana; and Sahota, 1968, on Brazil. See also Yap, 1977; Brigg, 1973; Todaro, 1976; and Berry and Sabot, 1978, for a review of the literature).

More recently, Cole and Sanders have sought to extend the model beyond its 'unidimensional' focus on the urban formal sector by elaborating an alternative framework in which rural workers may migrate not only to the urban formal sector but also to the traditional sector in towns. This is justified on the grounds that for many of those 'caught in the urban trek, the focus is not on the modern sector with its relatively high wages, but rather on the subsistence sector with its relative ease of entry' (1985:492).

At a more critical level, other authors have gone as far as questioning the relevance or realism of the model's assumptions: whether there exists a state of perfect knowledge, mobility of population, and of labour; whether individuals are the consistent and rational profit-maximising agents that the model portrays them to be; or whether the operation of the markets is anywhere near as competitive as the model assumes it to be. But rare are criticisms that go far enough to question the very framework in which migration is theorised from this perspective (see Amin, 1974, and Godfrey, 1979, for some criticism; Godfrey, 1973, too, disputes the application of this model in the context of migration in Ghana). The essential underpinnings of the model, therefore, remain unscathed even if its assumptions and adequacy are questioned.

Reflecting its neo-classical framework, this approach posits the question of the decision to migrate at the level of an individual person or household. Guided by a desire to maximise their 'permanent' income, these individuals respond to marginal changes in certain economic variables. Moreover, the machinery whereby they achieve their ends, after sufficient deliberation on the relevant costs and benefits, is entrusted upon the market system: it provides the relevant signals on income differentials, it indicates the existing job opportunities in the receiving areas, it oversees the allocation of the incoming migrants to the absorbing sectors, and it should accordingly decide how long each migrant stays in his/her new position.

The predictive sequence of the model, too, bears out this broad picture: any variations in the pattern and outcome of migration may be traced to variations in the net expected earnings of migrating individuals. All individuals, in other words, irrespective of their personal position and social strata, are subject to the compelling logic of the same 'iron law': details may vary, the logic stands.

By conceptualising migration at the level of the rational individual – the *homo economicus* – this 'equilibrium path' to migration suffers from the same inadequacy which characterises most discussions of labour transfer in general. It ignores the context in which individuals' decisions are made, and hence maintains the appearance of 'free choice' as a fundamental characteristic of the decisions to migrate. True, most migration decisions are individual (person or household) decisions. They involve, further, some kind of motivation on the part of the departing migrants: (short of forced migration) it would be difficult to envisage otherwise. Yet, the process which leads to the formation of these decisions is social. This arises out of conditions related to the socioeconomic structures in which individuals are situated and their perceptions of the costs and the benefits of migration are shaped. For a correct understanding of the dynamics of labour transfer, therefore, the structural context of development must be clearly understood.

Changes in property relations, an overview of rural transformations (whether the peasantry is consolidating or disintegrating), changes in the social division of labour (the extent to which the demand for rural labour is affected by the reorganisation of production and the introduction of new techniques), changes in the crop culture (the extent to which the cultivation of cash crops introduces monetary relations in the rural economy), and last, but not least, the development of gender relations (the extent to which the organisation of housework and growing women's participation in the wider rural context releases male labour time to urban areas) – these are but a few changes of a structural character with direct relevance in explaining the uneven and differentiating nature of the migration process. Considerations of the likely gains and losses of moving to towns are by no means inappropriate but misplaced in this context.These have to be situated and understood within the context of structural change and its dislocating effects on particular individuals and social classes affected by it. Todaro's view in effect, however, concentrates on the end result of migration, missing out its dynamic character and contradictory nature. Some of these are brought out in the following two stylised models of labour transfer, which focus on the diversity of its forms and mechanisms.

The dissolution/separation model

This type of labour transfer signifies a disjuncture in the nature of the relationship between labour and the means of production at the point of departure. The primary force behind this transformation may be located inside or outside the agrarian economy; its mechanism may be market-induced or institutionally propelled, yet the common feature in either case is its outcome: the permanent transfer of a part of the labouring population to other economic sectors.

Both Adam Smith's progressive extension of the market and Marx's primitive accumulation were based upon such a vision of labour transfer. Both saw the original impulse coming from the developments taking place on the land, and though for different reasons, both were in agreement over its 'liberating' character: Marx saw this as saving peasants from 'the idiocy of rural life' and Smith hailed it as a prerequisite for 'satisfying the other wants and fancies of mankind.'

In this model, in fact, the ultimate success of labour transfer depends on the extent of the rupture in the relationship between labour and the means of production. Both the quantity of labour released and the price at which it may be had by the receiving sectors depend crucially upon such a relationship. This is why policies aiming at either dejection/extrusion of labour from the land or its attraction/inducement to other sectors focus on a redefinition of this relationship. History attests to a variety of forms in which this may come about.

In the English enclosure movement, forced evictions and direct extrusion of labour from the common lands formed the basis for the formation of a rural proletariat and its subsequent transfer to the towns. In Africa, too, the history of the establishment of coffee, sugar and cotton plantations is written with blood and violence (Mennoune, 1981, on Algeria; Arrighi, 1970, on Rhodesia; Cliffe, 1977 and 1978, on Zambia and other parts of Africa). Whether intended to clear the land for cash crop production or whether aimed at generating the required supplies of labour, uprooting the indigenous peasantry was a common practice in the areas operated by the new settlers.

Although times may have changed, practices have not. Early indications from the introduction of the Green Revolution in the Indian subcontinent indicated an increase in the incidence of forced evictions of tenant farmers by landlords in a bid to convert their lands to the more profitable High Yielding Variety of seeds (Griffin, 1974:75, 215; George, 1977: 124–9). Subsequent studies too have stressed the trend towards increased peasant differentiation often with similar results (Byres, 1981). The same can be said of modern agro-industrial complexes (agribusiness companies), whose establishment in the fertile areas of some Third World countries has often been accompanied by similar dejections of the local population from their lands (see Chapter 5).

Yet forced eviction and extrusion are but one form of releasing labour from the land. Institutional change and state intervention may be another. The abolition of the Speenhamland system in England in the first half of the nineteenth century achieved results which were similar in nature to those of enclosures a century earlier (Hobsbawm, 1977:188, 202–3). In Africa the poll tax was a favoured policy used to force certain members of the family to enter the cash economy. This was particularly successful if combined with policies 'to limit possibilities for acquiring cash through independent commodity production' (Cliffe, 1978:328). In the interior regions, according to Samir Amin, 'the levying of taxes in money ... had the function of driving peasants towards the coast because there ... [had] been no alternative for them' (1974:95). Similarly, in Egypt, where feudal 'tax farming' was a common mode of exploitation of the peasantry, the optimum rate was 'loosely determined by the extent of village emigration' (Hansen, 1973, cited in Standing, 1981b:193). In some parts, such as in the Belgian Congo, employers even went as far as insisting on 'the labourer being accompanied if possible by his wife and family' in an attempt to sever their ties with the land (cited in Elkan, 1959:196). In Brazil, the withdrawal of the landlords' traditional obligations and goodwill, and in Iran, their refusal to maintain and repair irrigation canals, brought about much the same results (Galjart, 1974, for Brazil; Chapter 5 below for Iran).

Some agrarian reform programmes, too, have worked as a stimulant to rural-to-urban labour transfer in a number of ways. Where the development of large-scale capitalist farming has been the dominant motive for reforms (such as in Colombia in 1961), mechanisation and other labour-saving techniques have reduced the demand for agricultural labour. Elsewhere, with a redistributive emphasis (such as in Mexico in 1934–40, and the Dominican Republic in 1963), although the emergence of a peasant proprietor class might have actually retarded the pace of migration, the substitution of family labour for casual and permanent agricultural wage labourers has meant deterioration in the lot of the latter, thus paving the way for their departure from the land. In other countries, still, where tenancy contracts have been introduced (as in Argentina, Colombia, and Peru), landlords have resorted to mass evictions of tenants for fear of ceding the control of the land they owned (Peek and Standing, 1979:751–2). Thus, although the objectives, methods of implementation, and the context in which these programmes have been introduced have differed markedly, the results, in terms of labour release and transfer, have not been too dissimilar.

At times, market forces too have performed functions similar to those of eviction and institutional intervention. This has sometimes been the case with commercialisation and the increasing integration of agriculture into the wider structure of the home market. Falling terms of trade in areas of commercial farming may, for instance, result in a reduction of the area under cultivation and hence of the demand for labour. Fluctuations in the availability of food and/or its market price may exert similar influences on the rate of flow of labour out of agriculture. This was, indeed, the finding of one study, which found a negative relation between mining recruitment and food output in Nigeria in the 1950s: 'in five different years in which there were poor crops, the population of migrants who left in the succeeding January and February was on average 30.3 per cent of the annual figure, while after good crops in the other five years the corresponding figure was 18.2 per cent' (study by Hobart et al., 1952, cited in Standing, 1982:15).

Alternatively, the pursuit of a liberal food trade policy and the resulting inflow of cheaper imports may undermine domestic agriculture and precipitate farmers' departure for the towns. This appears to have been the main reason behind the international migration of Italians to Brazil in the last century (Roberts, 1978:94), and even today, it is argued that the 'cheap food' policy pursued by some Third World countries is responsible for undermining the viability of the domestic peasant agriculture, hence the perceived mass migration to towns (Lipton, 1977; de Janvry, 1981:ch. 4).

Finally, not all labour transfers of this type are 'compulsive' in nature. Although perhaps more effective as a means of stimulating short-term migration, economic incentives (rising income and employment opportunities) too can induce permanent labour transfer. The early growth of the city of São Paulo was based on a coffee boom in the last half of the nineteenth century (Roberts, 1978:94). The more contemporary Middle Eastern oil boom in the 1970s suggests a similar inducement mechanism at work which had, until recently, increased substantially the pace of international migration into the labour-deficient sectors of the region.

The involution/preservation model

Under this type of labour transfer the relationship between labour and the means of production is modified, not broken. In its seasonal form, traditional economic activity on the land or in the subsistence sector is combined with temporary sales of labour power for part of the year in the rural or urban wage labour markets. In its circular form, this results in dual residence in both the town and country and in periodic movements between the two (see Standing, 1985, for more on different types of circular migration).

Ironically, under this model, the success of labour transfer depends on the extent to which the acquisition of extra labour time is combined with the preservation, not disruption, of the relation between labour and the traditional means of subsistence. This is because the subsistence/agrarian sector provides the receiving sectors not only with labour but also keeps its production costs down by making available the necessary use-values for its reproduction (Meillassoux, 1981).

A further distinction of this model lies in its impact upon the post-transfer organisation of tasks and the division of labour within the remaining peasant households. Given the male-dominated nature of the departures, this usually raises the intensity of effort and the level of responsibilities for the remaining female workers in peasant households. Thus an ostensibly sectoral reallocation of male labour time is secured through an intensification of the females' work burden (Gordon, 1981; Standing, 1982:15–16).

As with the permanent form of labour transfer, this form too may be brought about by forces of compulsion, inducement or a combination of the two. The role played by institutional change and market forces may be similarly varied.

The South African contract labour system provides an example of this at one extreme. Here, the essential requirements of capitalist accumulation combined with a racialist ideology have produced a bizarre form of 'unlimited' supplies of labour in the formation of the Bantustans, where the state regulates the geographic division of labour along racial lines (Legassick and Wolpe, 1976:95).

Elsewhere, as in India and Thailand, it is poverty and destitution among peasant households which is the main drive behind the regular migration of some village women for prostitution in towns (Standing, 1981a:192, 1982:5). Similarly, a programme of institutional change (as in Ecuador after the agrarian reform in 1964) may result in an erosion of traditional incomes and thus drive impoverished peasants and farm labourers to towns in search of temporary jobs (Peek, 1980). Growing cash needs (as in the case of the transition to tenancy farming) may yet be another mechanism through which such a form of labour transfer may expand.

Improving employment opportunities and rising standards of living in the wake of regional booms may stimulate with equal force the recurrence of circular or seasonal migration. This seems to be the standard pattern of absorption/dejection in the construction industry in many Third World countries, and certainly that sparked off by the oil boom in the Middle East in the 1970s. The flow of 'guest workers' to Western Europe in the 1950s and 1960s seems also to have been encouraged and sustained as much by the booming nature of capitalism in receiving areas as by the relevant conditions in the migrants' countries of origin.

Studies from Iran

Labour transfer may thus take various forms and may be brought about in a variety of ways. This simple fact has been overshadowed by somewhat polarised thinking on the subject. Following Marx's special case and a tendency to view individual choice as subservient to structural necessity, the radical/Marxist tradition has emphasised compulsion, dejection, and extrusion. The economists, on the contrary, have relied on an individualist framework in which freedom and choice explain the induced nature of labour transfer. A successful theory, however, should transcend limitations of both these approaches. As Marx himself observed in the context of capitalist development: 'Part of the labouring population is . . . constantly on the point of passing over into an urban or manufacturing proletariat, *and on the look-out for circumstances favourable to this transformation*' (1867:601; emphasis added). Structural transformations may thus be supplemented with, not substituted for, an appropriate consideration of material incentives for migrating individuals. This can be said, with equal force, of the same tendency in the opposite direction.

Our case studies pursue this line of inquiry in relation to the experience of labour transfer in three important periods of Iran's economic development since 1900: the early part of the century, the 1960s and the 1970s. Given our critical review above, the book will focus on the following sets of issues:

1. The importance of labour transfer. This questions whether rural population has any significance for urban industry and, if so, in what respect.
2. The process which leads to the formation of surplus labour in the countryside and the wider context characterising it. The purpose here is to delineate the historical circumstances in which surplus labour is generated and its transfer is made possible.
3. The forces behind migration and the mechanism of labour transfer. Two such mechanisms are addressed in particular: institutional forces and the market mechanism. The role of each is examined in relation to the specificity of the historical conjuncture in which labour transfer is effected.
4. The features of the migration process. This focuses on the selectivity of the labour transfer process by examining its demographic and social composition, as well as examining its different forms.
5. Effects of labour transfer on the countryside. This is studied by focusing on two aspects of the rural economy in the post-transfer period: (a) agricultural output, and (b) the structure and pattern of labour use within the remaining agrarian economy.

6. Labour transfer in the urban context. This examines the quantitative contribution of labour transfer in towns and compares it with other sources of labour supply generation (natural growth and women's participation in the labour force).

Notes

1. The underlying assumption here is that wages are not only given and constant in terms of corn, but that they are also spent entirely on corn. Furthermore, the free movement of capital between different branches would ensure that at equilibrium the money rate of profit is equalised between agriculture and industry. With corn being both the input (wage outlay) and the output in agriculture, it will be through the movement in the prices of manufacturing goods that this equality will be achieved. See Kaldor (1956:84–7) for a concise statement of this.
2. The terms surplus labour and surplus population have a different significance in Marx's terminology. He used the former to refer to surplus value as the origin of profit: 'If the worker needs only half a working day in order to live a whole day, then, in order to keep alive as a worker, he needs to work only half a day. The second half of the labour day is forced labour; *surplus labour* (Marx, 1973:324–5; emphasis added). The terms, overpopulation, surplus population, relative overpopulation, and relative surplus population were, however, used interchangeably throughout the *Grundrisse* and the three volumes of *Capital* to refer to what is now more commonly referred to as surplus labour.
3. For a useful source book on Marx and Engels's writings on the Malthusian theory of population, see Meek (1971:part 2).
4. Leibenstein (1957a,b), for the 'critical minimum effort' thesis; Rosenstein-Rodan (1951), for 'balanced growth' and 'the big push' theories; and Hirschman (1958), for 'unbalanced growth' theory. Myint (1980:ch.7) provides a useful summary.
5. Before Nurkse, a 1951 UN report by a group of experts, which included economists such as Lewis and Schultz, had used the same term to refer to 'persons who work on their own account and who are so numerous, relatively to the resources with which they work, that if a number of them were withdrawn . . . the total output of the sector from which they were withdrawn would not be diminished.' This report was, however, quick to discard the term for being 'somewhat misleading' in favour of 'the less precise but more familiar term "under-employment" ' UN (1951:7). Even before this, Warriner had used a similar concept of overpopulation in her study of Egypt's agricultural problems (1948:32–3).
6. Having said this, Lewis went on to stress that zero marginal productivity of labour was a limiting case. This point was subsequently overlooked by many of his critics; see the discussion which follows later in this section.
7. Lewis was aware of the impediments to this process, among which he listed: (1) the price of subsistence goods may rise, or (2) their price may not fall as fast as subsistence productivity per head rises; and (3) capitalist workers may raise their standards of what they need for subsistence (1954:434).
8. Fei and Ranis define 'redundant' that part of the agricultural labour force

that has zero marginal productivity.Those whose marginal product is lower than their real wage rate are defined as 'disguised unemployment'. The latter thus includes the former.

9. For a more detailed summary of these two models and a general overview of other similar models, see Ghatak and Ingersent (1984:50–63). Another general survey of dualist models comes in Worrell (1980).
10. As mentioned earlier, Lewis treated this as a limiting case: 'Whether marginal productivity is zero or negligible is not, however, of fundamental importance to our analysis. . . . The supply of labour is therefore "unlimited" so long as the supply of labour at this price exceeds its demand' (1954:403). Reiterating this point emphatically in his 1972 reply to critics, he went as far as considering it 'probably a mistake to mention marginal productivity at all' (1972:77).
11. Fei and Ranis refer frequently to a 'pool of redundant labour' (1964:18–19, 35, 157). To the extent that this implies individually idle workers, they confuse open unemployment with disguised unemployment. Nurkse had unequivocally cautioned against this: 'There is no possibility of personal identification here, as there is in open industrial unemployment . . . we cannot point to any person and say he is unemployed in disguise' (1953:33).
12. See, for instance, Marx's statement that:

> In spite of the smaller number of its cultivators, the soil brought forth as much or more produce, after as before, because the revolution in the conditions of landed property was accompanied by improved methods of culture, greater co-operation, concentration of the means of production, etc., and because not only were the agricultural wage-labourers put on the strain more intensely, but the field of production on which they worked for themselves, became more and more contracted. (1867:697)

13. One such incidence was studied by Schultz (1964) in relation to the fatal influenza epidemic in India in 1918–19; for a critique of his methodology see Sen (1967) and a further follow-up discussion in Schultz (1967).
14. As Gibbon Wakefield observed: 'Where land is very cheap and all men are free, where everyone who so pleases can obtain a piece of land for himself, not only is labour very dear, but the difficulty is to obtain combined labour at any price' (cited in Dobb, 1946:221). Adam Smith made a similar observation when remarking that where 'uncultivated land is still to be had upon easy terms [as in North America], neither the large wages nor the easy subsistence which that country affords to artificers can bribe him to work for other people than for himself' (1776:482).
15. These ranged from earlier criticisms of import-substitution industrialisation to the more recent concerns about the ecological and environmental impacts of industrial development. What has united them is their common questioning of the identification of development with industrialisation.
16. Reflecting on this some thirty years later, Lewis remarked: 'I think the biggest mistake development economists were making in the 1950s was to underestimate the likely growth of population. We expected it to average 1.5 per cent. That the death rate might drop by 10 to 15 points per thousand over the next ten years never entered our heads' (Lewis, 1984:133).
17. On 'urban bias', see Lipton (1977). On the informal sector: ILO (1972); Hart (1973); Leys (1973); and Bienefeld (1975). Quijano (1980) provides a classic statement of the urban marginality theme. ILO reports of the early 1970s too reflect in a significant way this shift of emphasis (ILO, 1970, 1972, 1973).

44 Labour transfer and economic development

Kitching (1982:70-84) provides a useful summary.
18. Brenner reflects the general attitude taken in these replies toward the question of population: 'It is the structure of class relations, of class power, which will determine the manner and the degree to which particular demographic changes will affect long-run trends in the distribution of income and economic growth, and not vice versa' (1976:31). The problem with this, as Seccombe (1983) notes, is that it turns a discussion about where the emphasis should lie into an either/or debate. Another important contribution on the transition from feudalism to capitalism steers away from demography; see Hilton (1976).

3
Labour transfer in historical perspective
Persian workers in Southern Russia, 1880-1914

Introduction

This chapter studies migration and labour transfer in Iran at the turn of the century. Much has been said and written of the general political and economic developments of the period marking the Constitutional Revolution (1900-11), but the fact that these years also accommodated the embryonic phases of the formation of a wage-labouring class in the country has attracted little study. Numerous references in the existing literature have noted superficially that, at about this time, an increasing number of Persian labourers crossed the country's northern frontiers into Russia in search of employment.[1] The largest numbers departed from the northwestern province of Azerbaijan in Iran to the contiguous region of Transcaucasia in the Russian Empire to engage in short-term occupations. Unfortunately, few, if any, serious studies have looked into the specificities and determinants of the process, which was constantly on the increase towards the end of the nineteenth century.[2]

The first traces of migration were recorded as early as 1855 when the British Consul in Tabriz, K. E. Abbott, reported 'a great number of the peasantry of Salmas and other parts of Azerbaijan' to be in the habit of 'resorting to Erivan and Tiflis in search of employment'. Reflecting on the 'extraordinary number of these people', the Consul added: 'in the space of two months the Russian consulate has issued upwards of 3,000 passes' (Abbot to Thomson, dispatch 31 March 1855, FO60-205, cited in Seyf, 1982:161-2). The process gathered pace after the 1880s and by the turn of the century it had achieved a scale and consistency that was sufficient to win the attention of many scholars, travellers and commentators of the time.

46 Labour transfer and economic development

Viewed from a historical perspective, population movements had not been unknown in the Persian context. Either for the harshness of the natural environment, which kept large nomadic populations constantly on the move, or for the political expediency of despotic rulers, who resorted to periodic 'forced migration' in the settlement of border issues, Iran had appeared 'in all ages peculiarly liable to movements of population' (Balfour, 1922:22).[3] By the second half of the nineteenth century, however, there were also increasing, albeit limited, signs of movement among the sedentary population. While some of these appeared in resettlements of a permanent character – in quest of food[4] or for better economic climates[5] – others emerged in the form of internal migration of a seasonal type. Primarily farm-oriented, seasonal migration of peasants and village labourers, though still very limited, was most commonly observed in the northern province of Gilan (*PAP,* 1878: 701–2; Bouvat, 1913:183; Edmund, 1924:355) and, to some extent, in the opium cultivating areas of southern and central Persia (Wilson, 1925:189).

The development of labour migration to Russia, however, bore new significance. The sheer number of people involved and the regularity of their movements made this by far the most important form of labour transfer in Iran at the time. Besides, the root cause of the perceived migration, in the author's opinion, lay not in natural or political factors, but in structural changes of an economic character in both countries at the time. Until now, however, the migration's prime generating force has been commonly attributed to a constellation of 'push' factors, such as poverty and political oppression at home. This chapter, indeed, argues that this view, although describing well the context in which migration took place, fails to account for its trend, geographical concentration and short-term character. This failure arises from exclusive concentration on the domestic factors in areas generating migration and cannot be rectified unless proper account is also taken of the important transformations of the Russian economy at the time.

Given the unexplored status of the subject, this chapter begins with the basic questions concerning the scale and salient features of migration in order to establish a broad historical overview for its further analysis. Some thought is then given to migration's general determinants by examining critically the popular explanations as to how it was generated. Finally, its wider implications are discussed in relation to the social and political developments in Iran at the given historical conjuncture.

The scale of migration

By all accounts, the influx of Persians crossing Russia's Asiatic frontiers in pursuit of work was constantly increasing towards the beginning the

Table 3.1 Geographical distribution of Persians in the Russian Empire (by nationality and language, 28 January 1897)

	Persian subjects		Persian-speaking population	
	Male	Female	Male	Female
All Russia	53,268	20,652	24,071	7,652
European Russia	2,455	745	1,322	308
(Astrakhan)	(564)	(247)	(626)	(258)
Poland	1	—	12	1
Caucasus	42,080	18,325	12,607	4,138
(Baku)	(17,266)	(6,702)	(4,746)	(1,227)
(Tiflis)	(6,108)	(2,034)	(1,641)	(350)
(Erivan)	(5,065)	(3,158)	(174)	(61)
(Elizavetpol)	(8,134)	(4,542)	(257)	(81)
(Daghestan)	(1,287)	(564)	(1,295)	(425)
Central Asia	8,598	1,573	9,857	3,163
(Transcaspian)	(7,466)	(1,433)	(6,593)	(1,422)
(Samarkand)	(1,067)	(125)	(1,323)	(400)
Siberia	134	9	273	42

Source: Hakimian (1985:445).

twentieth century. According to some rough estimates, these movements encompassed some 200,000 to 300,000 Persians every year.[6]

More specific evidence on the number of Persians residing in various places in the Russian Empire comes in numerous travellers' accounts, political memoirs and other commentaries of the time. According to a variety of sources, for instance, the Persian residents of Baku amounted to some 50,000 (Nazem al-Islam Kermani, 1953:511; Arfa, 1964:41); the numbers for Tiflis were put at between 10,000 and 12,000 (Orsolle, 1885:49; Danesh, 1966:39); and those of the Transcaspian town of Ashkabad at 5,000 (Nazem al-Islam Kermani, 1960:vol. 2, 91) (see Figure 3.1, p. 52). Based mostly on casual observations and pertaining to various points in time, the picture emerging from these estimates is often inconsistent and contradictory. Hence, according to one source, the total number of Persians in Russia was put at 1 million while another count had it at only 90,000.[7]

Sparse and unreliable as the available information is, we have made use of two sets of historical data in order to establish a better and more accurate overview, the results of which appear in Tables 3.1 and 3.2. The former is based on the results of the first national census of the Russian Empire carried out on 28 January 1897 and shows the existing Persian population in various places inside Russia. The latter derives from the available Russian figures on the external passports and visas issued for the purposes of travel into Russia in her consulates at the time. The first refers to those actually resident in Russia at the time of enumeration, and the second indicates Persian travellers between 1900 and 1913.

48 Labour transfer and economic development

Table 3.2 Legal migration of Persians to Russia across Asiatic frontiers, 1900–13

Year	Entered Russia Passport	Entered Russia Permit	Left Russia Passport	Left Russia Permit	Total Entered Russia	Total Left Russia
1900	38,996	28,308	31,812	25,677	67,304	57,489
1901	51,158	20,751	38,030	17,419	71,909	55,449
1902	66,658	17,026	48,859	12,890	83,684	61,749
1903	74,186	19,199	52,681	16,642	93,385	69,323
1904	66,156	12,623	50,810	13,004	78,779	63,814
1905	51,550	16,416	45,786	14,245	67,966	60,031
1906	62,830	32,302	31,508	29,016	95,132	60,524
1907	56,267	38,349	41,772	36,031	94,616	77,803
1908	57,537	44,531	45,983	41,155	102,068	87,138
1909	63,899	52,357	45,464	49,990	116,256	95,454
1910	78,981	82,698	61,219	74,888	161,679	136,107
1911	82,687	108,582	61,984	95,721	191,269	157,705
1912	101,358	165,374	71,227	144,405	266,732	215,632
1913	124,966	149,589	88,238	125,135	274,555	213,373

Source: Entner (1965:60).

According to Table 3.1, some 74,000 Persian nationals were registered in the first census. This included about 21,000 (28 per cent) women. The largest concentration was in the Caucasus region which accommodated about 82 per cent of all Persians. Within this province itself, the four major towns of Baku, Elizavetpol, Erivan, and Tiflis saw, in the order of population, the heaviest concentrations of emigrant numbers: a total of 53,000 Persians in these towns accounted for as many as 72 per cent of all Persians in the whole of the empire.

Enumeration on the basis of mother tongue produced markedly different results: only 32,000 persons were registered as native Persian speakers. This reflected the overwhelming predominance of the Turkish-speaking Azerbaijanis among the migrants (Belova, 1956:11), a point forcefully brought out by Arfa, who observed, 'in Baku, I already felt myself in Iran as more Azeri Turkish was heard in the streets than Russian' (1964:41).

The limitations of these data, however, should not be overlooked. Conducted in the month of January, the census is clearly seasonally biased as it excludes all those people who returned home in the cold months of winter. Besides, the high incidence of illiteracy coupled with the illegal-alien status of many Persians could make a strong case for possible underestimation of the actual numbers.

Further information emerges from the data on the documented

Historical perspective 49

number of external passports and visas issued at the Russian consulates in Persia. There were four such consulates on the northern frontier in Tabriz, Mashad, Rasht and Astarabad.

According to one source, as early as in 1858 some 4,852 passports had been issued (Belova, 1956:113). The momentum rose clearly after the 1870s. An average of 13,000 Persians entered Russia each year between 1876 and 1890. By 1896, the number had reached 56,371 per year (Entner, 1965:60).

Table 3.2 gives a more comprehensive picture for the period 1900-13, which confirms the underlying upward trend. But equally importantly, it also sheds light on one of the most significant characteristics of migration: the two-way nature of the traffic to and from Russia. Each year thousands crossed into Russia for a certain period, while roughly comparable thousands set off for home. Seasonal or semi-permanent migration was, therefore, a salient feature of these mass movements: in 1913, for instance, over 274,000 Persians entered Russia, while as many as 213,000 returned home. Accordingly, in the first fourteen years of this century, an average of 126,000 Persians went to Russia annually against the 101,000 who departed from Persia. Assuming the number of Persian travellers from elsewhere – other than the Asiatic frontiers of Russia – to be negligible,[8] a total of 353,743 Persians seem to have remained in Russia during this period – giving an average net gain of about 25,000 immigrants for each year.

The passport data are not free from distortions. Firstly, given the financial attractions in issuing passports and travel documents, the procedure followed by the officials concerned was far from tightly regulated (Maraghe-i, 1974:28; Danesh, 1966:69-70). According to Arfa'd-Dawlah – an official of the Persian consulate in Tiflis in the 1880s and later its consul general – for many Russian subjects, purchasing false Persian travel identities had become a convenient practice in their attempt to escape military and other obligations at home.[9]

Besides, there was the more important question of illegal immigration by Persians, mentioned above. Much historical evidence suggests that thousands took liberties in overstepping the legal boundaries when traversing the international frontiers. For 1911 alone Sobotsinskii has indicated a total of 200,000 illegal migrants (cited in Entner, 1965:60). Belova, too, refers to the governor of Elizavetpol, who wrote in 1910 that the vast majority of Persians went to Russia without passports (1956:114).

In the face of such shortcomings, we can now make our own estimate – however approximate – of the number of Persian immigrants in Russia before the outbreak of the First World War. We may assume that Persians residing in Russia numbered some 100,000 by the beginning of

1900. This is not an overestimated increase on the 74,000 registered at the beginning of 1897 (Table 3.1), given the likely net natural growth and net immigration in the course of the following three years through to 1899. With an additional 'legal' net immigration of some 354,000 between 1900 and 1913 (Table 3.2)[10] it would be no exaggeration to hold that the number of Persians remaining in Russia ranged between 450,000 and 500,000 by 1913.[11]

The salient features of migration

We have seen that temporary stay, as reflected in the steady two-way traffic between the two countries, was an important aspect of Persian migration to Russia. It is believed that the largest numbers left Persia regularly in spring and autumn (around April and September) when agricultural work in Transcaucasus was at its peak; movements declined in summer and winter (Minorsky, 1905:206).

The available data on the social composition of migrants, although very limited, are illuminating. For 1904 alone, we have an indication from a collection of Russian consular reports that out of a total number of 59,121 passports issued in Tabriz (in the northwestern province of Azerbaijan in Persia) as many as 54,846 (93 per cent) went to workers. The ratio was far lower for Rasht: 794 out of 3,027 or about 27 per cent (Minorsky, 1905:205). But considering that the number of passports issued in Tabriz exceeded those of Rasht by over eighteen times, it should be apparent that an overwhelming majority of these migrants, and particularly those of Azerbaijan, were common labourers in pursuit of work. The rest came from a variety of social backgrounds and included merchants, traders, artisans and so forth, who travelled to Russia in greater numbers than before in the face of expanding economic relations between the two countries (Kasravi, 1967:85).

Geographically, too, the bulk of the traffic was concentrated in Azerbaijan. Again, according to Minorsky as many as 90 per cent of all permits in 1904 were issued in this province: 59,121 in Tabriz and 3,148 in Urumiah (see Figure 3.1). Then came Mashad with 5,459, followed by Rasht and Astarabad with 3,027 and 652 respectively (Minorsky, 1905:205). The importance of Tabriz is further sustained by another source, which estimates that permits issued in this town had gone up from 26,855 in 1891 to 32,866 in 1903 (Abdullaev, in Issawi, 1971:51).

Departure points and their proximity to Russian consulates should not be confused with the geographical origins of the migrants. Could not applicant travellers from other parts of Persia, for instance, obtain their permits in Azerbaijan? While this was theoretically possible, a number of considerations suggest otherwise.

There is no substantial evidence to indicate that in the period under discussion Azerbaijan was attracting any sizable permanent or semi-permanent populations from elsewhere in Persia. If anything, the 1890s saw the departure of Azerbaijanis for other parts of Persia. Moreover, given the underdeveloped transport system in the country, its vast and harsh terrain, and the difficulties of travelling in the mountainous areas of the international frontier, there is ample reason to believe that the seasonal aspect of migration strongly favoured populations close to Russia, namely those in the northern and northwestern provinces. This is vindicated by Table 3.3, which casts light on a rare aspect of the Azerbaijani migrants: their local origins, a point to which we return in the following section.

The overwhelming concentration of migration out of Azerbaijan, on the other hand, must not obscure the fact that migration was generally more extensive on both sides of the frontier. The existing evidence suggests that Persians also extended as far as the central Asiatic territories of the Russian Empire. Most of these went from the north-eastern province of Khurasan, as did, for instance, the 'thousands of Khurasan peasants', reported by Sir Percy Sykes, who went to 'work in Russian Turkestan during the winter' (Sykes, 1930:vol. 2, 392). Others also departed from as far south as the distant province of Sistan (Abdullaev, in Issawi, 1971:51-2). As we shall see, however, these were far fewer in number than those departing from Azerbaijan.

Being for most part common labourers, Persians took up simple manual jobs in the Russian towns or countryside. In Elizavetpol, the agricultural fields were almost exclusively operated by Persians who entered this *gubernia* in thousands every year. They took up occupations normally refused by local workers on the grounds of inferior pay and conditions of work (Belova, 1956:115). The situation was similar in the Baku *gubernia* where many local *kulaks* relied heavily on Persian workers, and in Tiflis where many Persians worked in the cotton fields on a seasonal basis (Belova, 1956:115-16).

Significant numbers also engaged in a variety of other occupations in the towns. As one contemporary witness described it: 'Baku swarms with Persians. They are seen everywhere – as shopkeepers, mechanics, masons, carpenters, coachmen, carters, and labourers all in a bustle of business, so different from Persians at home' (Gordon, 1896:8).

Demonstrating their personal capabilities, Persians had acquired 'the reputation of being the best masons in Transcaucasia' (Orsolle, 1885:49) as reflected in the observation that 'most of the new buildings in Tiflis were built by Persians' (Gordon, 1896:9). Various other manual works attracted them in large numbers. In the port of Baku, the loading and

52 *Labour transfer and economic development*

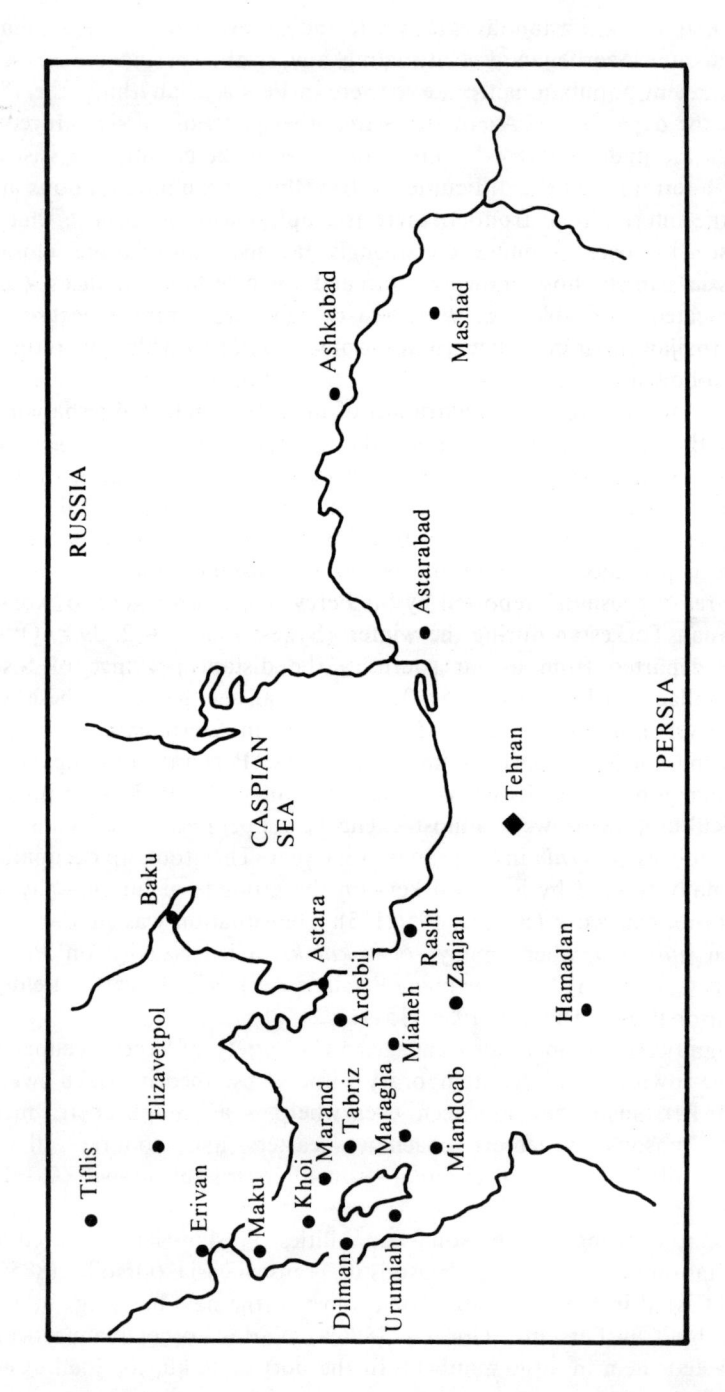

Figure 3.1 Russo-Persian frontier, circa 1900.

Table 3.3 The origins of migrants from Azerbaijan to Russia, 1904

Ardebil area		Trans-Urumiah area		Qarache-dagh		Tabriz-Julfa		Tabriz-Tehran		South and Southeast Urumiah		Kurdistan	
Ardebil	11,178	Urumiah	3,944	Qarache-dagh	8,539	Tabriz	3,425	Tehran	24	Sulduz	36	Kermanshah	38
Serab	6,020	Salmas	4,070	Khiriz	113	Marand	4,834	Ghazvin	31	Miandoab	55	Sunqur	2
Meshkin	80	Khoi	3,538	Udajan	852	Gerger	415	Khamseh	79	Maragha	638	Hamadan	119
Khalkhal	274	Irvanak	3,863					Zanjan	207	Tukharqan	724	Gyarus	277
Astara	188	Maku	1,195					Gyarmerud	3,019	Usku	333	Bijar	130
Alanbaraghush	119	Dilman	76					Khyamtarud	3,022	Isfahan	69	Afshar	466
								Tikmedash	35			Sain Kaleh	138
								Mianeh	67			Sauj-Bulagh	126
Total	17,859		16,686		9,504		8,674		6,484		1,855		1,296
Percentage of total	(29)		(27)		(15)		(14)		(10)		(3)		(2)

Source: Hakimian (1985:449) based on data in Minorsky (1905:207–9).

unloading was largely done by 'powerful porters, who come in numbers from the Persian districts of Khalkhal and Ardebil' (Gordon, 1896:8). Many others laboured on the roads and in railway construction, such as the 'thousands [who were] engaged in the construction of the Trans-Caspian railway' and the 'twenty thousand Persians, from the province of Azerbaijan and Hamadan working . . . on the new railway from Tiflis to Alexandropol and Kars' (Gordon, 1896:9).

Despite the temporary stay by most migrants, the human movements involved had reached such a scale and steadiness by the turn of the century that in many branches of production Persians amounted to a sizable proportion of the workforce. The oil industry in Baku demonstrated this best. In 1893, Persians accounted for 11 per cent of a total workforce of 7,000; in a decade's time, their share had risen to 22.2 per cent of a larger total (23,500). By 1915, as many as 13,500 Persians (29.1 per cent) constituted the largest national grouping in this industry (Abdullaev, in Issawi, 1971:51). Similarly, in the province of Elizavetpol, as many as 27.5 per cent of permanent workers in the copper smelting plant of Kedabek were from Persia (Belova, 1956:116).

The conditions under which the majority of these migrants toiled were very harsh indeed. Engaged for the most part as unskilled wage-labourers, their jobs were generally low paid and had little security. Belova mentions daily average earnings of 60–70 kopeks for unskilled Persians in 1904, regarding this as 20 kopeks less than the general rate of pay for other workers (Belova, 1956:118). Persian dock workers in Baku worked between 15 and 18 hours a day – sometimes even at night – ate badly, and many slept under trees and in gardens (Belova, 1956:116). According to Danesh, the fact that most Persians of Tiflis shared one room among three or four people hampered attempts to contain the periodic incidence of cholera in the town (1966:316).

The security of their occupations was no better. Very few had permanent jobs, and even the oil workers in Baku were no exception. Under a 1903 law, employers no longer held any responsibilities for accidents involving foreign workers (Belova, 1956:118). Moreover, the economic and political insecurity of foreign workers was further dramatised when, following the 1905 labour unrests throughout Baku, the Russian authorities resorted to forcible extradition of thousands of them (Belova, 1956:121). Harsh economic conditions at home and social indignity abroad formed the context in which a great many Persians found themselves on either side of the frontier.

Forces behind migration

Poverty and political oppression

Until now, the causes of the perceived mass migration have been widely attributed to a constellation of 'push factors' operating in Iran. A recurrent theme emerging in much of the critical writings of the constitutional period Persia is a vivid portrayal of popular grievances, rooted in economic hardship and political oppression, which beset the country at the time. In a context of sustained economic decline and political misrule, it was believed that traversing into foreign territories, notably the Russian Empire, became the only path to survival for the masses of overburdened peasantry, pauperised town labourers and craftsmen. One such source, *Siyahatnameh-i Ibrahim Baig,* acclaimed as an influential book in the movement for constitutional reforms, summarised the popular mood of the country as reflected in the mind of a fictitious traveller in foreign lands: 'In Iran, there is no security, no job and no bread . . . no wonder that the Iranians flee the country in large numbers to settle in Russia, the Ottoman Empire and in India' (Maraghe-i, 1974:24–5).

Another contemporary observer reinforced the same view – only in a more figurative style – when stating that: 'Nothing remains of Khurasan. Except for the holy shrine everybody has left for Ashkabad' (from the letters of Mirza Agha Khan Kermani, cited in Reza-Zadeh Malek, 1973:13). At a more theoretical level, this was how a leading member and theoretician (and himself a migrant) of the nascent Iranian workers movement saw the situation: 'Burdensome feudal relations on the one hand, and sustained immiserisation of traders and craftsmen [*pishevaran*] on the other, sent each year tens of thousands of cheap labourers from Iran to the labour markets in Transcaucasia and Turkestan (Soltanzadeh, in Chaqueri,: vol. 4, 99).[12]

There is no doubt that these general observations reflected deeply the economic and political climate of the country at the time. The condition of the peasantry, in particular, seems to have been critical. Either considering their sheer number in the total population, or else accepting, *prima facie,* statements that 'about 85 per cent of Iranian emigrants in Russia were of the peasantry' (cited in Chaqueri:vol. 1, 30), there is ample reason to believe that their material condition, in particular, had important implications for the dynamics of migration to Russia.

Some authors have maintained that the peasants' standard of living declined continually in the second half of the nineteenth century. Partial evidence for this observation has come from various Westerners' travel accounts. It has been noted that descriptions of peasants' lives became gloomier throughout the nineteenth century (Keddie, 1960).[13] Some have also enumerated specific mechanisms for this deterioration. Keddie has viewed the Western impact of encouraging large landholdings as responsible (1960:4); Lambton has sought the reason in the injudicious practice of the local administrations' placing 'the decision of land and other cases ... within the competence of the *tuyuldar* [land assignee] and landowners' (1953:143); whereas others have suggested the falling international prices of raw materials and the depreciation of the Iranian currency as the prime cause (Issawi, 1971:18; Bakhash, 1978:271).

There is no doubt that a fuller debate on the status of the peasantry in Persia is yet to take place. Meanwhile, we believe that *on the whole* (allowing for some differentiation of status) the bulk of peasants experienced a gradual but sustained deterioration in their living conditions. In this author's opinion, this was caused by the changing pattern of landed property relations, namely the concentration of land into large private holdings (*arbabi* lands) towards the beginning of the twentieth century.

As in Western Europe a century or so earlier, the growing commercialisation of agriculture and the development of cash crops for export, while still on a very limited scale, had increased the economic attractions of landholdings in late nineteenth century Persia (Pavlovitch, 1910:618; Issawi, 1971:208). The concentration of land into large holdings in Persia came about in two major ways: through *de facto* conversion of *tuyuls* into private property, 'inheritable and alienable by sale' (Lambton, 1953:139), and through the sales of the *khaliseh* lands (crown lands). The former was a direct result of the weakening political power of the state and the latter signalled its chronic fiscal crisis.[14] But unlike in England, which saw the rise of capitalist farmers as a new class, and in France, where the ranks of peasant proprietors were reinforced, expanding trade outlets for agricultural products in Persia swelled the ranks of the landowning class and raised its quest for income and authority. In conditions thus resembling that of the East European 'feudal reaction', Persian peasants were subjected to growing exactions and fiscal burdens, with their traditional common rights and communal privileges gradually fading into the background (Pavlovitch, 1910:620). In all, the substance of the new relations meant a 'more intensive exploitation of peasants ... than had been traditional' (Keddie, 1960:6).

General reactions of the peasantry testify to their worsening conditions in this period. Although major nationwide peasant rebellions appear to have been mostly absent,[15] a barrage of complaints sent to the Shah, frequent sit-ins in the sanctuaries, and mass village desertions – sometimes to Russian territory – were reportedly familiar aspects of rural life at least in some parts of Persia. The text of an important letter by *Taba-*

taba-i, a leading clergyman in the constitutional movement, sent to *Muzzaffar ad-Din Shah* highlighted the plight of the peasantry by mentioning 'the ten thousand *ra'iyats* [peasants] from Quchan [in Khurasan] who fled to Russia' (cited in Kasravi, 1967:85). The situation could have been no better for the 'Shahsavan tribe residing in Mughan [in Azerbaijan] of whom three thousand families escaped to Russia' (Reza-Zadeh Malek, 1973:12). Peasants' own accounts, in various complaints sent to the Shah, reinforced the same overall picture. For many overburdened peasants, flight into the Russian territory became a recurrent phenomenon in the face of economic hardship and political oppression at home (Adamiyat and Nateq, 1977:378-96).

What changing property relations had done for peasants, technical change and rising imports did for craftsmen. Apart from a few branches such as carpet-weaving, the state of the country's traditional crafts and local industries deserves particular attention in the wake of growing competition from abroad (Issawi, 1971:ch. 6). The decline of numerous branches left thousands of craftsmen in search of alternative employment, thus releasing considerable amounts of labour. But the generally restricted economic development at home could bring little relief either to the mass of overburdened peasantry or to the swelling ranks of impoverished craftsmen and town labourers. The domestic sources of demand for labour were severely limited as is clearly seen in the case of 'modern' indigenous factories where, by the early 1900s, total employment did not exceed a mere 850 workers (Floor, 1980b). It was in this context that foreign outlooks were beginning to appear more inspiring.

Other forces

The problem with these widely suggested sets of compulsive forces is that they are not so much inaccurate as insufficient explanations of migration. In the author's view, while they describe well the context in which migration took place, they fail to account for its timing or character. Poverty, political oppression, and lack of individual security were indeed integral aspects of Persian society at the time. Unpalatable as these were, however, none was new to the mass of common people throughout nineteenth century Persia. Even allowing for the aggravating trend towards the end of the century, the fact that none of these trends was exclusive to the areas in the north of the country, from where the majority of migrants departed, casts serious doubt on their explanatory power.

As far as poverty and destitution were concerned, some of the southern and central provinces were in no better – if not in much worse –

condition. This was the impression of the British Consul travelling in the south in 1894 who found the situation in Fars 'quite indescribable'. The damage inflicted by the tax collectors had been far greater than by locusts or the depredations of Arab tribes. As the Consul recorded: 'the people say that never in their recollection have they been so hardly treated, so utterly thrust down by oppression' (enclosure in Lascelles to Rosebery, no. 3, Tehran, 13 January 1893, FO60-52, cited in Bakhash, 1978:265).

Besides, expressions of popular grievances were not limited to northern Persia. Throughout the 1890s, in the wake of the rising movement for constitutional reforms, many Persian towns were commonly turned into scenes of anti-government riots and uprisings. In Astarabad and Hamadan, the governors were forced to flee by the local population. Similar mass agitations broke out in other major towns such as Shiraz, Isfahan, Mashad, and Tabriz. These were caused by 'genuine public grievances', and 'derived their main impetus from the powerful reaction produced among the people by the misrule of government and its officials' (Bakhash, 1978:288; also Seyf, 1982:137 for a list of such rebellions between 1881 and 1895).

Ivanov's interpretation emphasising the repeated incidence of hunger and famine in Persia as fuelling the mass exodus to Russia does not fare any better in this respect (1978:17). Firstly, the most devastating of Persian famines occurred in 1871-2, that is, generally before the rise in the momentum of migration in the coming decades. It is believed that after this date the gravity, or incidence, of famines declined (Seyf, 1982:137). Secondly, there is no reason to believe that famines would have had any greater impact upon the population in the northern provinces than in the centre and the south, where natural calamities were even more recurrent.

Ignoring the underlying trend of migration and side-stepping the relative importance of Azerbaijan in this regard, these views also underrate or ignore another, perhaps the most important, feature of migration. As we have seen, most migrants travelled to Russia on a short-term basis, returning home in large numbers. We also saw that on an average annual basis, net immigration of Persians into Russia did not exceed one-fifth of the total departures made to that country from Persia. For the bulk of migrants who did return home, periodic migration had the attraction of providing them with savings without severing their ties with their homes. No doubt this consideration militates strongly against those views depicting migration as a mass flight from economic hardship and political injustice at home. Such a view seems to have been widespread in the literature, as demonstrated in the following quotation: 'emigration from Iran [was] the only possible escape from the infinite oppression exerted by the State' (Reza-Zadeh Malek, 1973:12).

The temporary character of migration is also evident from another perspective. Sir T. E. Gordon, a high official of the British legation in Tehran in the 1890s, spoke of the migrants' motivation to 'save money steadily to enable them to return home' (1896:9). Similarly, according to Gad Gilbar, the migrants consisted of 'artisans, peasants, and nomads who left the country for a short duration only with the sole aim to save money' (1976:153). Presumably it was in this enterprising spirit that, in the eyes of the British observer of the time, H. J. Whigham, 'the Persian who works for four and a half d. a day in his native land wants 2 s. in Baku' (Whigham, 1903:402). This observation is consistent with an earlier remark by the French traveller Orsolle who, writing in 1885, attributed the rising tide of Persian migration to the accelerating momentum of 'fortune hunting' in the Caucasus (1885:49). Although somewhat exaggerated in tone and detached from the conditions of the domestic economy in Persia, these observations, nevertheless, point correctly to the changing nature of economic inducements which affected migrants.

This point is also brought out by some rare statistics on currency remittances by the saving labourers. Against all the odds – transport costs, passport fees, bribes and exactions by officials on both sides of the frontier, not to mention the higher cost of living and the incertitudes of life in foreign lands – migrants managed to accumulate savings that were far from negligible. Minorsky has estimated that in 1904 as much as 1.8 million rubles were brought home by the 60,000 or so Azerbaijani migrants (Minorsky, 1905:211). According to Entner, around 1909 the Russian bank was converting about 3 million rubles annually for homecoming workers, a figure which is most likely an underestimate given the many more millions which were being converted in the bazaars (Entner, 1965:61). Undoubtedly, the severe depreciation of the local currency (the *Qaran*) in this period gave migrants extra incentives to save the increasingly more valuable foreign currency.

Seen in this light, the impetus to migration came not solely from domestic forces of compulsion but also from the new and rising trend of economic and occupational attractions beyond Persia's northern frontiers. In sharp contrast to the conditions prevailing in Persia, the last quarter of the nineteenth century witnessed a sustained process of economic expansion in Russia, with her industrialisation well into gear by the turn of the century. Spearheaded by a strong state-oriented industrial policy – reaching its peak in the 1890s under the aegis of the finance minister Sergei Witte – Russia portrayed the monumental image of a constantly expanding industrial edifice. Some infallible symptoms of her industrial 'take-off' over these years were seen in an impressive expansion of her domestic industries, the development of massive mining projects, and a rapid extension of her railway networks (Falkus, 1972:44–6, 64–6).

The economic boom was particularly marked in the Caucasus, where the concentration of 90 per cent of the country's rapidly growing oil output (the second largest in the world, next to the USA's), had transformed the area into a centre of industrial production (Falkus, 1972:13, 59, 76). At its peak in 1901, Baku oil production exceeded its 1870 level by more than 450-fold, and despite severe fluctuations in employment, its workforce reached 30,000 in 1907 (Lane, 1975:177). Travelling in the area in the late 1880s, Lord Curzon wondered at the population of this town, 'no less than 90,000', reflecting that its growth was 'almost wholly that of the last 13 years . . . [the] exclusive creation of the petroleum industry' (Curzon, 1892:vol. 1, 66).

With such an increase in the pace of economic activity, labour deficiencies were becoming more recurrent. The situation was particularly acute in the Caucasus, where many branches of production had become heavily reliant on outside labour. Chief among these were agriculture and light, labour-intensive industries. Writing on the state of the tea industry in the region, in 1903, the British Consul referred to 'the question of labour supply' as 'anything but satisfactory', with severe labour shortages leaving 'much to be desired'. The report went on to warn that for the future development of the industry, 'considerable attention [had to be] devoted to the study of the question of importing outside labour' (*PAP*, 1903:5).

Belova's emphasis on the frequent incidence of labour shortages in this area as a contributory factor to Persian migration is also well placed. According to a Russian document quoted by her, the Baku governor stipulated that the area would suffer severely if the flow of Persian workers were suppressed. The local population could not on its own till and harvest the land in the face of an imminent threat by locusts (Belova, 1956:115–16). Political events around the Persian Constitutional Revolution brought out the same point. When the Russian authorities established a strict watch on border movements, the number of migrants dropped sharply, and wages rose in Transcaucasus as the tangible shortage of labour left large areas of land unworked. This led the Erivan governor to write in complaint stressing that far from being criminal elements, Persians were laborious workers, and hence very much in demand (Belova, 1956:115).

Rapid industrial expansion in Russia did not leave her southern neighbour unaffected. With production gathering momentum in what now resembled the 'industrial centre' in Russia, Persia was put under pressure to open up as the 'rural hinterland' for the supply of raw materials and a market for the products of her growing industries. This was also reflected in Russia's overall policy towards her borderlands and oriental neighbours, a policy – duly described by Entner as the 'Witte System in action' – that aimed at their economic absorption. In Persia, the essence of this new economic interest came in a spirit of active but quiet penetration after 1890. Utilising a variety of policy instruments to 'improve her position in Persia', Russian penetration had become so successful that, on the brink of the First World War, 'to a remarkable extent Persia had been drawn into Russia's economic orbit and was a functioning part of her economy' (Entner, 1965:39–41, 77).

The impact of economic integration was particularly manifest in the border provinces of Persia. At a time when Khurasan, Mazandaran and Gilan were gradually turning into cotton and rice growing and exporting areas for the Russian markets, Azerbaijan's contribution to the economic requirements of the centre came in the exportation of the commodity in which it was resourceful: its labour.

As we have seen, however, the importance of migration from Khurasan on the northeastern side should not be overlooked. In contrast to the other, more prosperous northern provinces of Gilan and Mazandaran, which even attracted working population from elsewhere in Persia, it has been observed that this province, like Azerbaijan, exported some labour especially into the Transcaspian labour markets. A Russian document quoted by Abdullaev shows that, in 1909, the number of villages in this province with offices for granting external passports rose from ten to twenty-five (Abdullaev, in Issawi, 1971:52). The essential difference, however, between northeastern and northwestern migration was that, despite its extensive occurrence, the former was far more limited than the latter. This was due primarily to the smaller demand for labour in the less-developed adjacent Russian territories (compared to the Caucasus) as well as to the difficulties and perils in crossing the vast desert terrain in these border regions.

The specificities of Azerbaijan in this context, therefore, merit closer attention. Described once by Lord Curzon as the 'granary of Northern Iran', the province was best known for its higher level of economic and social developments compared with other provinces. With an estimated 2 million inhabitants, it was also 'by far the most thickly populated province of Persia' (1892:vol. 1, 517). What mattered more, though, was not so much the larger number of people as their relationship to the productive capability of the province. It was in this respect that the relative position of Azerbaijan had been undergoing a distinct transformation.

Azerbaijan's leading position as the main commercial route to Europe had been severely undermined in the latter half of the nineteenth century. The rise of rival trade routes (the southern ports after the opening of the

Suez Canal, and Khurasan after the construction of the Transcaspian railway) had seriously shaken the once dominant position of the Tabriz–Trebizond route (Issawi, 1970:18–27).

The cultivation of cash crops for export in Azerbaijan did not tell a success story either: the performance of this province lagged behind the centre and the south (exporting opium) and other northern provinces (exporting cotton, rice and tobacco). Attempts at the development of cotton were short-lived and, after 1870, Russian imports of cotton from the province practically stopped (in favour of Mazandaran). Similarly, the attempt to develop tobacco exports proved to be unsuccessful as total exports of the province to Turkey (the main recipient) plummetted to a mere 20 cwt in 1901 from a high of 37,152 cwt in 1883 (Seyf, 1982:514).

It was this combination of long-term commercial decline and economic depression in the 1890s[16] that gave Azerbaijan the labour pool upon which the industrial expansion of the Caucasus drew. Needless to say, Azerbaijan's geographical proximity to the Russian territory, too, played an all-pervasive role in encouraging northbound migration – a matter of high significance, especially in the context of short-term movements.

Within the province itself, the heavy concentration of migrants in areas closest to the Russian frontier attested to this pattern. The valuable data in Table 3.3 on the origins of migrants from Azerbaijan show that as many as 56 per cent of all migrants came from the two areas of Ardebil and Trans-Urumiah, the former a mountainous region not considered particularly fertile, and the latter a resourceful area with a sizable Christian community of Armenians. The rest were similarly clustered in those localities of eastern and western Azerbaijan adjacent to the Russian frontier (Qarache-dagh and Tabriz–Julfa). Moving down to the south and southeast (towards Kurdistan and Tehran), the numbers declined dramatically.

Perhaps the best reflection of the scale of exodus from the Perso-Russian border towns and villages came in the words of the imaginary traveller whom we cited earlier in *Siyahatnameh-i Ibrahim Baig*. Spotting few adult males he paused to exclaim, 'it seems as if one has entered a city of women!' (Maraghe-i, 1974:28).

The social and political significance of migration

Apart from its quantitative importance, the transfer of labour from Persia to Russia had the added significance of putting many migrants in contact with new social and political environments. Even though short-term and of a temporary character, regular journeys to a more advanced industrial nation brought, in many cases, increased awareness of new social, cultural, and political horizons. This, for instance, was how socialist thinking was introduced to Iranian workers and intellectuals and how their understanding of political organisations widened. It was also in these years and among returning migrants that the foundations of Iranian social democratic and, later, communist movements were laid down; a consideration that also explains observations stressing the significance of migration in relation to the later emergence of an industrial working class in Iran. In the words of Abdullaev, 'without studying this question of migrants, it is impossible to understand correctly the essence of the birth of the working class in Iran' (Abdullaev, in Issawi, 1971:50).

Contact with the Russian revolutionaries and political activists seems to have had an impact on Persian workers in at least three important political phases of the period. These were the revolutionary situation in Russia around 1905, the Persian Constitutional Revolution of 1905 to 1911, and the events thereafter until the October Revolution in 1917.

Labour unrest was spreading throughout Russia in the early years of the twentieth century. The situation was particularly acute in the Caucasus where, according to the British Consul in 1905, 'labour troubles' had been felt in Baku 'more severely, perhaps, than in any other part of Russia' (*PAP*, 1906:159). This gave rise to a growing tendency of politicisation among Persian workers, thus implicating many of them in the events of the host country. In the 1906 strike in the copper mines and plants of Alaverdi in Armenia, for instance, about 2,500 Iranian Azerbaijanis were believed to constitute the core of the strikers (Abdullaev, in Issawi, 1971:51). By late 1905, Russian authorities began forcible extradition of thousands of Persians in Baku (Belova, 1956:121).

The first Iranian social-democratic organisation *Hemmat* (Endeavour) was founded in Baku in 1904 by activist migrants with the aid of their Russian revolutionary comrades. The influence of Russian social democrats was also evident in the establishment of different branches of the Iranian Social Democratic Movement (*Ijtima'yun 'Amiyun*) in various Iranian towns such as Tabriz, Rasht, Mashad, and Tehran (extracts from the memoirs of 'Amu Oghli in Chaqueri:vol. 6, 46–57). The most important of these was regarded to be the Baku committee, constituting its central committee (Chaqueri:vol. 1, 39). New ideas and organisational assistance did not go without material aid. According to Belova, before the introduction of printing facilities in Iran, the social democrats had their literature printed in the Caucasus for delivery into Iran (Chaqueri:vol. 1, 17). This was particularly important since at about this time (1906–11) strikes were spreading throughout Iran and workers' unions were coming into being (Ivanov, 1978:35). The first union, that of print workers, was established in 1906 (and reorganised later) and had by

1918 won the right for its members to work an eight-hour day.

Comradeship was also extended in the course of confrontations for constitutional reforms in Iran. According to an interesting article by the Russian revolutionary Tria (penname for V. D. Mgeladze) a brigade of militant workers from the Caucasus was sent to the siege of Tabriz to fight under the leadership of Sattar Khan. These trained and armed militiamen travelled long and hazardous distances from Tiflis. Although many lost their lives and others were arrested in the course of the battle, their presence was morally and materially beneficial to the defenders of the town. In particular, their use of bombs – introduced for the first time in Iran – proved an effective means of spreading fear among government forces (Tria, 1911:324–33).

In the course of the coming years, Iranians took part in other political activities in Russia. In 1914, Iranian workers residing in Baku participated in street demonstrations against the outbreak of war (Soltanzadeh, in Chaqueri:vol. 4, 48). Soon after the October Revolution, a group of Iranian workers in the Baku oil fields initiated the party *Idalat* (Justice), which was later to become the Communist Party of Iran in 1920. Sending active cadres to Iran for political propaganda, *Idalat* was closely linked to the Bolsheviks, and according to one of its leading activists, it 'acquired spectacular influence among Iranian workers in Baku in 1918 and 1919' (Soltanzadeh, in Chaqueri:vol. 4, 99).

In June 1920, when the first congress of the Communist Party of Iran was held in Enzeli, its leaders, who were aware of the embryonic status of their movement, looked to two factors to create an upsurge in its future growth: 'the desperate conditions of the peasantry on the one hand, and a lasting relationship with the proletariat in Baku on the other' (Soltanzadeh, in Chaqueri:vol. 4, 59–60).

Summary and conclusion

The most important type of labour transfer in Iran at the turn of the century was international in character. This involved the periodic movement of a considerable number of workers, mainly from the country's northern provinces to Russia's southern states. Compared to the other population movements of nineteenth century Iran, this had the distinct characteristics of being regular, involving considerable numbers, and being chiefly driven by economic forces. With an estimated half-a-million Persians in Russia, either residing for certain periods or engaged in annual movements, it is hard to imagine any Azerbaijani individuals or families who were left unaffected by the forces of migration in those years.

I argue that the views that place exclusive emphasis on the internal conditions of the country at the time disregard or discount to a large extent the important changes that were taking place inside Persia's powerful northern neighbour. By focusing exclusively on poverty and political oppression at home, these views fail to account for such essential features of migration as its trend, geographical concentration and short-term character. While these arguably formed the domestic context in which migration took place, it was the rise of new occupational opportunities elsewhere that made the expedition into foreign lands more attractive than before. Russia's powerful economic drive, in general, and the transformation of her borderland areas, in particular, provided the main impetus to the process that attracted thousands of Persian peasants and manual labourers each year to the more affluent provinces of the empire. This process was aided by economic and political hardship at home but cannot be fully explained by it. The fact that, for the greatest part, these migrants left from the nearby Persian border towns, stayed in Russia for short periods and then returned in just as great numbers best explains this view of migration, discounting the hitherto more popular conception which has seen migration in terms of massive peasant flights and village desertions.

Notes

1. Throughout this chapter, the words Iran and Persia are used interchangeably.
2. For a rare English source on the subject, see an abridged translation of Z. Z. Abdullaev (1963) in Charles Issawi (1971:42-52). For another excellent source, see Belova (1956) or its shortened French translation in Chaqueri (1979:53-62).
3. For a brief history of 'forced migration', see Perry (1975:199-215).
4. Subsequent to the famine in 1871-2, many thousands left the southern and central provinces for the Caspian littoral in search of food (Abbot to Alison, Rasht, 20 November 1871, FO60-338, PRO, referred to in Gilbar, 1976:152).
5. Like the many Azerbaijani families who left their province to settle in Khurasan (*PAP*, 1892:9).
6. The lower figure is suggested in Ivanov (1978). For the higher figure see Taqi-Zadeh's speech in the first *Majlis* (Iranian Parliament), cited in Nazem al-Islam Kermani (1960:vol. 2, 121). His figure is imprecise in the sense that it seems to include all emigration out of Iran. See also Belova (1956:114). Abdullaev, too, agrees with this higher estimate (Issawi, 1971:51).
7. See Nazem al-Islam Kermani (1953) for the higher figure. The lower estimate appears in Adamiyat and Nateq (1977:295).
8. Gordon mentions that in 1894-5, 20,000 Persian Passports were issued in the Persian Embassy in Constantinople, which 'would include pilgrims as well as home visitors' (1896:9). It is not unlikely that some of these travellers went to Russia.

66 Labour transfer and economic development

9. This practice was so recurrent that the consulate decided to reissue the travel documents. Arfa' was assigned the task of rewriting them, entitled in return to receive one-tenth of the revenue. Given the large number of Persians in the Caucasus, sometimes he had to 'write on until the early hours of the morning,' as a result of which 'his economic means expanded' (Danesh, 1966:70).
10. Dealing with the same passport data, Gad Gilbar has overlooked the national census, hence stating that: 'As there are no data for the number of Persians who returned from Russia to Persia before 1900, it is impossible to estimate the total number of Persian nationals who lived in Russian territories in the years immediately prior to World War 1' (1976:152). More importantly, Gilbar also commits an error in stating that, 'in the years 1900–13 about 1.765 million Persians left legally for Persia', and conversely that, 'over 1.412 million Persians left Russia for Persia' (1976:152). He arrives at these figures by adding up the relevant number of entries and exits for this period (see our Table 3.2), ignoring the fact that an 'individual Persian national' could have made recurrent entries to and exits from Russia – a common occurrence given the short-term nature of migration for the most part.
11. Gordon dismisses this figure as an exaggeration (1896:9).
12. Others regarded lack of 'individual's security, anarchy and widespread brigandage' as responsible for peasants' flight to Russia (Pavlovitch, 1910:625).
13. For a discussion of the limitations to this approach, see Nowshirvani (1980:552–4).
14. On the sales of *khaliseh* lands, see Lambton (1953:151–3); Pavlovitch (1910:618–19); Issawi (1971:208); and Bakhash (1978:280).
15. See Kazemi and Abrahamian (1978:294–5). The two regions of Hamadan in the west and Gilan in the north seem to have been the exceptions; see Adamiyat (1984:65–91).
16. On the economic depression of the 1890s, see various consular reports on Tabriz and Azerbaijan (*PAP*, 1895:5; 1897:5; 1906:4).

4
Agrarian change I: an outline of Iran's land reform

Introduction

This chapter and the next discuss labour transfer in the 1960s. Unlike the migration of Persian workers at the turn of the century, labour transfer in this decade was both internal and brought about by the domestic forces of change. Chief among these was a programme of land reform, introduced in the early 1960s, which marked the debut of the first systematic and nationwide set of institutional changes to sweep Iran's countryside in the coming decade and a half.[1] A clear understanding of this programme is, therefore, critical for a thorough understanding of labour transfer in this period.

For its part, the Iranian experience of land reform did not take the 'classic' form of the expropriation of the peasantry. On the contrary, it was designed (at least originally) to consolidate an independent peasantry by spreading ownership among particular categories of peasant. Nevertheless, by restructuring property rights in the countryside, the reforms played a key role in the process that subsequently released considerable supplies of agricultural labour to towns and other sectors of economic activity.

To study this process, the present chapter is devoted to a general description of the salient features and the results of this programme. It begins with an overview of the structure of landholding and tenurial relations prior to the land reform. This will be followed by an examination of the principal characteristics of the programme through its different phases and an evaluation of its main results. Some thoughts on the causes of the land reform conclude this chapter. In the following chapter, we focus on a detailed examination of the specific mechanisms through which the structural changes initiated by this programme affected rural labour.

Landholding and tenurial relations before the land reform

Prior to the land reform, there were four broad categories of landownership in Iran: crown lands, state lands, religious domains (*awqaf*), and privately-owned lands (*arbabi* lands). Of these, *arbabi* lands were the most prevalent. In the early 1960s over three-quarters of all villages were thought to be in the possession of private landlords; 4 per cent belonged to the crown; while the remaining 20 per cent were almost equally divided between the state and religious domains (Dehbod, 1960, cited in Ashraf and Banuazizi, 1980:17-18).[2]

Large landowners, of whom there were some four thousand, constituted the core of Iran's dominant class. They lived for at least part of the year in the towns and not, as in the feudal West, in castles or manors scattered throughout the countryside. Landownership gave this class social prestige, wealth and political power, as was evident from their distinctly privileged position in Iranian society: 1,000 families owned at least 1 village each, with 30 of them possessing between 40 and 200 villages each. The area controlled by large private landlords accounted for over 55 per cent of all arable land. Between them, the royal household, the large landowners and the tribal chiefs owned about 70 per cent of all arable land, pastures and forests in the country (Ashraf and Banuazizi, 1980:18).

Large landowners were particularly dominant in areas with difficult irrigation problems (such as in Kirman in central Iran). Here the technical complexity of the *qanats*[3] construction and the higher cost of their upkeep gave landlords almost exclusive control over the land. In contrast, small landowners were to be found in the less fertile districts around the towns (Lambton, 1969:24).

Regardless of the form of ownership, sharecropping was the principal mode of agricultural tenure in the pre-land reform rural Iran. This was based on an agreement between landlords and peasants to divide the crop according to their contributions to five elements of production: land, labour, seed, water and oxen. In practice, however, sharecropping was mainly regulated by local custom; hence the great deal of variation which was observed throughout the country. The nature of farming (whether dry or irrigated), irrigation methods (using river water, *qanat,* or well), and the type of crop grown, were some of the factors which influenced this practice (see Momeni, 1980:46-7 for a wide range of these variations in different regions of Iran).

Some sharecroppers enjoyed traditional occupancy rights over the land they cultivated. These rights, known as *nasaq* rights, were not tied to any specific plots of land. They acted rather as a privilege to operate *some* land, while all authority over the assignment of plots resided with the owners.

Production was organised co-operatively in work teams of peasants known as *bonehs* or *sahras*. Each *boneh* was run under the supervision of a team leader, known as *sarboneh*. These were chosen by the landlords, from among competent peasants, to take responsibility for all preparation and production works on the land assigned to *bonehs*. They retained generally their position for life.

Boneh lands were redistributed every three to four years among members. This practice reflected in part egalitarian traditions within the work team designed to safeguard members against undue variations in the quality of the soil, and in part the owners' apprehension lest peasants develop claims on the lands they cultivated.

There was, as yet, no overall tendency for the growth and expansion of large-scale capitalist farming in Iran. This type of farming existed only in embryonic form and was concentrated primarily in the two fertile provinces of Gorgan in the north and Khuzistan in the south (see Figure 4.1). The agricultural base of the former area had been transformed away from the traditionally strong wheat into rice monoculture by developments brought about by large-scale mechanised farming in the early 1950s. Similarly, in the latter area, large-scale irrigation improvements under the Dez Irrigation Project (DIP) in the late 1950s had encouraged cash crop cultivation, the expansion of orchards, and the development of the Haft-Tappeh sugar plantation (Okazaki, 1968, on the developments in Gorgan, and Salmanzadeh, 1980, on Khuzistan province).

In contrast to limited capitalist farming, sharecropping was prevalent but was mostly concentrated in the arid and semi-arid areas of central, eastern and southern Iran, where dry-farming wheat culture was predominant. The proportion of all lands operated by sharecropping peasants in the country reached 55 per cent, which accounted for 43 per cent of all holdings in 1960 (see Figure 4.2). In contrast, owner-cultivation was still very limited: it accounted for just over one-quarter (26 per cent) of the total area of arable lands, and even then it was confined to particular regions in the country. Over two-thirds of all owner-operated holdings were located in the fertile provinces of Gilan and Mazandaran in the north (Agricultural Census, 1960:table 103, p. 34), where a temperate climate and the better quality of the soil encouraged small-scale irrigated farming. It was in these areas and among this group of operators that the bulk of Iran's still limited peasant proprietor class were to be found before the land reform. Elsewhere, and for the most part, large landowners controlled economic and political life in the rural areas of Iran on the eve of the land reform.

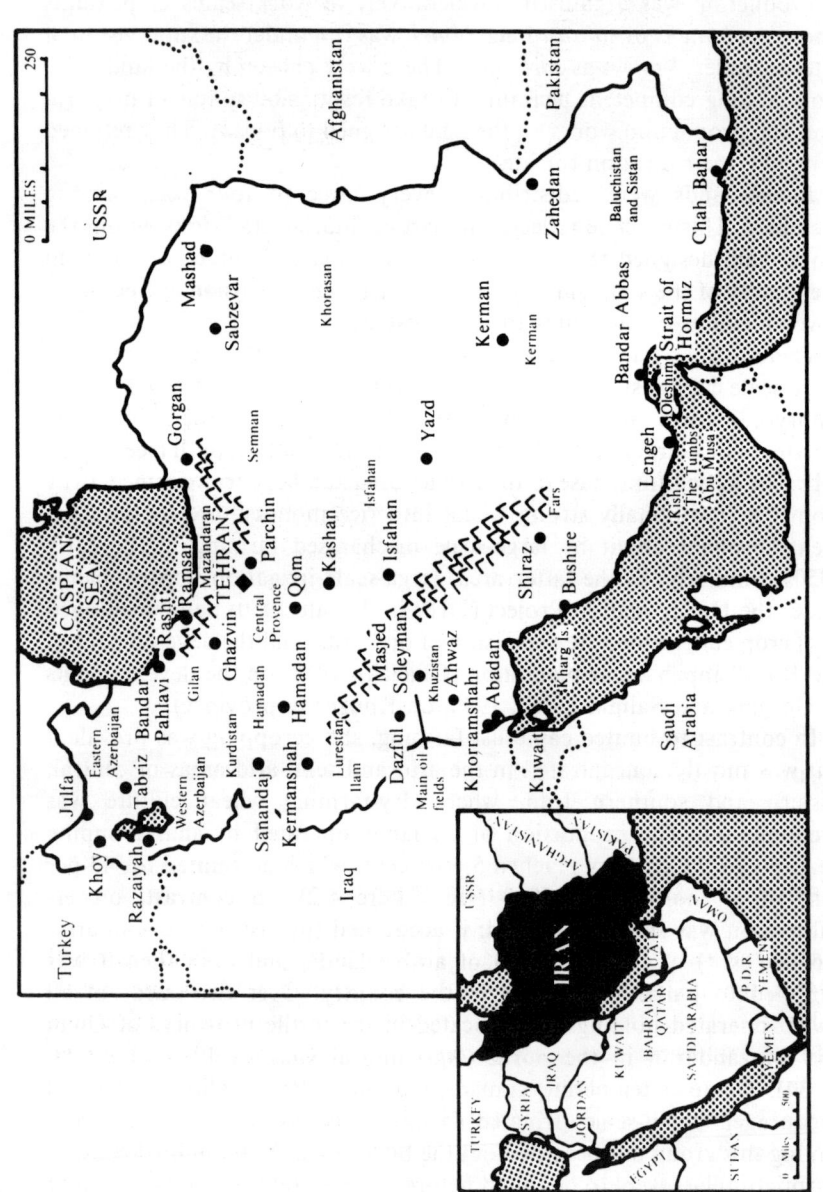

Figure 4.1 Iran – by geographical regions

Iran's land reform 71

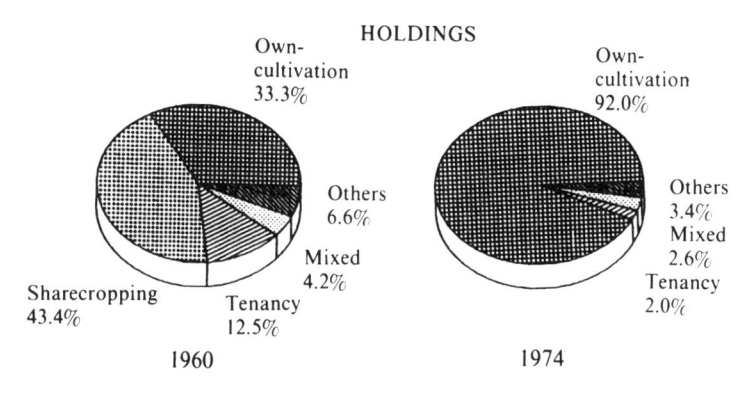

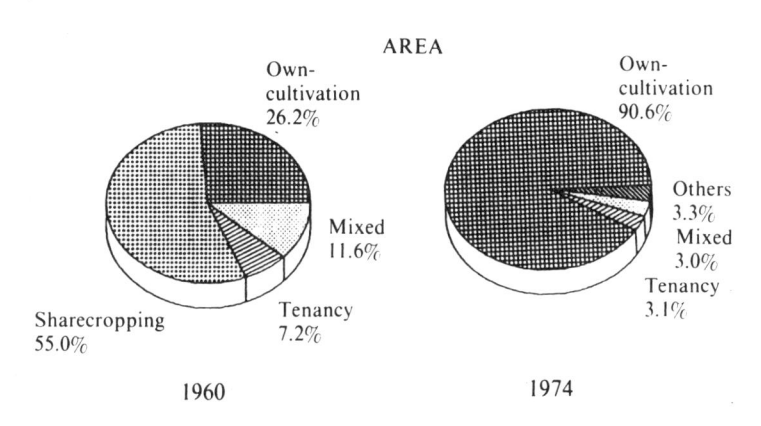

HOLDINGS

1960: Own-cultivation 33.3%, Others 6.6%, Mixed 4.2%, Tenancy 12.5%, Sharecropping 43.4%

1974: Own-cultivation 92.0%, Others 3.4%, Mixed 2.6%, Tenancy 2.0%

AREA

1960: Own-cultivation 26.2%, Mixed 11.6%, Tenancy 7.2%, Sharecropping 55.0%

1974: Own-cultivation 90.6%, Others 3.3%, Mixed 3.0%, Tenancy 3.1%

Figure 4.2 Land tenure before and after the land reform, 1960 and 1974.

General features of the programme

Iran's land reform was closely modelled on the Japanese land reform of 1945 in that it aimed at transforming sharecropping peasants into owner-cultivators (see Misawa, 1971:143–9, for a discussion of Japan's land reform). It thus excluded agricultural workers from the categories of land reform 'beneficiaries', but included peasants with *nasaq* rights.

The scope of redistributions in the first stage – described by Warriner as Persia's Original Strategy – was confined to the large landowners who possessed over six *dangs*[4] of a whole village or of different villages. Under the terms of the law of 9 January 1962, landlords were given the choice of retaining land to the equivalent of one whole village (six *dangs*). The remainder was to be transferred to the occupant sharecroppers through

72 Labour transfer and economic development

long-term credit arrangements underwritten by the government. However, special provisions were made for orchards and mechanised lands, which exempted them from redistribution.

By recognising peasants' customary rights and traditional land titles as a basis for redistribution, the land reform took the option of relying on the prevailing pattern of land use. In this way it avoided the need for fresh cadastral surveys to redefine new land boundaries. In the event, this aspect of the programme has been one of the most controversial. On the one hand, it has been praised for being practical and minimising disruptions to the field layout of the Iranian countryside; on the other hand, it has been assailed for being conservative and perpetuating the prevailing order of land use in the country.[5] But as the next chapter will demonstrate, this practice tended to discriminate against the young (as in general the older generation of peasants had better, established land rights) and the bottom layer of the peasantry (who operated insufficient lands and lands of inferior quality). Both these issues were to have important implications for the potential supply of wage labour in rural areas.

Despite ambiguities in design and a wide range of loopholes in its implementation, the first phase of the land reform has been widely hailed as its possibly most radical.[6] Official figures put the total number of peasants who received land under this stage at 753,258 (Table 4.1). According to another estimate, the net result of this stage was the transfer of some 17 per cent of all Iranian villages to about a quarter of the sharecropping peasants (Ajami, 1973:123) – a result which is not entirely insignificant considering the short-lived nature of this stage.

The drafting of the second stage laws (finalised on 25 July 1964) signalled the beginning of an important departure from the original spirit of the reforms. Under new legislation, the range of alternatives open to the landlords was broadened considerably by giving them any one of the following five options: (1) sale of land to peasants; (2) division of land according to the traditional practice of crop division; (3) renting land to peasants on a long-term basis; (4) establishing joint stock companies with peasants' agreement and participation; and most controversial of all, (5) purchasing peasants' occupancy rights.

Furthermore, the scope for evasion increased significantly. Two rulings by the Land Reform Council on 25 August 1963 and 7 February 1964 stipulated respectively that women and children under the care of the head of family, regardless of their family position, might hold land as independent persons up to the maximum acreage permitted (Lambton, 1969:68). This facilitated, in effect, predatory land transfers within landlord families, hence raising new possibilities for evasion.

Although given five options, the landlords opted for tenancy pro-

Table 4.1 Land redistribution summary, 1962–71

Total peasants with *nasaq* rights, 1962	2,100,028
Peasants acquiring land	
Under phase 1	753,258
Under phase 2	
Owner sale to peasants	57,164
Owner division with peasants	156,279
Under phase 3	
Purchase of 30-year tenancies	738,119
Owner division with peasants	61,805
Total	1,766,625
Peasants holding 99-year *vaqf* leases	172,103
Total beneficiaries of land redistribution	1,938,728
Peasants not obtaining land	161,300
Percentage of *nasaq*-holders obtaining land	92%

Source: Based on figures from the Land Reform Organisation, adapted from Hooglund (1982:table 4, p. 72).

visions (option (3)) in the overwhelming majority of cases. Over 1.3 million peasant households were thus turned into tenant farmers, accounting for as many as 80 per cent of all redistributions in this phase. The landlords clearly favoured this option on the grounds that it enabled them to continue to receive revenue from rents, while still preserving their property rights and titles. By affecting as many as three-quarters of all the estates in the country, this phase firmly established tenancy arrangements as a major form of agricultural tenure by the middle of the 1960s (Ajami, 1973:125; Ashraf and Banuazizi, 1980:33).[7]

By this time, however, growing peasant dissatisfaction with the 'tenancy reforms' of the second stage were beginning to make an impact. In some parts of the country, hostility towards landlords was on the increase, leading many peasants to withhold their rent payments (Momeni, 1980:239–40). To improve the situation, another set of amendments were introduced on 13 January 1969, which came to be known as the third stage of the land reform. These sought to terminate the arrangements for tenancy agreements by extending the provisions for sale and division of land (options (1) and (2) above). The implementation of this stage commenced in the spring of 1969 and continued until September 1971, when the land reform programme was officially declared to have been completed.

By this time, however, there emerged growing signs of a major rethinking by the government in its agricultural policy. Disillusioned with the sluggish performance of an agrarian structure dominated by scattered peasant farming, the state made a new bid at agricultural 'development' and 'modernisation'. As a result, by the early 1970s, it was evident that the development of large-scale commercial farming (farm corporations and agribusiness companies) had taken over as the new priority in agriculture. The main result of this turn-about in official policy, as will be shown later, was to erode some of the earlier achievements of the land reform.

General results

Figures released by the Ministry of Co-operation in 1973 suggest that in its third stage the land reform resulted in the transference of land to 1.2 million peasant households. This consisted of 752,000 cases of land division and 520,000 cases of land sale (Ashraf and Banuazizi, 1980: table 1, p. 34).

According to the Land Reform Organisation, however, at about the same time, land sales under this stage amounted to about 740,000 cases, whereas land division between peasants and landlords amounted to only 62,000 cases (see Table 4.1). Such data inconsistencies, and the fact that the land reform is widely known to have continued beyond its official date of termination, make an overall assessment of redistributions a controversial task. Such difficulty also applies to attempts to evaluate the broader outcomes of the programme.

Some estimates have put the total number of land reform 'beneficiaries' at about 3 million peasant households (World Bank, 1975:68; Amuzegar, 1977:221). This is broadly defined to include all peasants who acquired land either through purchase or the division of private or *awqaf* lands throughout the different stages of the land reform. More recently, Madjd has echoed this figure by referring to the total number of members of the rural co-operative societies by 1977. As membership of one of these societies was by law a prerequisite for receiving land, he has argued that a figure of about 3 million members should give an indication of the 'true' number of land reform beneficiaries (1983:10-12).

Two considerations, however, cast doubt on the validity of this argument. Firstly, as many as nearly 1 million new members (i.e. one-third of the total) joined after the land reform had been officially declared to be complete (that is, between 1972 and 1977). Secondly, after 1974 membership was extended to every rural inhabitant whose activities were directly or indirectly linked to agriculture, regardless of whether they held land, or whether they had received it before or after the land reform (Ashraf and Safaei, 1977:20).

Other estimates, though more conservative, appear to be more credible. Writing in 1973, Ajami cited a figure of 1.4 million peasants (70 per cent of total), while a later estimate by Abrahamian has put the number at 1.6 million (Ajami, 1973:126; Abrahamian, 1980:23). Hooglund, whose results have been reproduced in Table 4.1, subscribes to a figure of just under 2 million, approximately 92 per cent of the original *nasaq*-holding peasants. Furthermore, Ashraf and Banuazizi have argued that although affecting some 90 per cent of all villages, the scope of redistributions did not exceed 40 per cent of all arable land. This is thought to have benefited some 80 per cent of all sharecropping peasants (1980:36–7).

Whatever the true figure may be, it appears that the ultimate outcome of the land reform was to extend ownership among peasants in two principal ways: through the sale of land to occupant sharecroppers, and through division of plots according to the traditional practice of crop division between sharecroppers and landlords.

Despite these redistributions, the land reform left the overall size distribution of landholdings virtually intact. Prior to the reforms, this structure had been heavily dominated by a myriad of small plots: as much as two-thirds of all holdings consisted of units below 5 hectares (Table 4.2). Paradoxically, this feature survived remarkably well: more than a decade later, a similar proportion of all holdings (64.4 per cent) was still below 5 hectares, though in terms of the total area, their share had fallen to 14.8 per cent from 18.7 per cent. Ironical though this may appear, it was brought about by reliance on the existing land boundaries as a basis for redistributions.

Perhaps the land reform's most marked success was the exclusion of the landlords' influence from the countryside. This was evident from the elimination of sharecropping as an institutional practice in Iranian agriculture.[8] Prior to the reforms, this had been customary on as many as 43 per cent of all landholdings which stretched over 55 per cent of the total area of arable land in the country (see Figure 4.2). But with new forms of land tenure and agricultural organisation emerging, it was not long before this practice began to fade away.

Two trends, in particular, emerged in Iranian agriculture in the aftermath of the reforms. On the one hand, spreading peasant proprietorship extended and consolidated family holdings on small and medium farms. This feature, as will be shown, was perhaps the most prominent outcome of the programme.

On the other hand, the land reform encouraged simultaneously the development of commercial farming on large landholdings. This trend had been evident ever since the exemption from redistribution of mechanised lands under the first stage, but was reinforced in the early 1970s, when new directions in government agricultural policy began to

Table 4.2 Size distribution of holdings by number and area, 1960 and 1974

	1960					1974				
	Number		Area		Average size (ha)	Number		Area		Average size (ha)
Size of holding	('000)	(%)	('000 ha)	(%)		('000)	(%)	('000 ha)	(%)	
Small										
Under 1 ha	493	26.3	199	1.7	0.40	734	29.6	260	1.6	0.35
1–2 ha	256	13.6	372	3.3	1.45	322	13.0	444	2.7	1.38
2–5 ha	474	25.2	1,554	13.7	3.3	542	21.8	1,733	10.5	3.2
Under 5 ha	1,223	65.1	2,125	18.7	1.74	1,598	64.4	2,437	14.8	1.52
Medium										
5–10 ha	340	18.1	2,413	21.2	7.1	428	17.2	2,953	18.0	6.9
10–50 ha	301	16.0	5,264	46.3	17.5	428	17.2	7,501	45.7	17.5
5–50 ha	641	34.1	7,677	67.5	12.0	856	34.4	10,454	63.7	12.2
Large										
50–100 ha	8.5	0.5	564	5.0	66.7	16.3	0.7	1,074	6.5	65.9
100 ha and over	4.1	0.2	991	8.7	242.5	9.5	0.4	2,453	15.0	258.2
Over 50 ha	12.6	0.7	1,555	13.7	124.0	25.8	1.1	3,527	21.5	136.7
All holdings with land*	1,877	100.0	11,356	100.0	6.05	2,480	100.0	16,417	100.0	6.6

*Totals may not add up due to rounding.
Sources: Agricultural Census (1960:table 101; 1974:table 15).

Table 4.3 Size distribution of owner-cultivators by number and area of holdings, 1974

Size of holding	Holdings ('000)	(%)	Area ('000)	(%)	Average size (ha)
Under 1 ha	678	29.7	237	1.6	0.35
1–2 ha	292	12.8	402	2.7	1.38
2–5 ha	495	21.7	1,584	10.6	3.20
5–10 ha	400	17.5	2,755	18.5	6.90
10–50 ha	396	17.3	6,923	46.5	17.50
50–100 ha	14	0.6	941	6.3	67.20
100 ha and over	8	0.4	2,035	13.7	254.40
All holdings*	2,282	100.0	14,878	100.0	6.52

*Totals may not add up due to rounding.
Source: Adapted from Agricultural Census (1974:table 88).

place the emphasis on large-scale, plantation-type agribusiness companies and farm corporations.

The extent to which peasant proprietorship developed as a direct outcome of the land reform is clear from Figure 4.2. By 1974, owner-cultivators accounted for a staggering 92 per cent of all landholdings, or the equivalent of 90 per cent of all arable land in the country. This was a remarkable increase over the pre-reform period when this type of tenure had accounted for only 33 and 26 per cent of the total number of holdings and their area of operation respectively. Not all of these, of course, consisted of peasant proprietors; included in this category were also private holders such as the large commercial owners who survived the reforms. A closer look at the size structure of lands operated by owners sheds more light on this point.

Table 4.3 shows that an overwhelming majority of owner-cultivated holdings consisted of small plots: nearly 65 per cent were under 5 hectares, and as many as 82 per cent under 10 hectares. Predominance in terms of numbers, however, was not matched with a proportional share in the total area: over 1.4 million units of the former size group accounted for as little as 15 per cent of the area operated by all owner-cultivators. Similarly, the share of the latter group did not exceed one-third of the total. Peasant family-holders were predominant among these two size groups of lands but some were also established on medium-sized farms of between 10 and 50 hectares. Altogether it would appear that there were in the region of some 2 million peasant family proprietors in Iran after the implementation of the land reform, operating between one-third and one-half of the total area of arable land in the country.[9] This confirms the point made earlier that, despite the anomalies of the second

78 Labour transfer and economic development

Table 4.4 Marketing agricultural surplus by size of holdings, 1974

Size of holding	Annual crops			Perennial crops		
	A (%)	B (%)	C (%)	A (%)	B (%)	C (%)
Under 1 ha	55.5	25.9	18.6	47.7	25.5	26.8
1-2 ha	39.5	28.5	32.0	47.5	22.5	30.0
2-5 ha	51.1	26.6	22.3	51.2	26.5	22.3
5-10 ha	59.2	26.5	14.3	52.8	25.2	22.0
10-50 ha	48.4	28.2	23.4	54.4	24.5	21.1
50-100 ha	1.0	1.9	97.1	2.8	2.6	94.6
100 ha and over	3.0	0.2	96.8	0.0	0.4	99.6
All holdings	51.0	26.7	22.3	49.5	24.9	25.6

A = Marketing no produce at all.
B = Marketing less than half of their produce.
C = Marketing half or more of their produce.
Source: Agricultural Census (1974: table 9).

stage, the land reform had firmly established small family-holders at the heart of Iran's structure of land tenure by the early 1970s.

For the most part, these small farms were subsistence operations with a limited degree of market integration. According to one source, although small farms below 10 hectares produced 40 per cent of gross agricultural output, their share of the total marketed surplus in 1972 was no more than 19 per cent (Aresvik, 1976:116). For large farms, in contrast, specialisation for the market was an almost universal rule. This picture is also confirmed by the data in Table 4.4.

It can be seen that 97 per cent of the largest holdings (in excess of 50 hectares) which produced annual crops, reported sales of half or more of their produce. Small units, on the contrary, were self-sufficient family-enclaves whose production was largely oriented towards meeting their subsistence requirements. Of all units below 1 hectare, more than half (55.5 per cent) produced too little to sell anything on the market; about one in four reported sales of less than half their produce; while fewer than one in five (18.6 per cent) were engaged in sales exceeding one-half of their produce. In the intermediate range, too, market specialisation appears to have been very limited: 70-85 per cent of all farms up to 50 hectares sold either no produce at all or less than half of it. Also reflecting this inward orientation was the fact that peasant-holders relied heavily on family members to meet their labour requirements – a point which is taken up in more detail in the next chapter.

Polarisation was not confined to tenure structure as a closer look at changes in the average size of holdings will reveal. The earlier-mentioned constancy of the overall size distribution of holdings concealed an undercurrent of consolidation and centralisation in which the average size of small farms was getting smaller, while that of large commercial farms was growing. A close look at Table 4.2 shows that the mean size for the smallest plots (those below 1 hectare) declined from 0.40 hectare in 1960 to 0.35 hectare in 1974; and for those between 1 and 2 hectares, it declined to 1.38 hectares (from 1.45 hectares). The average for farms of over 100 hectares, in contrast, grew by about 6.5 per cent to reach 258.2 hectares, increasing considerably their share in the total arable area (from 13.7 to 21.5 per cent). For farms in the intermediate range (2–100 hectares), however, there was no notable change.

Thus, if in its implicit objective of breaking down the power of the landowning class the land reform had been largely successful, in its stated objective of spreading the benefits of landownership to peasants, the balance sheet was far less impressive. Less than fifteen years after its implementation, the general pattern of landholding in the country was more unequal than before.[10] This was perhaps a paradoxical outcome for a programme which had originally set out to extend ownership among the peasantry.

Some reflections on the causes of the land reform

Most explanations of the causes of the Iranian land reform fall into one of two broad categories: situational/conjunctural, or structural analyses.[11] The former focuses on the timing of the land reform and the specific conditions surrounding its introduction – most notably, the crisis of the early 1960s, the Kennedy Administration, and the alleged threat of peasant rebellions – whereas the latter attributes its implementation to the deeper structural undercurrents of Iranian capitalism necessitating the removal of any fetters to its future advance. That these two approaches have been generally presented as competing paradigms points to an unfortunate gap in the literature in what is possibly its most widely debated aspect to date.

There is little doubt that, from a long-term or strategic point of view, some form of land reform was necessary for the future development of capitalism in Iran. This is because a 'successful' agrarian reform plays the historical role of laying the foundations for a new socioeconomic order in a number of important ways: breaking down the traditional bondage of peasants to landlords, extending specialisation and the division of labour, deepening the home market, attracting investment funds into agriculture, and providing the required supplies of labour – in all, the removal of any obstacles to the expansion of capital in the town and country.

It was this historical setting that, translated into the Iranian context, required the dislodging of the economic and political influence of the all-powerful landowning class in the country. Their firm grip over social and economic life in rural areas had to be broken if capital accumulation were to proceed unhindered, if resources were to flow between towns and the countryside, and if archaic relations on the land were to give way to new, revolutionary methods of production.

This is why, in its initial drive under the first stage, the state made considerable efforts to transform the landlords either into commercial farmers by providing them incentives to mechanise their land, or to turn them into successful entrepreneurs by offering them, as recompense, shares in industrial establishments in towns. The considerable political fervour aroused among the peasantry, aimed shrewdly at disarming the landlords and breaking down any possible resistance put up by them. The tactical nature of this course of action became clear as soon as the first major signs of 'success' emerged: the popular climate surrounding the reforms subsided swiftly, giving way to a far more measured pace of events.

'Inevitable' though this may be considered from a long-term point of view, however, it does not provide an adequate explanation of the character and timing of the reforms. Paradoxically, there is no evidence to suggest that agricultural production in general, or food output in particular, experienced any major difficulties around this time. Nor, as discussions in the next chapter demonstrate, were there any signs of labour shortages to necessitate labour release from the countryside. In either case, even if any such conditions did exist, it could be argued that a stream of stable and growing oil revenues since the mid-1950s could have been used to alleviate the situation by allowing for greater importation of food and, if necessary, labour from abroad.

If exclusive concentration on the structural level fails to capture the detail and the timing of the reforms, to judge them solely by the conjunctural setting would be equally unsatisfactory. Firstly, the deeper structural underpinnings of change are lost sight of at the expense of concentration on the surface. Secondly, the evaluation of the outcome must necessarily be favourable: there is no doubt that judging by the economic crisis of the early 1960s, or by the American pressure, the reforms went through with a great deal of success.[12] But this is far from the truth.

Ultimately, it is a synthesis of the above two approaches that is capable of offering a satisfactory explanation of the origins of Iran's land reform. Such an approach must be based on the recognition of the structural roots of these reforms, but must allow also for the specificity of the circumstances which saw their introduction and implementation. The breadth of the reform package itself attests to this: ranging from the extension of suffrage rights to women to a programme of land redistributions, the package manifested in part its strategically reformist overtures, and in part its *ad hoc* nature in response to the specific conditions of the time.

Summary and conclusion

This chapter examines some of the main characteristics and outcomes of Iran's programme of land reform. The first stage began in 1962 with the Land Reform Law which required all landlords to sell their holdings in excess of one village. The redistribution of the purchased properties among sitting peasants was a key factor in the government's bid to curb the political and economic power of big landlords. This phase came to an abrupt end, when, reflecting a major rethinking of the programme, the Additional Articles of July 1964 were introduced. Signalling major concessions to landlords, peasants were offered security of *tenure* rather than *ownership* under the second stage. These amendments gave rise to growing peasant dissatisfaction, as a result of which open hostility towards the landlords and their property increased. Apprehensive of this potentially destabilising situation, the government decided finally in 1969 to introduce another stage, known as the third, under which tenants were given the opportunity to purchase directly from the owners the land which they rented.

Over a decade, up to 2 million peasant households acquired land – representing 80–90 per cent of all *nasaq*-holding peasants. Of these, about one-third purchased land during the first stage, when conditions were more favourable for them. The remainder consisted mainly of land sales or divisions in the third stage.

Two main trends emerged as a direct result of these changes. Firstly, peasant proprietorship was established as a major feature of the new system of land tenure in the countryside. Some three-quarters of all holdings were operated by small and medium family-cultivators, accounting for one-third to one-half of all arable lands in the country. Growing in number but shrinking in average size, these were largely self-sufficient production units with a limited degree of market integration.

Secondly, the land reform also consolidated extensive farming on large capitalist farms. This was evident from the first stage with important concessions granted to large commercial owners, but the main thrust came in the late 1960s and early 1970s with new directions in the government's agricultural policy.

The next chapter takes up the impact of this programme on rural

82 Labour transfer and economic development

labour by focusing on the ways in which changes in property rights affected the demand for and the supply of rural workers.

Notes

1. This programme consisted of a six-point package of wide-ranging reforms dubbed 'The White Revolution'. Apart from the land reform, other items included were: (1) workers' participation in the profits of industrial enterprises, (2) setting up education, health, and development corps, (3) nationalisation of water and forest resources, (4) extension of suffrage rights to women, and (5) a number of administrative reforms.
2. See the discussion in Chapter 3, which traces the rise and consolidation of a private landowning class in Iran to developments at the end of the nineteenth and the beginning of the twentieth centuries.
3. A *qanat* is the traditional underground channel that brings water to the surface.
4. *Dang* commonly refers to any one of the six parts into which village agricultural land is divided.
5. See Ashraf and Banuazizi (1980:30), for the former view. Most of the radical critics of the programme would come under the latter group. Platt (1970) has also expressed similar criticism, though from a technical point of view.
6. Lambton (1969) and Warriner (1970) for the most explicit formulation of this point of view. The Fedaii Guerrillas also seem to accept this point to some extent: 'The division of land in this [first] stage, compared with subsequent stages, had a rather decisive impact on the eradication of large-scale land ownership – although in practice some landlords managed to find ways of dodging the reforms' (OIPFG, no. 1:32).
7. Next most popular with the landlords was the option for division (10 per cent of all), whereas sales of land under this stage accounted for a mere 3.7 per cent of all redistributions (Denman, 1973:338–9).
8. *Instances* of sharecropping were still observable throughout the 1960s and were in fact accentuated by the labour shortages of the post-1973 period, a point discussed in Chapter 6. It was sharecropping as an *institutional* practice which was brought down with the fall of the old system.
9. Based on Table 4.3 and Figure 4.2. This is most probably an underestimation given the extensive parcelling of lands under the medium and large categories.
10. This is seen by estimates of the Gini coefficient on size distribution of landholdings, which increased from 0.6 in 1960 to 0.65 by 1974 (Azimi, 1982:161–3).
11. There is a large body of literature dealing with this aspect of the land reform. For a typical statement of the former school, see Mahdavy (1965), and to some extent Lambton (1969). For the latter school, see Halliday (1979), Momeni (1980), OIPFG (no. 1), and Sodagar (n.d.), among many others. For a condensed, though rhetorical, review of the position taken by the various groups within the Iranian Left, see *Kando Kav* (1977:8–9).
12. Even less persuasive is the argument that the land reform in Iran sought to contain the 'threat' posed by the peasantry. It is hard to find credible evidence for any challenge – actual or potential – posed to the authorities by the peasantry at the time. For a history of 'non-revolutionary' peasantry in Iran, see Kazemi and Abrahamian (1978).

5
Agrarian change II: labour and the land reform

Introduction

The impact of the land reform on rural labour was not realised until the programme was well under way. Even then the effect was not uniform throughout the various stages.[1]

As in most programmes of change and reorganisation, the full and immediate impact was first made on those traditional occupations, some of them centuries old, which had been the pillars of the old regime.

The elimination of the landlords' influence, for instance, undermined, directly or indirectly, the position of a host of landlord-related functionaries, who had acted as indispensable elements of the old system. Chief among these were *mubashirs* (bailiffs), *zabets* (landowner agents and/or harvest controllers), and to some extent even *kadkhudas* (village headmen), whose position, though not necessarily their personal influence in village life as elder trustees, was gradually undermined by the expanding organs and apparatus of the state.[2]

Various other traditional functions and occupations on the land succumbed to the process of change, which affected the organisation of production and tenurial system. The utilisation of tractors, for instance, did away with the jobs and responsibilities of *somkars* and *rabanis* (permanent farm hands with primary responsibility for ploughing and threshing) in the Khuzistan plain, while irrigation improvements in the same province eliminated the customary function of *sarbildars* (canal cleaners) (Salmanzadeh, 1980:78, 188, 193). Elsewhere, *dashtbans'* (harvest overseers or field guards) traditional functions gave way to new developments as, according to Hooglund, the new peasant proprietors camped with their families in their fields in order to protect their own produce at harvest time (1975:166).

The overall impact of the land reform, nevertheless, went well beyond these changes: restructuring property rights and reshaping tenurial relations, its implementation had far-reaching effects on the general mode of economic activity in rural areas. This chapter seeks to demonstrate that, as a result of this programme, rural employment opportunities deteriorated substantially – a process which contributed decisively to the release of considerable supplies of labour from agriculture as a principal sector of economic activity. There were two mechanisms behind this. Firstly, by spreading landlessness among some rural sections, it expanded considerably the size of a relative surplus population on the land. Secondly, through a contraction of the demand for wage labour, it paved the way for the subsequent transfer of this population to the urban areas.

These two processes are studied in turn below. A final section questions the extent to which such results may be considered to have been the intended objectives of the land reform.

Factors affecting the supply of labour[3]

Despite spreading landownership among certain categories of peasant families, as discussed in the previous chapter, the land reform also accentuated a growing trend of landlessness among some other sections of the rural population. Chief among these were agricultural workers, who proved to be the main 'non-beneficiaries' of the programme. Their outright exclusion since the first stage made them legally and finally landless. Next were those peasant families who were eligible to receive land although they never did, followed by those who were given some land but could not subsequently maintain it.

It was essentially among these groups, as well as those who continued to operate small plots, that a substantial pool of rural labour took shape in the decade following the reforms. With declining labour demand in the agricultural sector, conditions were ripe for the release and transfer elsewhere of this surplus population. Let us first consider how labour was cut loose from the land.

Agricultural workers

Few observers of Iran's land reform would disagree that ultimately it was agricultural workers who had to bear the main burden of economic and social dislocation caused by the land reform. Their situation deteriorated decisively in the post-reform period, partly because of an increase in their numbers, and partly because their raised expectations of receiving land were quickly dashed. The combined effect was particularly harsh at a time when the demand for their services started to decline.

In the traditional village stratification before the reforms, agricultural workers were known to be an important section of the *khowshneshin* population.[4] These workers lived and worked in the village but did not own any land. They were hired to carry out specific tasks on the land in return for a wage. Those who were paid in cash were known as *kargaran-e keshavarzi;* those who received wages in kind (as a share of produce) were referred to as *barzegaran*. What united them with the rest of the *khowshneshins* at large was their status of being landless. They were also distinguished from occupying peasants by the fact that they did not entertain any customary rights or titles to land, nor did they own any other 'elements' of agricultural production than their labour. According to one estimate, the total number of these workers and their families amounted to some 6 million which accounted for 80 per cent of all *khowshneshins,* 'fully one-third of Iran's total rural population' at the time when the land reform went into effect (Hooglund, 1973:236).

Under Article 16 of the original Land Reform Law (January 1962), persons living in a village who were not engaged in the cultivation of the soil were virtually excluded from the categories of persons entitled to receive land. A further amendment in the second stage similarly excluded vegetable growers and summer croppers who were not domiciled in the village (Article 28 of this stage; see Moridi, 1979:207). Some hopes were, however, raised in March 1962 when a ruling by the Land Reform Council made it a matter of agreement between the peasants of a village and its *khowshneshin* inhabitants to include the latter among those holding a share in village ploughlands. Under these circumstances, interested parties could, by agreement, revise and change the *nasaq* of the village before proceeding to the transfer of land. These hopes were, however, undermined rapidly with a further ruling on 27 January 1963, which barred daily labourers working on the land growing pistachio nut trees from receiving any benefits from land redistributions. It was the spirit of this latter ruling that continued to guide the theory and practice of land reform in the coming years: non-sitting peasants and workers were systematically excluded after that (Lambton, 1969:75; also Maclachlan, 1968:694-5).

The fate of agricultural workers in Iran thus compared unfavourably with similar groups in other UDCs with a comparable land reform programme. Whereas some form of a minimum protection was granted elsewhere,[5] in Iran they were given 'no protection – no minimum wage, no unemployment compensation, no gleaning rights on the now private fields, and no land' (Keddie, 1972:392).

Although some commentators have justified the exclusion of

agricultural workers from the framework of Iran's land reform either on practical or financial grounds,[6] the potential implications of this for the labour situation in the countryside cannot be ignored.

Agricultural workers and non-sitting peasants formed a substantial labour pool from which the labour requirements of Iranian agriculture could be met. To have pursued a policy of uniting them with their means of production (land) could have arguably had deleterious effects both on the availability of labour and its price in the years to come. Even though not of immediate practical concern at that conjuncture, a measure of such foresight cannot be denied of Iranian policy-makers.[7]

Evictions and general departure from the land

At the same time as aggravating the economic position of farm labourers, the land reform programme also accentuated a general trend of landlessness among some sections of the peasant population. This stemmed not so much from the outright exclusions as from the manner in which the programme was implemented.

There were two main mechanisms in which peasant expropriations took place. Firstly, from the existing loopholes within the framework of the land reform law and the landlords' bid to exploit them. In such cases peasants who were legally entitled to receive land were evicted from their lands by landlords in a variety of ways ranging from coercion to enticement. Secondly, the ability to operate and maintain land often fell short of the initial optimism surrounding the new ownership of land. A number of factors were crucial in this respect: the size and quality of land received and the means of production available. Thus the pressure to leave land could be as compelling for peasants who received inadequate or poor quality lands as for those who did not receive any land at all. Both these mechanisms merit closer attention.

The first group of peasants affected adversely were those who, by misfortune, happened to work the lands that the landowner chose to retain for himself – a practice that was allowed under provisions specified by the original Land Reform Law. Losing their land rights, they either became agricultural labourers working in the village or had to leave it in search of jobs in nearby towns and factories (Craig, 1978:145, for a case in Shiraz province). As seen in the previous chapter, further legislation under the second stage increased possibilities for evasion by allowing the transfer of land ownership to landlords' wives and children. Unfortunate peasants who worked on these lands were denied their tenancy rights and were subsequently evicted. This practice was greatly enhanced by further abuses on the part of the landlords who resorted to ante-dating the transfer or sale of some lands. In some areas (notably in Kirman and to a lesser extent in Isfahan) this was seen to be a thriving practice by the landlords, 'possibly with the connivance of officials' (Lambton, 1969:147).

Provisions for mechanised lands created yet another set of loopholes. Firstly, the earlier-stipulated ceiling of 500 hectares was effectively relaxed in the second stage. Secondly, ambiguity surrounding the definition of 'mechanised' lands enticed many unscrupulous landowners to try to place their land outside the operation of the land reform by ploughing it by tractor once, hence declaring the peasants to be agricultural labourers (Lambton, 1969:196; OIPFG, no. 3:29). This practice was widely observed in many parts of the country, often facilitated by peasants' ignorance of their rights.[8]

Aside from loopholes and evasions, the terms under which lands were redistributed enhanced differentiation of the peasantry. In its extreme form this process caused the ejection of some peasants from the land.

The fact that redistributions were based on peasants' customary tenancy rights meant the system carried an in-built differentiating element from the start. The quantity and quality of land operated by peasants varied widely across the country, and to have used the prevailing patterns as a basis inevitably meant the institutionalisation of ownership disparities. Where new ownership of land fell well short of securing for peasants an adequate living, the pressure to leave land could be as strong as that of receiving no land at all (Lambton, 1969:146; OIPFG, no. 4).

Related to this, the fertility of the soil varied on different lands. Under the traditional system, periodic redistribution of land especially among *boneh* members had been a common practice. This took place every three to four years and provided peasants with a degree of social protection against variations in the quality of the soil.

The attitude of the land reform towards this well established agricultural practice was unsympathetic. Under the terms of the original law, peasants had to content themselves with the piece of land they happened to be working on that particular year. Besides, the same law abolished altogether the periodic redistribution of peasant lands (Lambton, 1969:75, 132). A combination of these two rulings struck hard against those peasants who were, by bad luck, operating the more infertile lands at the time.

As in the case of peasants with insufficient land, inferiority of land quality often posed serious problems for peasant families struggling to meet their subsistence requirements (Craig, 1978:146). The situation was made better if some family members had access to short-term occupations on nearby farms or in towns. In many instances, however, selling land rights appeared to be a more practical, albeit temporary, alternative to poverty and destitution among peasant families, who departed to towns in quest of a new livelihood.

In this, peasants were aided by landlords, who resorted to a variety of methods to secure the purchase of their land titles. In some instances, they would go as far as discontinuing water supplies, or even withholding seed from peasants in order to sabotage their production. In other cases, landlords enticed peasants by promising to continue to employ them as agricultural workers if they agreed to sell them their (insufficient) lands (Lambton, 1969:253-5).

Given the strategic importance of water in Iranian agriculture, it is perhaps not surprising that the ultimate success or failure of the land reform depended closely on the distribution of water rights.[9] In northern provinces, particularly those along the Caspian littoral, land reform seems to have progressed more smoothly with generally more favourable results for the peasantry than elsewhere. Here a combination of temperate climate and plentiful rainfall increased peasants' motivation to work hard from an early stage: the result was often an extension of the area under cultivation (Warriner, 1970:609-10). Elsewhere, the outcome was more varied as the peasants' struggle over the provision and control of irrigation sources turned into a bitter struggle for survival.

In general, in those villages which depended on a stream, river, or spring, peasants usually continued to observe the traditional water schedules. The situation was also similar in villages which had been traditionally dependent upon *qanat* irrigation, but where the whole of the village passed into peasant ownership after the land reform. Here they could combine to meet maintenance costs of *qanats* formerly paid by the landowners; or they could carry out some of the repairs themselves.

More serious problems, however, arose in places where the landlord continued to hold part of the village for himself. This put him in a formidable position to exert pressure on peasants by charging exorbitant water fees (Hooglund, 1975:149), or reducing its rotation time (Lambton, 1969:287), or even withholding its supply.[10] The impact was particularly damaging to those peasants who had leased their land under the second stage. Similarly, where land was divided up, the sinking of power-operated deep wells exerted adverse pressure on the contiguous peasant plots (see Lambton, 1969:289; OIPFG, no. 4:19, 98-9, for instances of this in Kirman villages).

The decay and ruinous conditions of many *qanats* also worked against the interests of peasants in many parts of the country. According to the original Land Reform Law, it was incumbent on the landlords to pay for the repair and upkeep of *qanats* and other irrigation works in keeping with the local customs. In practice, uncertainty governing property rights checked new investment by landlords, culminating in widespread peasant outcries against landowners who allowed *qanats* to lie in ruin and decay (Lambton, 1969:284–5 reports cases in the province of Isfahan).

To sum up, it was a wide range of practices governing the distribution of lands, combined with the outright exclusion of agricultural workers, that exacerbated landlessness in Iran's countryside. The result was a constantly expanding surplus population in floating form, ready for transfer to other economic sectors.

Factors affecting the demand for labour

The picture would be incomplete without an examination of the conditions determining the demand for agricultural labour. Had, for instance, the absorptive capacity of the rural farm or non-farm sectors been expanding sufficiently, the surplus population thus created could have been taken up elsewhere in the rural economy, thus reducing the pressure of departures to towns. The resulting labour transfer in this case would have been limited to an intra-rural sectoral allocation of labour rather than rural-to-urban migration.

Quite the contrary, this section argues that deteriorating demand conditions after the reforms in general accentuated proletarianisation in the countryside, paving the way for the ultimate departure of landless households throughout the 1960s. The demand for wage labour, in particular, declined appreciably as a result of the same process of institutional change, which brought about new forms of production relations in the countryside.

This study will be conducted in two ways: firstly by looking at intensive family farming on small and medium farms; secondly by an examination of extensive farming on the large capitalist farms and agricultural joint-stock companies (agribusinesses and farm corporations).

Intensive family farming

The type of labour use prevalent on lands operated by Iran's new class of peasant proprietors mirrored their limited overall market integration. Table 5.1 shows that an overwhelming majority of these holdings relied heavily on family members for their labour requirements: as many as 94 per cent of all holdings in the country were either wholly or predominantly based on family labour. The extent of this reliance varied, of course, with the size of holdings. Large units were, in general, less dependent on this form of labour, whereas small holdings were almost entirely dependent upon it. The use of wage labour, in contrast, seems to

90 Labour transfer and economic development

Table 5.1 Labour use by size of holdings, 1974

Size of holding	Wholly based on family labour ('000)	(%)	Predominantly based on family labour ('000)	(%)	Predominantly based on wage labour ('000)	(%)
Under 1 ha	549	74.8	153	20.8	33	4.4
1–2 ha	197	61.2	111	34.5	14	4.3
2–5 ha	331	61.1	185	34.2	25	4.7
5–10 ha	235	54.9	174	40.7	18	4.3
10–50 ha	189	44.2	207	48.4	31	7.3
50–100 ha	3	17.8	7	45.4	6	36.8
100 ha and over	1	10.5	3	27.4	6	63.0
All holdings*	1,506	60.7	841	33.9	133	5.4

*Totals may not add up due to rounding.
Source: Agricultural Census (1974:table 7).

have remained very limited: in general only one in twenty (5.4 per cent) of all holdings in the country were predominantly based on wage labour. Although the proportion rose to about two-thirds on the large units (in excess of 100 hectares), for the greatest majority of holdings this ratio was no higher than about one in twenty.

Moreover, in Iran as elsewhere, smaller family farms were characterised by intensive methods of farming (see, e.g., Kautsky's 'Agrarian question' in Banaji, 1980:74–7). Table 5.2 provides some broad indications of this by farm size in 1974. It may be seen that the proportion of fallow land for small plots (below 1 hectare) did not exceed 11.4 per cent of their total area. This proportion rose consistently with farm size, reaching 40–45 per cent for holdings above 50 hectares.

Similarly, there was a wide variation in gross output per hectare of different sized operations. For wheat and barley, which are mainly dry-farmed in Iran, this tendency was most marked: indicating a proportionately higher input of human labour, output per hectare on the smallest farms was between two and three times the average. At the other end, on the largest farms (over 100 hectares, most notably), gross output per hectare also increased, but this time possibly as a result of greater use of fertiliser and machinery. Rice, in contrast, showed a more stable relationship between yield and size of operation.[11]

Prior to the reforms, small farms relied, albeit to a limited extent, on casual wage labour for simple tasks (such as weeding and hand harvesting), especially at peak harvest times. This practice was reportedly disrupted after the reforms as family members took over functions previously performed by wage-labourers.

Labour and the land reform 91

Table 5.2 Broad indicators of the intensity of cultivation by size of holdings, 1974

Size of holding	Fallow land as % of total arable land	Wheat kg/ha	Wheat Ratio to average	Barley kg/ha	Barley Ratio to average	Rice kg/ha	Rice Ratio to average
Under 1 ha	11.4	1,594	3.3	1,424	2.7	2,719	1.2
1–2 ha	18.5	973	2.0	995	1.9	2,466	1.1
2–5 ha	26.8	659	1.4	611	1.1	2,291	1.0
5–10 ha	34.3	480	1.0	460	0.9	2,301	1.0
10–50 ha	37.9	346	0.7	385	0.7	1,909	0.8
50–100 ha	40.0	530	1.1	574	1.1	2,703	1.2
100 ha and over	44.5	690	1.4	1,073	2.0	1,746	0.7
All holdings	36.3	483	1.0	535	1.0	2,337	1.0

*Excluding fallow land.
Source: Agricultural Census (1974:tables 15, 140, 164, 188).

This new development reflected a deeper current of social change in the countryside. As some sociological studies of Iran's villages have reported, there were growing signs of a deepening social rift between the new peasant proprietors and the excluded agricultural workers in the aftermath of the reforms. In his study of the *Sheshdangi* village in the Fars province, for instance, Ajami documents a growing trend of mutual distrust between these two social groups. Agricultural workers resented having been left out of the framework of the land reform. For their part, peasants exercised caution in employing wage workers – a reluctance which revealed not just cost considerations, but also their apprehension lest farm workers develop *nasaq* rights on their lands (Ajami, 1977:46–7, 91, 112).[12] This situation contrasted sharply with the village solidarity prior to land reform, when *nasaq*-holding peasants reportedly offered landless farm workers casual employment not infrequently out of altruistic considerations.[13]

Competition over non-farm casual work could only exacerbate this rift. With possibly as high as 65–85 per cent of Iran's peasantry in need of supplementary income, such competition was particularly fierce in areas nearer towns, factories or other sources of temporary wage-paid employment.[14]

Finally, at a time when agriculture as a whole was losing population, small family plots were seeing an increased concentration of the rural workforce.

As Table 5.3 suggests, between 1960 and 1974 the concentration of

Table 5.3 Farm population per hectare of land by size of holdings, 1960 and 1974

Size of holding	Working-age population* 1960	1974	Total population 1960	1974
Under 1 ha	5.40	7.56	10.90	11.70
1–2 ha	2.25	2.25	3.50	3.50
2–5 ha	1.16	0.99	1.60	1.60
5–10 ha	0.50	0.48	0.77	0.77
10–50 ha	0.24	0.21	0.37	0.34
50–100 ha	0.11	0.07	0.17	0.12
100 ha and over	0.03	0.02	0.04	0.02
All holdings	0.58	0.48	0.87	0.89

*Refers to those 10 years of age and over.
Sources: Agricultural Census (1960:tables 101 and 301; 1974:tables 3 and 15).

population in general, and population of working age in particular, either stagnated or declined on most lands with the exception of small holdings. In 1960, the population/land ratio on small plots (of less than 1 hectare) had been 5.4 persons per hectare, already eight times higher than the overall average density on all lands. By 1974, this ratio had gone up to 7.6 persons per hectare, exceeding by fourteen times the average density of working-age population on all lands. As noted by an ILO study in the early 1970s, this trend reflected 'the absorption on small family plots . . . of farm children reaching labour force age who have no more rewarding employment opportunities elsewhere' (Bartsch, 1970a:17).

In summary, the formation of a peasant proprietor class in Iran had the major effect of displacing casual wage labour with family labour, creating a social rift between these two rural groups, and intensifying their competition over casual non-farm work elsewhere in the rural economy. Under these conditions, the greater burden of adjustments fell upon agricultural workers, whose general response was often to depart for towns in large numbers.

Mechanisation and extensive capitalist farming

Increased possibilities for evasion under provisions allowed for mechanisation since the inception of land reform combined with an active government policy of promoting the use of agricultural machinery in later stages explain the consistently growing trend of mechanisation in Iranian agriculture.

Table 5.4 The distribution of lands ploughed by tractor by size of holdings, 1960 and 1974

Size of holding	Number of holdings*				Area‡		
	1960		1974		1974		
	Total ('000)	% of total	Total ('000)	% of total	% change over 1960†	Total ('000)	% of total
Under 1 ha	13	2.6	110	15.0	761	44	16.8
1–2 ha	25	9.7	104	32.4	318	109	24.8
2–5 ha	53	11.2	255	47.0	380	652	37.6
5–10 ha	37	11.0	273	63.9	635	1,420	48.0
10–50 ha	49	16.0	315	73.6	548	4,205	56.0
50–100 ha	2	28.0	15	91.5	522	783	73.0
100 ha and over	3	64.0	9	96.0	248	2,034	83.0
All holdings	182	9.7	1,081	43.6	495	9,247	56.0

*Refers only to those units which had reported the use of tractors.
†Accurate estimates. Rounding errors eliminated.
‡Data for 1960 are not available.
Sources: Agricultural Census (1960:table 127; 1974:table 260).

This trend is seen in two ways: growing tractor imports and the diffusion of their usage in Iranian agriculture. As for the former, data suggest that, allowing for some annual fluctuations, there was a clear upward trend between 1964/5 and the early 1970s. By 1972/3, the annual value of tractors imported had risen to almost three times their initial level in this period. The biggest increase came in 1972/3, when expenditure on imports more than doubled in one year (Nowshirvani, 1976:25–7).

A similar picture emerges from an examination of data on the actual spread of tractor use in the countryside (Table 5.4). In 1960, less than one in ten holdings reported the use of tractors for ploughing land; by 1974, the proportion had risen to one out of every 2.3 holdings – a staggering increase of about 400 per cent. Although lack of data prevents a similar point being verified with respect to the area of land affected, it seems almost certain that the extent of increase must have been substantial. By 1974, indeed, over half of the total area of arable land in the country was ploughed by tractors.

The rate of diffusion was even more impressive on small holdings. On holdings below 1 hectare, tractor use increased by as much as 750 per cent – well above the increase for any other size groups. Although low base-levels are to some extent behind these high growth rates, all indications are that tractor *use* was nevertheless, spreading fast.

Joint ownership of tractors seems to have contributed to this trend, as

94 Labour transfer and economic development

by 1971 it affected more than one-third of all tractors in the country (Nowshirvani, 1976:21). Such ownership enabled small farmers, sometimes assisted by government loans, to spread the initial purchase price and subsequent operating costs among themselves. It also increased the machines' capacity utilisation. Moreover, aided by stable tractor rental prices, contract work was also spreading rapidly. This was, in turn, brought about by a combination of factors such as increased government subsidies, stable fuel costs, and the greater availability of spare parts and maintenance services. As a result, throughout the decade following the land reform, the tractor rental rates remained stable in the region of about 450–600 Rials per hectare, depending on the geographical location of the lands and the type of machinery used (Nowshirvani, 1976:23).

This said, however, the impact of mechanisation on labour cannot be taken for granted on an *a priori* basis. A more widespread use of machinery may, for instance, increase, rather than decrease, the demand for labour if it increases (sufficiently) the area under cultivation. Instances of this have been reported in areas such as the Indian state of Punjab (Sinha, 1973:406–7, 416–18) and indeed in the Gorgan province of Iran prior to the introduction of land reform (Okazaki, 1968:42). Similar results may be achieved if mechanisation improves the possibilities of multiple cropping by speeding up the harvest and minimising attrition in yields. Alternatively, however, mechanisation may be dislocating labour through substitution of machinery. Even then labour replacement in a particular operation or for a particular crop is not to be identified with the displacement of labour from agriculture in general (Abercrombie, 1972:26). The outcome would depend on the type of mechanisation, the type of agricultural operations affected, and the type of land covered.

To start with, mechanisation is not limited to increased use of tractors. It may include a host of other manual or power operated equipment and tools ranging from fruit and seed dryers, seed drills, and threshers to combine harvesters and fertiliser distributors. Besides, agricultural production varies greatly in nature involving such detailed operations as ploughing, sowing, interculture, irrigation, harvesting, threshing, and so on. The net result of mechanisation would thus depend not only on the type of machinery used but also on the nature of operations involved. The use of combine harvesters, for instance, is generally known to make operations much less dependent on labour. In contrast, tube-well irrigation is widely recognised as being capable of increasing the area under cultivation and hence possibly increasing the demand for labour (see Agarwal, 1981, for the Indian experience).

In Iran, ploughing on small and, to some extent, medium farms was traditionally carried out by draught animals. To this effect, the spread of tractor use on these holdings must be regarded as primarily animal- rather than labour-replacing. Indicating this, the proportion of small holdings without draught animals increased between 1960 and 1974 from 86 to 92 per cent for lands below 1 hectare, and from 65 to 73 per cent for those between 1 and 2 hectares (*Kando Kav,* 1978:40).[15]

On the large lands, however, available indicators point to considerable displacement of labour brought about by a greater use of agricultural machinery.

One study of three villages in Azerbaijan in 1970 found that the introduction of new machinery had resulted in the loss of about 120 days of labour-time, about one-eighth of the total labour input in the preceding year (Hooglund, 1975:154-9). According to another study, full mechanisation of wheat production in the Marvdasht plain (in Fars) in the early 1970s reduced labour requirements by 131 hours per hectare per year. This was a considerable loss of demand for labour considering that, altogether, wheat and barley accounted for over 82 per cent of the total hectareage in the region (Soltanie, 1974:46-8). Similarly, in most villages operated by ex-landlords in the province of Fars, which were surveyed by the Organisation of Iranian People's Fedaii Guerillas (OIPFG), plough- ing and harvesting were reported to have been almost totally mechanised. This led many agricultural workers to complain about the loss of their jobs (OIPFG, no. 3:32-3, 43, 192).

Still in this province, the case of a large farm in the late 1960s perhaps best illustrates the situation prevalent on many mechanised lands in the country. Before the land reform, the landlord drew his labour require- ments from a total of about sixty sharecropping families. After the reforms, with two tractors ploughing the entire land and all the wheat and barley harvested by combines, no more than two drivers and four other full-time members of staff were necessary for running the same farm (Hakimi *et al.,* 1969:33-4).

A general belief in the inherent advantages of very large mechanised farming formed the basis of two other government policies introduced in the latter stages of the land reform. Both aimed at creating fully mechanised and highly integrated farming units. The law for the formation of Farm Corporations (1967) sought to do this on the holdings previously distributed to peasants, while the law for the establishment of agribusiness companies (1968) was aimed at areas newly brought under irrigation through the construction of large dams. A separate study of the labour and employment impacts of each one of these two schemes is necessary before the overall effect of extensive farming can be concluded.

Agribusiness companies

Agribusiness companies, initiated as public or private joint ventures with foreign capital, were the clearest examples of the uprooting of the peasantry from their traditional lands. In what appeared to be integrated programmes in selected areas, whole villages were razed to the ground with the intention of setting up large-scale mechanised farms specialising in a wide range of operations in agricultural production and industrial processing. Each unit covered a minimum area of 5,000 hectares and its activities varied from poultry and fish farming to the production and/or processing of fruit and vegetables, oil seeds, forage crops, cuttings, seeds, flowers, and sometimes even food processing.

Earlier ideas of this programme dated back to the late 1950s, when the Dez Multi-Purpose Project was initiated in Khuzistan province. This was a regional development programme, assisted by the IBRD, which involved the construction of a dam and a hydro-electric power plant, the development of a new irrigation system in the Dez area, and the setting up of a sugar cane plantation at Haft-Tappeh (Richards, 1975:12–13). A new law concerning 'the establishment of companies for the utilisation of lands downstream of dams', passed in 1968, paved the way for the establishment of agribusiness companies. Accordingly, government agencies were empowered to purchase land from the villagers to be leased under thirty-year agreements to interested companies. In its embryonic stage this involved a purchase of some 68,000 hectares of land in the DIP area (Salmanzadeh, 1980:45). By the middle of the 1970s, 100,000 hectares had been carved up between six agribusiness companies in Khuzistan affecting 58 villages with a farming population of 40,000 (*Financial Times*, 21 October 1976). In addition, agribusiness enterprises were operating 25,000 hectares of land in Giroft (in Kirman province) and 20,000 hectares in Mahabad (in Kurdistan) (Moridi, 1979:303).

Although in percentage terms the area under their operation was still very limited, the significance of agribusiness activities is seen partly in the regional context in which they operated and partly in their rapid proliferation in a relatively short period of time. By early 1975, the Ministry of Agriculture had signed letters of intent with 300 foreign investors to undertake commercialised farming projects in Iran (Nowshirvani, 1976:47).

From the beginning, however, the programme proved to be highly controversial. Two sets of issues, in particular, overshadowed the operations of these companies. Firstly, the 'human element' involved in the depopulation of villages in the affected areas and their resettlement into newly constructed *shahraks*. Secondly, the limited labour absorption capacities of the new production units, which constrained their contribution to local employment generation.

Peasants were from the start extremely reluctant to part with their lands. Bitterness at lost ownership raged particularly high among those who had only recently acquired their land titles. Moreover, there was the question of compensation. Under the 1968 law, land prices had been fixed at 40,000 Rials per hectare for farming land and 250,000 Rials per hectare for orchards.These prices came under criticism from informed observers for being 'not really of much use to a farmer who has one, two, or even more hectares because having sold his land to the government he has no further interest in the village and must move to urban centres' (Rabbani, 1971:159). In practice, peasants did not receive even this price and had to settle for a much lower sum in the region of 16,000 Rials per hectare (Marzi, n.d.:6).

The conditions of housing inside the new *shahraks* left a great deal to be desired. Despite a foundation area of only 40 square metres, each living unit was planned for as many as ten persons. Besides, according to an engineer responsible for their design, the rooms were constructed deliberately small so as to prevent the villagers from living with and rearing animals in their homes as had been the tradition (Richards, 1975:14).[16]

It was initially anticipated and stipulated in company law that each unit would have to employ at least 1 person for every 10 hectares of land leased. In practice, however, a state of near total mechanisation on these units resulted in employment levels far below this target.

Government policy actively promoted mechanisation on agribusiness lands in two major ways. Firstly, by the provision of long-term, subsidised credit, which lowered the effective price of capital to them. In 1973, out of 310 projects approved by the Agricultural Development Bank of Iran, 13 agribusiness units took a lion's share of 49 per cent in the total value of loans disbursed with an average size of 56.8 million Rials (Nowshirvani, 1976:46). Furthermore, while 2.7 million peasant families altogether received slightly over 2.4 billion Rials in 1976, 4 of these companies alone received total loans of over 2 billion Rials (Moridi, 1979:304). Secondly, agribusinesses enjoyed exemptions from import restrictions including customs duties on imported machinery.

The resulting high degree of mechanisation had adverse effects on the local population's employment prospects. According to one case study of four such companies in Khuzistan, as much as 76–94 per cent of the active population in the region would have remained unemployed between 1971 and 1973 had they not left the area after the commencement of agribusiness operations (Rachidzadeh, 1978:103–4). Similar results were reported by another study in the same province, according to which at best only a quarter of the traditional labour force could have been employed by the companies (Ehlers, 1977:92–3).

The trend was expected to deteriorate yet further as activities such as the initial land-levelling and related work were gradually phased out. Ultimately, it was expected that each person would work an estimated area of between 50 and 100 hectares of land. With such bleak employment prospects, it was no wonder that in the areas where these companies operated, large-scale unemployment and outward migration were found to be endemic features of life for the villagers concerned (Rachidzadeh, 1978:103-5; Salmanzadeh, 1980:238-43).

Farm corporations

Farm corporations were agricultural joint stock companies whose shareholders comprised peasants and other landowners who turned over their land in return for a proportionate share in company ownership. These units differed from agribusiness companies in at least three respects: (1) they were not outlets for private investment (foreign or Iranian) from outside the villages; (2) their management was government-controlled by design, and (3) peasants were not dispossessed from their landholdings nor were their villages razed to the ground. The improvement of peasants' income was in fact a stated objective of the original law concerning the establishment of the Farm Corporations in 1967.[17]

Accordingly, farm corporations were to be set up in areas surveyed and selected by the Ministry of Agriculture subject to the approval of the majority of peasants (51 per cent of those eligible to vote). Agricultural land belonging to several villages would be turned into single large tracts, and peasants, although still nominally entitled to their land, would become shareholders in the companies in proportion to the amount of their land contribution. The management would be appointed civil servants - usually graduates of an agricultural college - who would run them on the basis of modern farming techniques. Peasants would receive profits proportional to the amount of their shareholdings and, should they wish to supplement their income, they could also work for the corporations as day labourers. In this way, it was envisaged that the consolidation of land into enlarged production units would overcome problems associated with excessive fragmentation and parcelling of land, increase possibilities of agricultural mechanisation, and thus ultimately, improve land productivity and peasants' income.

By early 1977, a total of 89 farm corporations with over 33,000 shareholders had been set up across the country. These covered 401,448 hectares of land stretching over 813 villages with a total population of about 300,000 (*Salnameh-e Amari-e Keshvar*, 1356:292).

Of these, 15 were reported to be operating in Fars, 11 in East Azerbaijan, 9 in Kermanshahan, and 6 in Central Province.

The actual size of farm corporations varied widely across the country: a typical corporation would normally embrace eight to ten villages. Yet at one extreme, they could be as small as a few in Gilan which consisted of only a single village. At another extreme, as in Giroft, a corporation could include as many as forty-five villages within its boundaries (Hooglund, 1982:87). Like agribusiness companies, the national importance of these corporations in percentage terms was still very limited (only about 4 per cent of all cultivable land was operated by them), but their wider importance derived from the fact that their number had increased rapidly in a fairly short period of time and was still rising in the early 1970s.

Similarly, the use of agricultural machinery in farm corporations was actively promoted by the government in a variety of forms. These ranged from outright capital grants and interest-free loans to the provision of technical services.[18] As a result, the spread of mechanisation in these corporations was rapid. Before their establishment only 20 per cent of these areas were ploughed by tractors and 5 per cent were harvested by combines. By 1974/5, the corresponding ratios had risen to 100 per cent and 95 per cent (Ashraf and Banuazizi, 1980:41). A typical farm corporation now maintained and operated a wide range of agricultural implements from tractors and combine harvesters to ploughs, discs, levellers, trailers, seed drills, sprayers, and so on.

As with agribusiness companies, in their area of operation farm corporations promoted capitalist relations by weakening or destroying the self-sufficient basis of the independent peasantry. This was generally brought about through a two-pronged expansion of market relations. On the one hand, peasant families were drawn into the growing network of the commodity market as they became dependent on these corporations for the supply of their subsistence goods. Thus, food traditionally produced within the confines of the farming peasant households now had to be procured from the companies at market-determined prices. On the other hand, farm corporations turned into principal employers of the local peasant population. But with vast areas of land operated with the aid of sophisticated agricultural machinery, the labour requirements of the farm corporations could be met by a handful of temporary and permanent staff only. It was no wonder that in these areas, too, unemployment and outward migration were established as major features of the consolidation programmes. There is indeed ample evidence to support this.[19]

Agrarian reform and the labour constraint

To have argued that land reform marked a turning point in Iran's recent history of labour transfer does not mean, and should not be taken to imply, that this was indeed a primary objective of the reforms. True, the implementation of the land reform helped the creation of a sizable relative surplus population on the land. Combined with a simultaneous overall reduction in the demand for wage labour, this paved the way for rural-to-urban labour transfer on a scale unprecedented in the country's history. But by no means can this be interpreted to suggest that the programme had as its preconceived and intended objective the immediate release of an important section of the rural population to urban areas.

This latter view is indeed part of an orthodox interpretation of Iran's land reform, which has placed primary importance on the generation of a stable supply of labour as a conscious policy objective in the urban setting. The remainder of this chapter challenges this view, arguing that it ignores the specific conjuncture in which the programme was introduced. As a result, it is argued, this interpretation confuses the final *outcome* of the programme with its initial *objectives*. In what follows, a brief overview of this school is presented, followed by a critical evaluation of its adequacy.

Formulations of this viewpoint, although also prevalent in more heuristic observations surrounding the manner in which the reforms went through,[20] have featured more prominently in theoretical discussions of the development of capitalism in Iran (Dana, 1979:85, 87; Sodagar, n.d.:178, 180; Momeni, 1980:221; OIPFG, no. 1:introduction).

Accordingly, for industrial capitalism to expand, workers must be made 'free' in the double sense of being separated from the means of production and the means of subsistence (i.e. being 'free' to hire themselves out as wage workers). This in turn implies, firstly, the creation of a relative surplus population, and secondly, the mobility for the 'freed' workers to move and migrate from their villages to areas of new industrial ascendancy.[21]

Translated into the Iranian context, this argument holds that the land reform package had the task of creating just such unfettered labour markets for the advance of capitalism:

> In a feudal society, the overwhelming majority of the labour force is deployed in agriculture, whereas imperialism needs more and more labour for work on assembly lines. The increase in the supply of labour thus attained will lower the general wage level. Nothing could achieve this better than the land reform which has dispatched masses of bankrupt farmers and landless peasants to the factory gates. (OIPFG, no. 1:9)

Similarly, the motivation behind the so-called emancipation of women, which also accompanied the reforms, has been attributed to the growing labour requirements of capitalism: 'The granting of votes to women and related reforms were designed to benefit imperialism. Here the aim of imperialism was to exploit a cheaper source of labour, which was devoid of any economic role by feudal traditions, and which was needed by the bourgeoisie' (OIPFG, no. 1:11).

A more substantive discussion of the women's question is deferred until Chapter 8, but as far as the general orientation of the wider argument is concerned, two problems may be pointed out.

Firstly, it overlooks the fact that in Iran, unlike in the feudal West, peasants were not tied to the soil before the land reform. Thus, given a relative degree of mobility by peasants, it is conceivable that greater labour supplies could have been secured through a combination of harsher fiscal exactions and/or greater monetary inducements (i.e. without the necessity to resort to a massive programme of institutional change).

Secondly, and more importantly, while recognising the *strategic* importance of stable labour supplies to the advance of capitalism, this interpretation misjudges the specificity of the historical *conjuncture* in which the programme was put into effect. As is widely recognised and duly emphasised in the literature, in the period 1961-4, when Iran's land reform was prepared, ratified and implemented, the country was in the grip of a deep economic recession. This was in the main triggered by the introduction, in 1960, of an austere Stabilisation Programme which was designed to curb domestic inflation and the worsening trade deficit.[22] As a result of the vigour with which the programme was pursued, 'the economy was led into about three years of almost complete stagnation' (Bharier, 1971:95). Thus, many urban industries were brought to a standstill for lack of credit; various urban construction sites were abandoned incomplete; and there was a spate of bankruptcies in the bazaar. This meant that a situation of mass urban unemployment – rather than chronic labour shortages – beset the country. Not only was there no 'scramble for cheap labour', but to provide jobs for the mass of unemployed workers in the towns was itself a major task confronting policy-makers. In brief, the adopted policy of restraint and the ensuing economic recession thus created could hardly call for measures to further expand the urban labour supplies.

Although mild recovery followed the lifting of many of the restrictive prescriptions of the Stabilisation Programme after 1964, it was not until the Fourth Development Plan in the late 1960s that the economy fully recovered. As a result, the demand for labour, though gradually increasing, remained generally slack for a good part of the decade.

A broad overview of this situation appears in Table 5.5, which is

102 Labour transfer and economic development

Table 5.5 Demand for and supply of labour in the urban labour markets, 1964–69

Year	Job-seekers	Vacancies	% of job-seekers finding jobs
1964	71,870	34,851	34
1965	48,303	26,785	39
1966	51,155	24,450	38
1967	54,154	27,358	39
1968	52,173	35,949	54
1969	36,901	33,349	62

Source: Ministry of Labour and Social Affairs (1970b:table 1).

compiled on the basis of returns from the various Employment and Exchange Offices of the Ministry of Labour and Social Affairs throughout the country. Although limited in scope (it only includes those who reported to these offices for jobs), the overall trend is, nevertheless, very clear. In 1964, the number of job-seekers was at its peak, thereafter somewhat lower but stable until 1967, when there was a sudden drop of some 30 per cent. As the number of unfilled vacancies remained generally stable, the proportion of successful job-seekers increased steadily from a low of one-third in 1964 to nearly two-thirds by 1969.

Considerations of the wage trend reinforce the same point. Not only were there no signs of spiralling wage increases at the time of the promulgation of the land reform, but nominal and real wages in urban industry and construction were actually declining at the height of the recession. Taking 1962 as the base year (=100), the real wages of operative workers in industry fell to 97.4 in 1963 and 97.1 in 1964, only to rise to 99.2 by 1965. Similarly, the real wages of construction workers, in whose case available data go back to a slightly earlier date, fell consistently between 1961 and 1967. By 1968 their wages in real terms were only just what they had been in 1959.[23]

To summarise, neither considerations of the urban labour market on the eve of the land reform nor developments throughout the 1960s lend support to the theories that view labour, implicitly or explicitly, as a serious constraint to Iran's economic development around the time when the reforms were introduced. The persistence of extensive urban unemployment and falling real wages would indeed suggest otherwise. Rather than alleviating pressing labour shortages, the land reform in fact exacerbated the excess labour situation in the urban areas. This was to a large extent a by-product of a programme which had sought to replace the old tenurial system of landholding with a mixture of peasant farming and commercial agriculture.

Summary and conclusion

This chapter argues that the institution of Iran's first nationwide land reform programme in 1962 led to the release of considerable supplies of agricultural labour. This was brought about in two ways.

First, the land reform created a surplus population in the countryside by inflating the number of those who were detached from the soil. This comprised:

1. Non-*nasaq* holding agricultural labourers, whose outright exclusion from the categories of land reform 'beneficiaries' from the first stage made them finally and legally landless.
2. Peasants who were victims of eviction and evasive practices of those landlords who tried to place their lands outside the operation of the land reform.
3. Those peasants who received some land – but of insufficient quantity and/or inferior quality. Pressured by poverty and the difficulties of making a subsistence living on small plots, they had a similar fate: to give up their land and to leave for towns.

Second, the reorganisation of the land tenure and the related changes in the technique of production affected adversely the demand for wage labour in agriculture. On the one hand, increased peasant proprietorship gave rise to a more widespread use of family labour on small and medium farms. This substitution, although making economic sense in relation to the more abundant labour resources of peasant families, reflected also the new proprietors' concern lest 'outside' workers develop *nasaq* claims on their lands.

On the other hand, mechanisation exacerbated the labour-replacing tendencies of the land reform. On large private lands this had always been a popular course with unscrupulous landlords, who tried to escape the provisions of the land reform from its earliest days. In the late 1960s, mechanisation received further government support by the encouragement given to the development of agribusiness giants and farm corporations. This type of policy promoted capitalist relations in agriculture by weakening, and often destroying, the self-sufficient basis of the independent peasantry. This chapter shows that, in their areas of operation, open unemployment was established as an endemic feature of rural life.

The net result of the land reform was to limit employment opportunities in the agricultural sector. With no visible improvements elsewhere in the rural sector, the way was paved for massive rural-to-urban migration in this decade. With this, 'major outlets' were opened which released substantial supplies of rural labour to the towns.

Despite this unambiguous *outcome,* however, it is disputed whether considerations of labour supply could have been an immediate factor behind the initiation of the programme. A study of the general economic situation as well as the specific conditions of the urban labour market at the time cast doubt on the validity of such an interpretation.

Notes

1. In the words of Warriner: 'Whereas the first stage had no effect on utilisation of labour and may have had some positive effect on the extent of cultivation, the effects of the second stage were deleterious' (Warriner, 1970:623).
2. According to Salmanzadeh: 'The *mubashir* and *zabet* have, of necessity, been forced to seek other employment, but the *kadkhuda* still continues although the remuneration originally supplied by the landowner has not been replaced by any other source. His position is in fact slowly being eroded and may well disappear in the future' (1980:120).
3. This is not a study of the determinants of the aggregate supply of rural labour. Such a study would require a wider examination of the effects of population growth, its composition and sectoral distribution, as well as the labour force participation rates of various age groups. By looking at the growing trend of landlessness, we are examining one important aspect in the composition of labour supply which was directly affected by the implementation of the land reform.
4. *Khowshneshins* (literally, those who sit comfortably) designated not a homogeneous group but a collective of diverse occupations. According to Hooglund, these consisted of three broad groups: the rural bourgeoisie, the non-agricultural workers, and the agricultural labourers. Their only common characteristic was their landless status (1973:229).
5. The 1952 land reform in Egypt allowed some agricultural workers to become tenant cultivators or even to own some land, while giving the rest minimum wage protection. In India, agricultural workers were excluded from land redistribution, but various special schemes for the creation of alternative employment were envisaged for them. Although the actual success of these schemes may be disputed, the fact that these workers were not outrightly excluded from rural reform policies distinguishes their case from those in Iranian villages. See ILO (1969:77) for Egypt; and Chaudhuri (1979:143) for India.
6. Lambton speaks approvingly of this for two reasons. Firstly, restricting the programme to occupying peasants was practical and did not involve any change in the field layout of the village. Secondly, agricultural workers 'did not have the means to cultivate the land; and to have required the cooperative societies at the outset of the reform to provide them with the draught oxen, agricultural implements, and seed, would have placed an additional burden upon these societies' (1969:74).
7. Dobb quotes one nineteenth century English writer, who shrewdly remarks: '[Under capitalism] farmers, like manufacturers, require constant labourers – men who have no other means of support than their daily labour, men who they can depend on.' Another one puts the case even more forcefully: 'The greatest evils to agriculture would be to place the labourer in a state of independence (i.e. by allowing him to have land) and thus destroy the

Labour and the land reform 105

gradations of society' (1946:222). It is not suggested that these observations acted as the guiding principles for Iranian policy-makers, but some foresight on their part cannot be a far-fetched assumption.

8. In Tasooj (near Shiraz) the landlord falsely declared that 200 hectares of his lands were mechanised and peasants, unaware of the consequences, wrongly confirmed this to the land reform officials who were investigating the case (OIPFG, no. 3:62–3). In another case in Ghazvin plain, the landlord utilised a 'variety of methods' ranging from intimidation to enticement in order to remove the population of one of his villages to another belonging to himself; elsewhere, but nearby, he went as far as bulldozing an entire village to secure the departure of the local population (Mahdavy, 1982:54).

9. Over two-thirds of the total cultivated lands in Iran are dependent on rainfall. Further, mean annual precipitation in the country is only one-third of the average for the globe (Vahidi, 1968:7; Khosravi, 1969; and Bowen-Jones, 1968:587, for a general overview of water and irrigation issues in Iranian agriculture).

10. In Kuhpayeh-i Darakhtingan (in Kirman province), the landlord cut off the water supply so as to drive out the peasants, mechanise their lands, and hence declare them exempt from the land reform. See Lambton (1969: 285–6), and Warriner (1970:622) for instances of such practice.

11. Limitation of scope deters us from a more in-depth treatment of the so-called inverse relationship between farm size and productivity of resource use in agriculture. For a good source book on the subject, see Berry and Cline (1979). A concise treatment may be found in Ellis (1988), and some aspects of the problem in relation to India, the most extensively discussed country in this context, are brought out in Barbier (1984) and Bhalla (1979). Moghadam (1985) pursues this question with reference to Iran.

12. Even on the large farms, landowners preferred to take on contract farmers (*Jaliz-karan*) from other provinces (such as Isfahan and Qom), not just to benefit from their greater farming skills, but also to minimise any risks of facing prospective claims to their land; see OIPFG (no. 4:28).

13. One such incidence in the village of Shater-Abad in Kermanshah province is discussed in *Tahqiqat-e Eqtesadi*, (1348:vols 17/18:196–7).

14. A figure of 7 hectares is suggested by Hooglund to be the minimum required for an average farming family's subsistence (1982:77, 93–8). This figure, largely accepted by Iranian agronomists, is based on the assumption that about one-half of the crop land is left fallow annually; wheat is grown on 2 hectares to cater for the annual bread supply, and other fodder and cash crops are grown on the remainder to trade for necessities such as clothes, tea and sugar. Clearly, such 'average' figures have to be used cautiously against the background of wide-ranging geographic and climatic variations in a country as large as Iran. The type of product no doubt also greatly influences this 'minimum' viable size of land.

15. Reflecting on a similar point in a village in Ghazvin plain, Mahdavy observes that due to complete mechanisation, 'one can no longer find even a single bull in the village' (1982:62).

16. The official justification, on hygienic grounds, overlooked the financial importance of this practice for many poor peasant families. Goodell (1986:ch. 7) too provides interesting insights on the organisation of life in a typical *shahrak*.

17. The other stated objectives were: (1) to mechanise and expand the scale of

operations; (2) to acquaint shareholders with modern methods of agriculture; (3) to lower the man/land ratio and compensate for the displacement of labour by regional planning of resources between agriculture and industry; (4) to end the fragmentation of holdings, and (5) to expand the area under cultivation to cover lands previously barren and unused; see Richards (1975:10); Denman (1973:209-11).

18. Farm corporations were charged an interest rate of 2.5% per annum on loans advanced for the purchase of tractors assembled in Iran, compared with 6% for peasants (Nowshirvani, 1976:40).

19. In Dargazin Farm Corporation full mechanisation of operations increased the area under cultivation to 1,410 hectares from 820 hectares, but reduced at the same time the required labour force by as much as 80 per cent, 'a laying off of some 300 shareholders' (Denman, 1973:224). Elsewhere in Farah Corporation, only 40 per cent of the shareholders managed to find jobs within the corporation, but over 90 per cent of them worked for less than nine months only (Moridi, 1979:293). The establishment of Baghain Corporation in Kirman reduced by as much as 90 per cent the number of peasant households engaged in agricultural occupations (down from 1,046 families to less than 100). In Aryamehr Corporation in Fars no more than 55 per cent of the local labour force could be employed by the company, but even then for three months only. Finally, the unemployment rate in the area where Dariyush Corporation operated was observed to be as high as 96 per cent for eight months of the year, never falling below 77 per cent for the rest of the year (OIPFG, no. 2:96-7, 144-5, 179).

20. There is some circumstantial evidence in support of this viewpoint, namely some early public pronouncements by the designers and implementors of the land reform. For instance, Hassan Arsanjani, the then Minister of Agriculture and the chief architect of the reform, is reported to have stated that: 'Our progressive aim from the implementation of the Law of Land Reform is to gradually transfer the unnecessary people from villages to other productive activities' (cited in Momeni, 1980:380). This issue was also raised in a number of background studies and consultative documents leading to the formulation of a strategy of land reform for Iran. According to the preliminary report of the Third Development Plan: 'A pre-requisite for the progress of the country is that large sections [of rural population] gradually leave their rural occupations and be drawn into other occupations' (Momeni, 1980:216). Similarly, this was the general line of argument, which emerged in a number of studies by a group of Harvard economists acting as consultants to the Iranian government, see Kristjanson (1960) and Webster Johnson (1960). As stated above, however, the evidence in support is circumstantial. The more theoretical argument, therefore, merits closer scrutiny.

21. As observed by Maurice Dobb in his study of the historical development of capitalism: 'The commodity labour-power had not merely to exist: it had to be available in adequate quantities in the places where it was most needed; and here mobility of the labouring population was an essential condition' (1946:274).

22. See Bharier (1971:106); Pesaran (1985:20); Mahdavy (1965:135; 1970:440) for an extended discussion of both the boom in the late 1950s and the slump following the austerity programme in the early 1960s.

23. For construction wages, see Table C.1 in Appendix C; for a more extended discussion of the wage trends in Iran in this period, see Hakimian (1988).

6
The onset of the oil boom in the 1970s

Introduction

For the third and final of our case studies, we move to a discussion of labour transfer in the 1970s. According to a well established and popular view, the oil boom marking the beginning of this period dealt a decisive blow to the country's ailing rural economy in general, and its agriculture, in particular. The wealth and accumulation of these years allegedly precipitated rural poverty and decay, while growing landlessness and marginality of peasants pushed the once-thriving agricultural sector along a path of 'destruction' and 'depredation'.[1] This 'immiserisation' theme has inevitably influenced existing perceptions of labour transfer out of agriculture, broadly depicted thus far as a mass migration of a permanent character.

This chapter challenges both this 'destruction' theory of agriculture and its implications for labour transfer by exploring in a new light the difficulties experienced by this sector, and offering an alternative explanation. It is shown that the traditional interpretation is rooted in an inadequate understanding of the specificities of the oil boom period. This is why the use of 'push factor' concepts – although relevant to the analysis of the structural transformations in the land reform period – prove to be inappropriate in this context.

Firstly, a discussion of the dominant strand is presented and scrutinised against the background of the important structural changes which swept the rural economy in the post-boom period. Secondly, our discussion focuses directly on the mechanism of the interaction between the boom and the constituent sectors of the rural economy (farm and non-farm), and explores its effects. It will be shown that it was changes in the relative 'effort-intensity' of income against participation in agricultural production which intensified participation in (rural and urban) wage labour markets. Rather than being an outcome or *effect* of the 'depredation' of agriculture – as depicted in conventional thinking – labour outflow was, in fact, a constant *source* of difficulty to this sector in the period under study.

New circumstances, old ideas

Iranian agriculture had to adapt to new circumstances following the dramatic rise in petroleum income in the early 1970s.[2] Associated with this were a marked improvement in urban employment opportunities on the one hand, and a growing urban demand for food, on the other.

Despite these radical changes, images of deepening rural poverty and destitution – reminiscent of the earlier period after the land reform – have persisted among some Iranian scholars. Three developments, in particular, explain the widespread projection of this 'monolithic' perspective from the 1960s onto the 1970s:
1. Accelerated urban growth and the concomitant rapid decline in the relative share of rural population. Between 1966 and 1976 urban population grew six times faster than rural population (compared to three times faster in the earlier intercensal period).[3] This expansion was largely due to a new tempo of rural-to-urban migration, which quickened considerably with the onset of the oil boom. As a result, the share of rural population in the total declined consistently: from 68.6 per cent in 1956 to 62 per cent in 1966, reaching a low of 53 per cent by 1976.
2. The growing inability of Iranian agriculture to meet the rapidly expanding domestic demand for food, which became even more apparent in these years. Average annual imports of wheat, amounting to about 300,000 tons per annum between 1962 and 1972, increased to over 1 million tons per annum between 1973 and 1977 (FAO, *Trade Year Book:* various issues). Similarly, annual imports of barley, rice and corn shot up by as much as nine to ten times in the same period. Undermined by rising domestic consumption, Iran's agricultural exports, too (with the exception of rice), dwindled to near-negligible levels. Once self-sufficient in major staples, and to some extent even a net exporter of some products, Iran now portrayed a country heavily dependent on foreign imports for its basic food requirements. Despite its simplistic ramifications, this type of evidence is freely used by critics as another indication of the 'failure' of the country's agricultural sector.[4]
3. Illusions surrounding the state's modernisation programmes in agriculture had largely waned by the mid-1970s. It was increasingly

apparent – though not openly admitted – that, after a short-lived experience, the much-publicised agribusiness policy had been socially a disaster and financially a complete failure. New projects had largely ground to a halt, while existing ones went through a critical phase in which foreign participants were intent on pulling out. Similarly, farm corporations – the official spearhead for agricultural modernisation – failed consistently to produce the much-sought revolution in agricultural production.

In the light of these developments, most discussions of Iran's agriculture – scholarly and popular – have been characterised by a firm belief in the continued degeneration of rural life in the oil boom years. Rare indeed are discussions of the period which do not depict the rural economy as being on the verge of 'decay', 'disintegration' or 'decline'.[5]

It is a central proposition of this chapter that this misconception stems from an inadequate periodisation, which groups together the two decades of the 1960s and the 1970s as one and the same ('The Shah's') period. Although correct from a political, legal, and perhaps even an administrative point of view, there is little doubt that this approach cannot be defended from the perspective of the distinct socioeconomic developments which took place in the rural areas in the aftermath of the oil boom. More specifically, three considerations cast doubt on the validity of this approach.

Firstly, the urban boom of the 1970s was *not* accompanied by a slump in rural areas, as the popular view would have us believe. There was indeed a simultaneous, and distinct, process of urban *and* rural economic expansion. The underlying confusion here derives from an unwarranted, though widespread, identification of *agriculture* as a sector of economic activity with the *rural sector* as a geographical space accommodating a host of these activities.

It is true that agriculture was put under strain in this period. But this was mainly brought about by developments in the urban construction sector and to some extent by the revival of rural non-farm activities. By no means did this indicate a downturn in the pace of rural economic life. On the contrary, there was a certain revival of economic activity in Iranian villages as some home industries, crafts, and a host of other light industries flourished, competing away agricultural labour.

Secondly, the nature of developments within agriculture differed radically in each of the two periods. After the oil boom, endemic labour *shortages* (particularly at peak harvest times), rather than labour *surplus*, beset Iranian agriculture. Reflecting this, agricultural wages began to rise significantly for the first time since the land reform. Preoccupied with the depressing effects of the oil boom, the conventional wisdom has all too often ignored this important feature of the period. It would indeed be a matter of interest to see how an all-round and major upturn in real agricultural wages may be reconciled with this gloomy picture of the countryside.

Finally, the structural characteristics of the two periods were also substantially different. The decade following the land reform was marked by a period of intensive institutional change which altered the structure of property rights in the countryside. This exacerbated differentials between those who received land and those who were rendered landless. For the former, conditions improved generally, while the plight of the latter weakened considerably their desire or motivation to stay on the land. This fate was also shared by those peasants who received land, but of insufficient quantity and/or inferior quality. Many thousands of landless agricultural workers and poor peasant families left rural areas as a result. Although urban economic prospects were not particularly bright as yet, to have stayed behind would have meant subjection to intolerable poverty and hardship. As shown in the last two chapters, by the time of the oil boom there had indeed emerged a new structure of landholding and tenurial system in the countryside, within which the broad terms for 'success' were largely set by the institutional framework of the land reform.

The coming of the oil boom changed the situation dramatically. The explosion in urban wages (particularly in the construction sector) affected even the 'self-sufficient' peasantry by broadening the range of options to which their aggregate family labour input could be allocated: either to ignore new opportunities offered by the labour market, or to divert (at least part of) their households' human resources to cash-earning activities outside the farm sector. Given the radically improved terms of exchange for labour, it was not surprising that the latter course of action often took precedence over the former. Interestingly though, the resulting labour outflow from agriculture did not, in all instances, entail rural-to-urban migration, or a severing of peasants' ties with their lands, and perhaps least of all, their 'bankruptcy' or 'destitution', though wrongly identified with all of these so far.

The oil boom and changing 'effort-intensity' of income in the labour and agricultural produce markets

Developments in the Iranian economy in the aftermath of the oil boom altered the 'effort-price' of income significantly in favour of participation in the labour market. Expressed in simple terms, this meant that from a material point of view, it was now far more rewarding for the peasantry at large to participate in the sale of labour power than to engage in the

The onset of the 1970s oil boom 111

production of agricultural products (cash or subsistence).[6] This simple, though generally neglected, mechanism accounts for the remarkable increase in the pace of labour outflow from agriculture and the subsequent difficulties encountered by it in this period.

There were two underlying causes: the rising urban construction wages on the one hand, and sluggish agricultural commodity prices, on the other. The former pushed up money and real wages in the labour market, whereas the latter, although rising, failed to secure a similar inducement in agricultural production. On balance, this resulted in considerable disincentives to participation in the produce market. Each of these processes is studied below.

The urban construction sector

Urban construction activity had been growing at a steady rate ever since the middle of the 1960s. This trend was boosted in 1968 with the introduction of the Fourth Development Plan (1968–72), which placed particular emphasis on building up a number of heavy industries in Iran (such as petrochemicals, steel, and machine tools). As a result, construction value-added grew at an average annual rate of 7 per cent in real terms, with real investment expanding by 12.7% per annum between 1968 and 1972. Similarly, private investment in urban construction grew at about 11% per annum in real terms, while in nominal terms its value almost doubled in the same years (Bank Markazi, 1351:141, 210).

This phase of expansion benefited from a more moderate pace of price rises compared with the oil boom period. Given extensive underutilisation of resources and the plentiful supplies of urban labour after the initiation of the land reform, the growth of this sector was made possible in the absence of undue inflationary pressures. The wholesale price index for metallic and non-metallic construction materials rose on average by 8.7 and 3.2% per annum respectively, while unskilled construction workers' nominal wage index grew by 11.8% per annum (5.9% in real terms) in the course of these five years (Bank Markazi, 1351:213; also Table C.1 in Appendix C). Although securing the economy on an upswing, the Fourth Development Plan largely managed to avoid the disturbing effects of a spiralling inflationary process, which was to emerge later with new developments in the oil sector.

The onset of the oil boom shook the entire urban construction sector. Speculation in the urban property markets sent the price of land and residential construction sky-high, while a major boost to the government's oil income expanded considerably its scope for initiating major construction projects. As the private sector widened its lead in urban residential construction, the state embarked upon major programmes of expansion and improvement in basic infrastructure so as to alleviate massive pressures building up on the country's ports, roads and the railway network. As a result, Iran – like many other oil exporting countries experiencing a similar expansionary phase – turned into a giant and constantly expanding construction site. Construction investment in 1974 alone shot up by some 50 per cent, its volume almost quadrupling in the four years from 1973. Similarly, by 1977 investment in urban private construction sextupled over its 1973 level. Although spiralling inflation was partially responsible for this, real value-added in construction grew at no less than an average of 14.4% per annum – that is, twice as fast as in the preceding plan period (1968–72) (Bank Markazi, 1356:94–5).

Characteristically, this extraordinary surge in construction activity boosted the demand for simple labourers. Employment in this sector increased by 133 per cent between 1966 and 1976, to reach nearly 1.2 million people. As a result, this sector's share in the total employment of the country almost doubled: from 7.2 to 13.5 per cent (Hakimian, 1981:table 1).

Buoyant demand also raised the wages of construction workers dramatically. These rose by as much as 32 per cent in 1974 alone and almost doubled in nominal terms in the course of just two years between 1973 and 1975 (a real improvement of some 56 per cent). By the end of the period in 1977, the money wages of unskilled construction workers were three and a half times their 1973 level (almost five times that of 1971). In real terms this represented an improvement of some 100 per cent over 1973, or 230 per cent over 1971. A similar increase for the period 1968–72 had been 27 per cent only.

Agricultural prices: trend and policy

By contrast with construction wages, the evolution of major agricultural commodity prices was more gradual both before and after the oil boom.

Prior to 1974, these prices were primarily market-determined. For wheat and barley, however, the government had maintained a somewhat interventionist posture since the early 1960s, which aimed at price stability while ensuring continued food supplies to urban areas. This policy was based on an active food imports and exports scheme, coupled with the operation of a domestic floor price system. The latter authorised the Cereals Organisation to purchase surplus wheat and barley from producers at officially declared minimum prices. In practice, however, this scheme was not followed vigorously: annual government purchases of wheat between 1960 and 1974 averaged only 1.9 per cent of the total production, never exceeding 5.4 per cent in any individual year (Aresvik, 1976:144). Besides, official prices remained constant throughout the entire period: at 6,000 Rials/ton for wheat, and 4,000 Rials/ton for barley, these were no more than notional prices.

Although limited storage capacity curtailed to some extent annual wheat purchases, far more important was the government's general attitude which did not oblige it to buy all the wheat offered to it at the floor price.[7] Reflecting a general breakdown of this policy, farm gate prices varied widely from year to year, and from season to season. In nominal terms, the price of wheat fluctuated between 5,500 and 8,400 Rials/ton between 1962 and 1972 with an underlying trend which was generally stagnant. There were similar oscillations in the prices of barley, cotton, sugar and rice, but the underlying trend was moderately upwards (see Figure 6.1; more detail in Table C.1 in Appendix C).

Soon after the oil boom had got under way the government showed signs of apprehension about the state of domestic production. Firstly, it embarked upon a major revision of its agricultural pricing policy. Purchase prices of wheat, barley, corn, sugar beet, meat and milk were raised by as much as 50–80 per cent in January 1974. This meant prices at 10,000 Rials/ton for wheat, 7,500 Rials/ton for barley, and 9,500 Rials/ton for corn. As a further step, the price of wheat to farmers was raised to 12,000 Rials/ton in 1977 (US Agricultural Attaché, IR8002:1); prices to consumers were still to be kept constant via subsidies (Bank Markazi, 1352:69–70).

Further, to boost domestic production, the 'wheat impact programme' was stepped up and widened to include a number of other major products. This policy – originally put into effect during the Fourth Development Plan – aimed at expanding wheat production through the introduction of improved varieties of seeds and a more intensive use of fertilisers. Under the terms of this programme, participant farmers were provided high-yielding seeds at half the cost, fertilisers and pesticides at 20 per cent discount, technical assistance, free land levelling and irrigation works, as well as soft loans to cover production costs and new investment in agricultural machinery. By 1976, a significant proportion of the rice and corn area had been brought under the operation of this programme, though coverage for wheat and barley still lagged behind.[8]

Disincentives to agricultural production

Despite the above measures, the government's commitment to lower urban food prices thwarted any substantive price support scheme that it operated for the benefit of agriculture. The massive importation of

114 *Labour transfer and economic development*

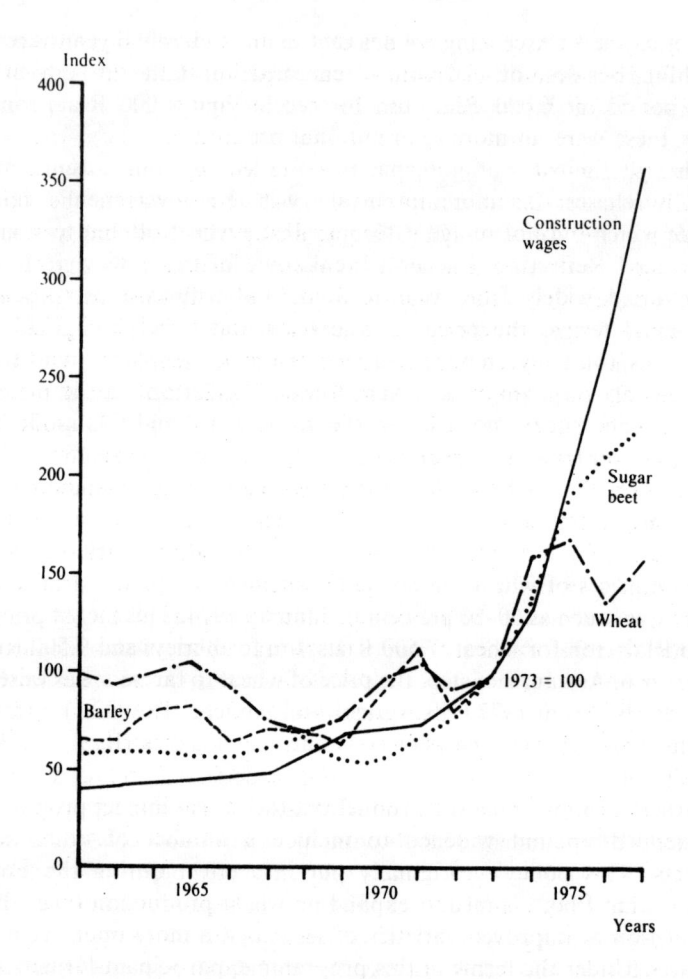

Figure 6.1 'Effort-price' of agricultural production in Iran, 1962–77.

foodstuffs exerted a powerful dampening effect on the market price of agricultural commodities, turning once again their official prices into notional prices. This was exacerbated by a lack of the required administrative machinery, widespread official corruption, and apathy on the part of the state to see through the successful implementation of its agricultural pricing programme. Despite the official price rises, therefore, these were either insufficient or ineffectual in encouraging domestic production. This tendency was aggravated by the rising opportunity costs of production in agriculture. Frantic land speculation, for instance, discouraged investment in agriculture, particularly in the case of the large commercial farms situated near the urban centres.[9]

It was against this background that the massive rise in construction wages tilted the balance in favour of participation in the labour market. An indication of this tendency can be seen in Figure 6.1.

Before 1973 the underlying trend for agricultural prices was either stagnant (wheat) or moderately improving (barley and cotton). With gradually but consistently improving construction wages, the 'effort-price' of income was already moving against agriculture, but was as yet insufficiently strong to act as a serious disincentive to agricultural production. After 1973 the situation altered radically with the take-off in construction wages comfortably outpacing the trend in agricultural prices. This is visibly demonstrated on the same graph for wheat and sugar beet (the only products for which post-1973 data are available – the former a subsistence and the latter a cash crop). Taking 1973 as the base year (=100), the index of wheat prices had gone up to almost 160 by 1977 and that of sugar beet to 226.4; for construction wages a similar index had reached about 360.

This undoubtedly had serious implications for the pattern of comparative earnings in agriculture and construction. In some parts of the country it was reported that income from five months' work on the land amounted to 3,000 tomans, whereas a similar job on an urban construction site would bring in 5,000 tomans. Likewise, a twelve-hour working day in rural areas would earn an agricultural worker 35 tomans, whereas a shorter working day of eight hours would secure up to 70 per cent more in towns (Khosravi 1979:86, 112–13). Not so atypical was indeed the case of a young shepherd in a Caspian village in the north, who could previously 'be employed for 2,000 tomans a year; now the lowest wage offered is 30,000 and, even at this salary, young men are reluctant to accept the hardship of a shepherd's life and to be absent from the village for the larger part of the year' (Mir-Hosseini, 1987:406).

Although a more substantive discussion of the impact of this development on the agricultural sector is deferred to a later section in this chapter (pp. 119–23), two observations are, nevertheless, relevant here.

For the large commercial farms, which relied on hired labour, rising wage costs, *ceteris paribus,* eroded profits. The resultant tendency in their case was increased mechanisation and replacement of local labour with Afghani immigrant workers, if not a reduction altogether in the area under cultivation. For subsistence holdings, by contrast, rising wages came not as direct costs but as rising foregone opportunities of earning cash outside agriculture. Although the mechanism varied, the result was similar: their incentives to agricultural production were weakened. This resulted in a considerable transfer of family labour from small and medium farms operating especially near the more prosperous urban centres to temporary wage-earning occupations outside agriculture. In some cases, this form of labour migration was so well established that peasant proprietors found it profitable to rent out their land 'on a sharecropping basis' while they themselves joined the urban labour markets (Madjd, 1983:23).

Some of the earlier-criticised conventional theories have sought further support for their 'rural decline' hypothesis in the widening urban/rural gap, which persisted throughout the entire period from the early 1960s. In 1963 private rural per capita expenditure as a ratio of the countrywide expenditure was 0.71; by 1968 this had fallen to 0.66; by 1973 to 0.5; and by 1978 to an all-time low of 0.4 (Katouzian, 1981b:25). This argument, however, overlooks a number of important points.

Firstly, this trend conceals the possibility of a marked absolute rise in rural per capita consumption expenditure, as was indeed the case after the oil boom. Secondly, it masks possible variations in sectoral earnings and expenditure *within* rural or urban sectors. The fact that agricultural wages began to rise considerably in the aftermath of the oil boom is also largely neglected from this perspective.

Given the predominant presence of the agricultural sector in rural areas, a deterioration in the relative effort-price of agricultural income would be reflected in the widening urban/rural gaps. But there is no general case for treating both trends as being identical. The latter, for instance, continued to widen throughout the 1960s in Iran even though the trends for relative income effort of agricultural production and wage labour participation were only gradually pulling apart. After 1973, in contrast, both gaps widened dramatically. This reflected not only the fact that urban incomes were improving much more significantly, but also the more important point that income from agricultural-based occupations was falling markedly behind that from wage employment in general.

The rural non-farm sector

Difficulties experienced by agriculture in this period have also overshadowed the stimulating effect of the rise in petroleum income on the rural economy at large. At a time when rural economic activity entered a new upturn phase, the traditional concern with 'rural decline' continued to emphasise the 'rapidly declining handicraft and non-farm occupations' (Kazemi, 1980b:260). On closer examination these observations, too, turn out to be unsubstantiated projections from an earlier period.

Judging by the rural consumption trend, the situations before and after the oil boom were markedly different (see Figure 6.2 and Table C.2 in Appendix C). The monthly budget expenditure of an 'average' rural household remained generally stagnant throughout the 1960s up to 1973. In nominal terms, it grew at a rate of 1.9% per annum only, while in real terms it remained virtually unchanged. These were years of mass departure of landless families from the rural areas, moderate economic expansion in towns, and above all, a relatively limited degree of interaction between the rural and urban economies.

After 1973 the pace of rural economic activity visibly surged forward. The colossal rise in oil revenues broadened the dimensions of the home market, contributed to its growing monetisation, and as a result, boosted demand for commodities produced in, as well as trade between, rural and urban areas. Buoyant urban incomes, in particular, increased the demand for rural commodities (including labour), contributing in turn to an all-round rise in rural incomes. The average monthly budget expenditure of rural households increased by as much as 85 per cent in nominal terms and 60 per cent in real terms in just one year (1973 to 1974). This trend reached its peak in 1975 in real terms and, although declining somewhat thereafter, it grew by an average of 23.6% per annum in nominal terms and 9.3% per annum in real terms until 1977 (Figure 6.2).

Reflecting this resurgence in rural economic activities, employment in non-agricultural occupations expanded by almost 50 per cent between 1966 and 1976. This expansion – clearly at the expense of agricultural employment, which declined by 13 per cent – came about through a sustained increase in both wage and non-wage employment opportunities. Growing by 58.4 and 40 per cent respectively, these activities now competed with agriculture for its labour resources. Both categories of employment in agriculture in fact declined in absolute terms (by 18 and 3 per cent respectively) (Census, 1966:table 19; 1976:table 21).

Brickmaking is a good example of the many rural activities which flourished in this period. Traditionally, this industry had been concentrated near urban centres. With growing demand for construction materials and improvements in the transport system, there took place a 'relocation' of brickmaking to rural areas. This process was facilitated by the nature of brickmaking technology, which was highly labour-intensive and relied on simple raw materials such as clay, water and fuel (Madjd, 1983:24).

Expansion in services had a similar stimulating impact on rural areas near the Caspian littoral. Mir-Hosseini, who has studied the changing economy of one such village (Rudbarak) found that 'major shifts' in the economic structure of this village in the early 1970s 'coincided with the increase of tourism in the area, the purchase of land by Tehranis, and the beginning of villa construction' (1987:403–4).

Another impetus to Iranian village life in this period came from a revival of a number of rural crafts and home industries. Traditionally,

118 *Labour transfer and economic development*

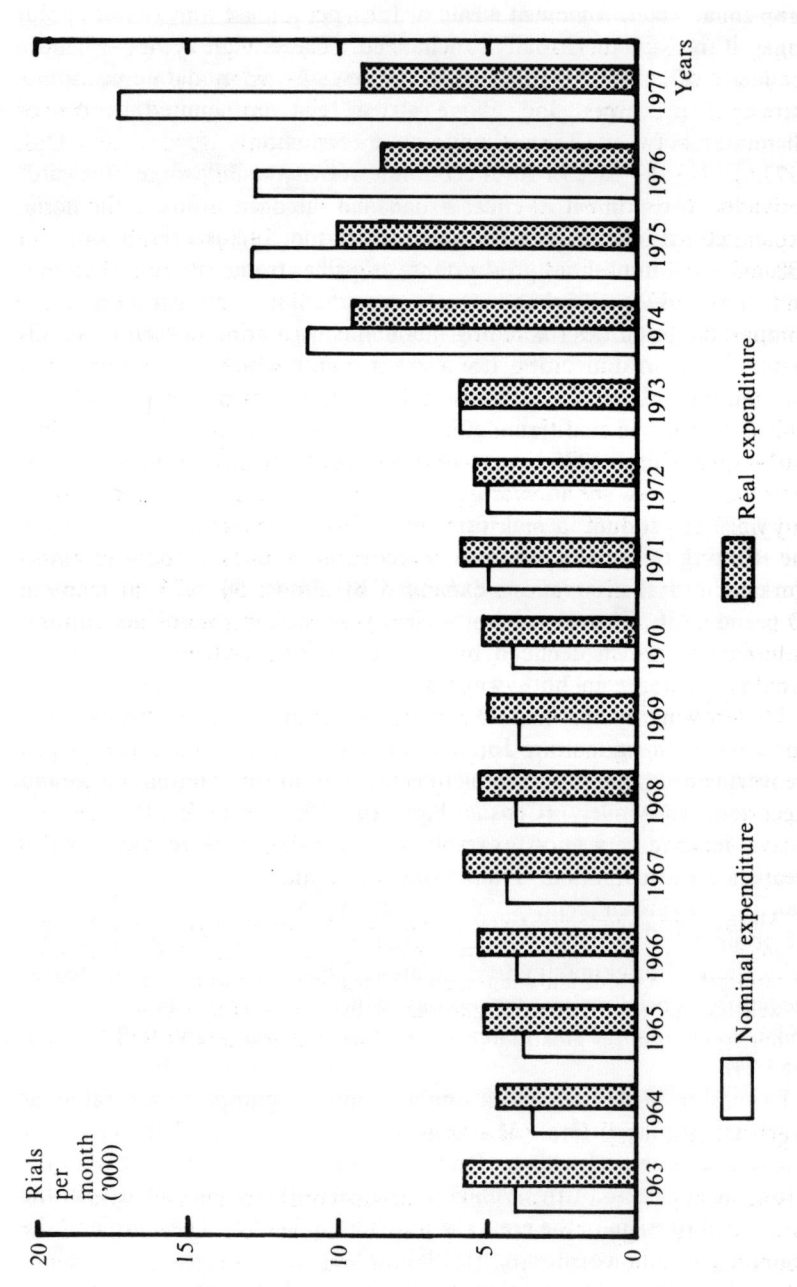

Figure 6.2 Trends in monthly budget expenditure of rural households, 1963–77.

most peasant families engaged in a number of subsidiary activities to supplement their incomes. The proportion of all rural households engaged in some such activities was reportedly as high as 79 per cent in the late 1960s. Rural crafts, including textiles, carpet- and rug-weaving, were by far the largest single home industry, accounting for 30 per cent of all non-farm labour force (including construction) (Heydari and Das, 1977:6). The 1970s saw a further increase in the importance of such activities. The number of rural households engaged in home industries expanded by 110 per cent between 1966 and 1976, to embrace over 700,000 rural households. Even more impressive was the rise of carpet- and rug-weaving activities, which expanded by 154 per cent on a comparable basis. This was brought about by a combination of strong export demand and rising domestic incomes which had significantly boosted the demand for high-priced Iranian carpets since the late 1960s. This industry was traditionally organised along the lines of the 'putting-out' system. Carpet merchants 'commissioned' the rugs, by providing raw materials, design specifications, and cash advances, and undertook to buy finished products at specified prices. Given the lucrative rewards and the relatively low risks involved, many rural families introduced carpet workshops on their premises (Madjd, 1983:26-7). By 1976, as many as 80 per cent of all rural households who engaged in some kind of home industry were involved in carpet- and rug-weaving (up from 65 per cent in 1966) (Census, 1976:178; 1966:143).

The coming of the oil boom acted as an extra bonus to this industry, boosting the demand for its products. As a result, wages of carpet-weavers began to rise, often to the chagrin of capitalist farmers. According to Madjd, in the summer of 1976 the wages of a teenage weaver reached between 400 and 500 Rials per day, while the more skilled weavers could command up to 700 Rials per day:

> All the large commercial farmers roundly condemned carpet-weaving as a social evil to be curtailed by government legislation. They stressed the long-term health hazards and the foregone educational opportunities caused by weaving, not to mention the reduction in the supply of agricultural labour during the summer months and the resulting higher wages. (1983:27)

Agriculture and the oil boom

Rising occupational attractions in urban construction and rural non-farm sectors began to exert a powerful impact on agriculture. Once abundant in labour supplies, this sector was now subjected to endemic labour shortages and witnessed, for the first time since the land reform, a significant rise in the wages of simple farm labourers.

Agricultural wages came under pressure in two ways. Firstly, remuneration in this sector had to take account of the improved income-earning opportunities elsewhere (both inside and outside the rural economy). Secondly, there was a remarkable coincidence in the seasonal pattern of activity in agriculture and construction: peaking between spring and autumn, but tailing off in the winter. This compounded agriculture's labour problems by bidding away farming hands at a time they were most needed. As a result, the dearth of farming hands and the associated rise in wage costs emerged as 'one of the most persistent complaints by farmers' after 1974.[10]

Even in the areas of operation of the agribusiness companies, where heavy mechanisation had substantially reduced the demand for labour, adequate labour supplies were not always a foregone conclusion. Blaming the new situation on improved alternatives outside agriculture, a senior Mitchell Cotts executive in Khuzistan told an interviewer in 1975 that this province was not like Africa, 'where labour is forthcoming at very low wages'. In Iran, he is reported to have complained that, 'peasants didn't want to work for the agribusinesses because they weren't faced with absolute economic necessity. They can "pick and choose" ' (response in an interview by Richards, 1975:17; see also Khosravi, 1979:138-9 on the labour shortages of these companies).

As noted earlier, rising wages had two effects on agricultural operations. For cash crops (such as sugar beet and cotton), where labour enters directly into production costs, a rise in wages, *ceteris paribus*, eroded profitability, and therefore the incentives to increase production. For subsistence products (such as wheat, barley and rice), it was not the direct cost considerations of a rise in wages but the foregone alternative income in the construction sector that affected production decisions. In either case, both for small and large operations, rising wages in agriculture and construction acted as a major disincentive to increasing agricultural production.

This widespread tendency has been noted by a number of studies. Madjd who has studied problems faced by the sugar beet producers, has found that it was 'in response to rising labour costs' that a substantial number of these producers abandoned production, 'despite the market and institutional advantages of growing the crop'. Thus even the relatively high levels of protection given to the industry in this period, 'were not sufficient to offset the structural problems of the industry' (1983:41 and n.49).[11]

Similarly, regular reports by the American Agricultural Attaché in Tehran, who monitored Iranian agriculture, conveyed the same message about the damaging effect of labour shortages on potential agricultural output in the country:

A factor of uncertainty in future expansion of wheat (and barley) is the loss of labour brought about by continued rural migration to the cities, affecting particularly the dry-land areas. One must realise that about 50-65 per cent of Iran's total wheat and barley area is still harvested by hand.[12]

Table 6.1 shows the adverse impact of this tendency on the area under cultivation. Until 1973 there was a gradual expansion in the cultivated area for most crops. In the short period between 1973 and 1978, this trend was reversed: allowing for exceptions (both for individual years and crops), the aggregate area under cultivation of major crops declined by about 20 per cent. This tendency was as true for subsistence products as for industrial crops. Harvest area for wheat, barley and rice shrank by 11-26 per cent, and for sugar beet and tobacco by as much as 13-21 per cent. Sugar cane, which enjoyed an expansion in cultivated area, was the only exception to this rule, while worst hit was another cash crop, cotton, which lost one-third of its total cropped area.

A similar picture emerges from a study of agricultural output. Reflecting the combined effects of contraction in area and labour supply difficulties, the production of major annual crops suffered a set back. This is clear from Table 6.2 which shows that the earlier moderate expansion in the production of several main crops during the 1960s was by and large arrested, and in some cases even reversed, during the period covering the oil boom years. But the important point is that far from being the *cause* of migratory labour movements in this period, the decline was in fact a major *manifestation* of the pressures built up on agricultural labour supply. It is in this respect that the analysis of the strains experienced by agriculture presented above differs from that put forward by the conventional viewpoint.

Agriculture's labour shortages were indeed so significant that they led to a revival of some modified forms of sharecropping in parts of the country. Once a major target for the country's land reform in the 1960s, this traditional practice of crop division began to flourish once again, albeit in different forms and for different reasons. Reflecting labour supply difficulties, many commercial farmers initiated some kind of sharecropping agreement with farming peasants as a means of meeting their labour needs.[13] This was also observed in the areas of operation of farm corporations: where the supply of a sufficiently motivated workforce was a major problem, the management tried to involve peasants in a share of the final produce. Thus in the four farm corporations studied by Salmanzadeh in the Dez Irrigation Project (DIP) area, 'the corporation provides the seeds, land, water, and machinery and the peasants provide the labour. The harvest is then divided according to a mutually agreed rate. The adoption of this centuries-old practice has

Table 6.1 Index of area under cultivation for major annual crops, 1960–78 (1973=100)

	1960	1967	1968	1970	1971	1972	1973	1974	1975	1977	1978
Grains											
Wheat	75.8	73.3	84.5	—	100.5	100.9	100	105.7	101	—	—
Barley	63.4	68.6	75.9	84.2	88	86.5	100	94.4	88	76.6	74
Rice	72	45.9	64.1	83.6	87.3	91.7	100	84.8	86.9	87.4	85.4
	97.3	77.2	94.1	143.2	101.8	111.5	100	104.4	118.3	91.1	88.7
Pulses	31.3	43.6	37.9	—	49.8	52.1	100	113.5	77.7	—	—
Vegetables	31.1	41.1	38.4	—	43.7	56.9	100	86.7	72.8	—	—
Industrial crops											
Sugar beet	69.2	72	80.9	—	87	88.2	100	106.4	97.2	—	—
Sugar cane	28.3	79.5	89.1	101.8	90.4	87.9	100	95.8	106.6	84.3	78.9
Cotton	—	44.4	44.4	44.5	55.5	77.7	100	100	111.1	100	144.4
Tobacco	41.9	90.4	88.7	101.8	93.4	93.1	100	114.8	85.2	93.7	65.1
	175	125	106.2	87.5	118.7	131.2	100	131.2	81.2	81.2	87.5
Total	60.2	57.5	65.6	—	83.1	86.1	100	94	89.3	81.4	81.3

Compiled from *Salnameh-e Amari-e Keshvar* (1356:270) and Azimi (1982:table 6, p. 181).

The onset of the 1970s oil boom 123

Table 6.2 Production index for major crops, 1960–78 (1973=100)

	Wheat	Barley	Paddy rice	Sugar beet	Sugar cane	Cotton
1960	64.3	69.9	75.7	17.3	—	58.6
1967	84.7	50.2	115.6	69.3	—	67.5
1968	84.9	83.1	125.1	83.5	—	97.3
1970	93.7	93.5	144.0	94.8	48.6	91.6
1971	79.4	73.5	93.6	92.3	53.8	83.2
1972	96.7	106.0	107.6	89.1	77.3	78.6
1973	100.0	100.0	100.0	100.0	100.0	100.0
1974*	63.5	64.8	88.1	91.7	102.0	115.7
1975	96.0	88.0	109.2	110.0	102.6	77.8
1976	—	—	—	129.0	76.4	76.1
1977	85.7	97.6	80.3	88.4	89.8	94.8
1978	83.4	97.8	79.1	87.0	118.1	72.3

*Adversely affected by lack of sufficient rainfall.
Compiled from Azimi (1982:table 7, p. 182). For 1970 and 1976: *Salnameh-e Amari-e Keshvar* (1356:209; 1360:273).

contributed towards the "financial success" of these farm corporations' (1980:234; see also Hooglund, 1982:70–1; and Madjd, 1983:n.33).

Where possible, commercial farmers resorted to mechanisation in a bid to mitigate the damaging effects of labour shortages and mounting agricultural wages. As a result, in the period 1974–7, average annual sales of tractors by the Organisation for the Expansion of Agricultural Machinery rose by 2.5-fold over the 1967–73 period.[14] To some extent, this arose from the favourable attitude shown by the government towards mechanisation. But objectively, too, it reflected capitalist farmers' bid to replace labour with machinery, where and when its price was prohibitive or the continuity of its supplies was uncertain.

Summary and conclusion

According to Marx, 'Part of the labouring population is . . . constantly on the point of passing over into an urban or manufacturing proletariat, *and on the look-out for circumstances favourable to this transformation*' (1867:601; emphasis added).

In Iran, in the period studied in this chapter, the impetus to these 'favourable circumstances' came from outside the agricultural sector. This comprised mainly the urban boom and the concomitant increase in the demand for labour, rather than rural poverty, peasants' destitution, and marginality – as sustained thus far by conventional wisdom.

124 Labour transfer and economic development

By stressing the depressing effects of the oil boom on rural life, conventional characterisations of Iranian agriculture have misconceived the nature of developments within the rural areas as well as between the town and country in the 1970s.

This chapter demonstrates that the much-stressed downward march of agriculture was a mere manifestation of a wider structural problem emerging in this period. Rapidly rising wages (mainly sparked off by developments in the construction sector) induced greater participation in the urban labour market, to the detriment of participation in agricultural production. This affected not only agricultural workers who were drawn into temporary construction and non-farm employment but also peasant proprietors and their families, whose relative self-sufficiency had until then left them largely protected from market vicissitudes. With a marked rise in alternative income opportunities, an increasingly large number of owner-operator peasant families were also drawn into the market orbit: by diverting more of their labour resources into non-farm rural and urban activities, their commitment to agriculture declined. The ensuing labour shortages and the rise in real wages were significant departures for Iranian agriculture from its traditional setting since the inception of the land reform. Both of these aspects have been seriously neglected in the conventional characterisations of Iran's agricultural development.

Notes

1. The following quote summarises some of the popular sentiments expressed against the *ancien régime* in this regard: 'Our agriculture has suffered because Muhammad Reza [the Shah] has sold himself and our country to the Americans, to give them our oil money and store up their useless metals' (anti-Shah preaching by a religious leader during the Revolution, cited in Dehqani-Tafti, 1981:8). Also reflecting this, 'the destruction of agriculture, animal husbandry, and forestry' was one of a total of sixteen charges cited by the Islamic prosecutor in the trial of Amir Abbas Hoveida (the Shah's longest-serving prime minister). He was subsequently executed. See Iran's two major national newspapers, *Keyhan* and *Ettela'at* (24 Esfand 1357/ March 1979). For scholarly formulations of the 'destruction' thesis, see n.5 below.
2. The international price of oil nearly quadrupled as a result of the OPEC agreement in late 1973: rising from $1.85 per barrel to $7 p.b. By the end of 1974, the figure had climbed to $10.21 p.b. As a result, the government's oil revenues in 1973/4 rose to $4.6 billion, an increase of 65 per cent over the previous year. For 1974/5, the rise was even more phenomenal: reaching $17.8 billion, it had increased by 278 per cent over 1973/4 (Bank Markazi data). This period of Iran's economic development, although much talked about, is little studied. For some background information, see Graham (1978) and Razavi and Vakil (1984).

The onset of the 1970s oil boom 125

3. Based on census figures; for more details see Hakimian (1987).
4. See Afshar (1981:1098, 1101-3). Many others also erroneously identify the wider performance of agriculture with the trend for food imports. In the context of discussions about Iranian agriculture, in particular, this approach overlooks the upward trend of per capita domestic food consumption at a time of rising 'average' incomes. As observed by the US Agricultural Attaché in Tehran in the heyday of the boom:

> It is apparent that the trend towards greater consumption is continuing, even for wheat, rice and pulses, products which might be expected to decline in an affluent society where the quality of the diet is changing. Cereals are said to account for about 80 per cent of the Iranian diet at present, but with little decrease noted. (IR6004:1-2)

5. See, for instance, Kazemi, whose study of migration into Tehran in the heyday of the oil boom, largely disregards the overall impact of the boom on the urban economic environment. His explanations are thus couched in terms of 'the importance of push factors', 'flight to the city', and 'marginality and landlessness' (1980a:30-2). Similarly, Katouzian speaks of 'the rapid destruction of Iranian agriculture in the past fifteen years' (1978:347), attributing it in the main to the state's 'adventurous strategy . . . *vis-à-vis* the agricultural sector', which 'technologically and institutionally devastated [it] all the time' (1981a:305-6). His treatment of migration as *prima facie* evidence for widespread rural poverty is also questionable:

> The assertion that the high rate of rural–urban migration reflected in part the poor state of the agrarian economy is strongly supported by the evidence on rural poverty. If migration were in fact inspired by growing employment opportunities in towns, one would not expect to find widespread poverty in rural areas. This is precisely what one finds. (1981b:30)

His identification of the roots of such poverty is also unreservedly clear: 'the plight of the Iranian peasantry is a *direct consequence* of the increase in the oil revenues' (1978:347; emphasis added). See also Afshar (1981:1103-6), and Dana (1979) among others. Madjd (1983), Mahdavy (1982), and Mir-Hosseini (1987) are, however, exceptions to this otherwise general rule.

6. The concept of 'effort-price' or 'effort-intensity' of income was first used by Arrighi (1970). This may be expressed either in terms of the working time required to earn a given unit of income or the amount of income which can be earned in a given unit of time in a particular occupation. In this way, it can give an indication of the comparative incentives to engage in different occupations.

In the labour market, where remuneration is in terms of cash income or wages, this is more straightforward as wages or salaries per a suitable unit of time (hour or working week) may be taken as an indication of this. For participation in the agricultural produce market, this is somewhat more complicated as, firstly, peasant families may engage in the production of more than one product and, secondly, only part of this may be offered for exchange in the market: the remainder being used up in family consumption. In both cases, however, a suitable valuation of net output (in farm gate prices) should give a comparable index for effort-intensity of income, allowing for the fact that the time cycle of agricultural production is normally about one year.

126 *Labour transfer and economic development*

Assuming homogeneous labour and similar working conditions, unchanged technique of agricultural production over time, and constant factor costs (fertilisers, pesticides, tractor rentals, and so on) effort-intensity of agricultural income is inversely related to the price of agricultural products, and positively related to the wage rate in the labour market. Thus wage increases in the labour market which outpace increases in the price of agricultural products would, *ceteris paribus*, alter the effort-price of income in favour of non-agricultural occupations. With reasonable mobility, this should encourage labour away from agriculture towards wage employment occupations. Conversely, significant real improvements in agricultural prices compared to wages should increase incentives of farmers to expand production rather than work in the labour market.

7. According to Kaneda:

> The Cereals Organisation is virtually impotent to have any effect on the encouragement of wheat marketing. The Organisation's buying price has tended to be either lower than the free market price (e.g. as in 1971) or, when the price has been realistic, the Organisation has been provided with insufficient resources to make any significant intervention. It appears common for farmers to sell their wheat for as little as Rl 3,500 per ton, some 30 per cent less than the nominal minimum price. (1973:43)

8. The corresponding share of the total area was 15 per cent for wheat compared to 84 per cent for rice and 66 per cent for corn (US Agricultural Attaché, IR6031:2–5).

9. Similarly, higher direct costs of production (such as the prices of technical inputs) exacerbated such disincentive effect. Partly for lack of data and partly for the sake of simplicity, our analysis will assume constant costs, although its real force would be strengthened by a proper consideration of the costs trend.

10. *Kando Kav* (1977:6). Unfortunately, there are no systematic data on agricultural wages either before or after the oil boom. The table opposite constructed from various scattered sources (including newspaper reports) gives a rough but clear indication of the upward trend especially after 1973/4.

11. By concentrating on the rising wage costs, Madjd's analysis remains limited to the large commercial farms, which relied on hired labour. The greatest majority of peasant farmers, for whom rising urban wages came as a rise in opportunity costs of agricultural production, are therefore left out from his analysis.

12. US Agricultural Attaché (IR6004:2). Two years later, his reports were confirming that 'the continued migration of rural workers' was responsible for the reduction in the area of barley; while for rice, the outlook appeared as 'somewhat pessimistic': 'The area is said to be down from 1977–8 due mainly to the effect of industrialisation on [*sic*] outward migration on labour availability' (IR8011:2, 4). Khosravi (1979:88), too, discusses disincentives to agricultural production which led 'even the rich peasants' to reduce their area of cultivation.

13. One particular form of this (known as *Nesfeh Kari* or 'half-and-half' cultivation) had become particularly common in some areas from the early days of the land reform. Under this practice, large owners contracted out land to skilled farmers – usually coming from outside the village from Yazd, Qom and Isfahan – providing them with water and contributing half of the other costs of production (seed, fertilisers and ploughing). The latter

Average agricultural wages, 1969-76 (Rials per day)

Source	Year	Men	Women and children
Keyhan (Khordad 1348)	1969	40–80	20–40
Tehran Economist (4.5.1354)	1970	70–90	50–60
Agricultural census 1350 and 1351*(a)	1971	89	48
	1972	98	52
Tehran Economist (Mehr 1353)	1973	100–120	—
	1974	220–300	—
(4.5.1354)	1975	250–300	150–200
Ettela'at (22.12.1355)	1976	500	—

*Average for the country.
Source: *Kando Kav* (1977:6).

provided labour and contributed the other half of the costs, retaining a share in kind from the final produce. For the owners of land this practice had several advantages: it would secure them the badly needed local skills for the cultivation of the more profitable cash crops, it would bring in some cash, and above all, it would wrest away potential claims of property from the local population by entrusting responsibility to 'outsiders'. See Mahdavy (1982:55); Ajami (1977:46–7).
14. Average annual sales reached 3,377 and 8,342 tractors in these two periods respectively. See *Salnameh-e Amari-e Keshvar* (1356:265; 1360:312).

7
Labour transfer and the rural economy

Introduction

This chapter has three objectives: to quantify migration and labour transfer of the 1960s and 1970s, to examine its main characteristics, and to gauge its impact on the wider rural economy. Our discussion has focused on the main determinants and mechanisms of this process. As a result, a number of important issues remain to be explored, which are taken up in this chapter.

The first of these is the actual significance of migration and labour transfer in each of the two periods studied. What was the scale of movements involved and what implications did this have for the rural economy? To tackle this question, this chapter presents detailed estimations of both population and labour flows and situates them within the rural framework so as to assess their relative importance.

The second set of issues pertains to the features and the characteristics of these flows. Who were the migrants and where did they come from? To tackle these, there will be estimates of the composition of migrants by age and sex and some reflections on their social composition.

The third and final point relates to the impact of these flows on the rural economy. Two areas of analysis are specified: the impact on agricultural output and implications for the pattern and structure of labour use within the remaining agrarian workforce.

In what follows, first comes a general discussion of the decline in the country's farm population, followed by an examination of its principal constituents: intra-rural labour transfers as well as migration to urban areas. This discussion is used as a background to assessing the magnitude and the characteristics of the generated labour flow. The ensuing section

Labour transfer and the rural economy 129

studies the impact of labour displacement, with the final section summarising the results.

The decline of farm population

Sustained labour outflow from Iranian agriculture, for reasons discussed in the previous three chapters, led to a gradual diminution in the country's farm population. Initially, this was only a relative decline, but by the end of the period there also occurred an absolute decline in the number of people occupied on the land. Accordingly, agriculture manifested all signs of losing significance in the structure of national output and employment.

On the production side, although continuing to grow in absolute terms, agriculture's share in gross domestic value-added was reduced drastically: in the early 1960s this sector contributed about one-third of national output; by the late 1970s the figure had fallen to about one-tenth. A similar proportion of agriculture in non-oil GNP had shrunk to 13.8 per cent in 1977 from 36.1 per cent in 1959 (Bank Markazi Iran data).

On the employment side, too, the number of workers engaged in agricultural production was on the decline. While the size of the rural workforce expanded constantly, the population working on the land first grew slightly and then declined in absolute terms (see Figure 7.1). In 1956, there were nearly 3.3 million agricultural workers accounting for 54 per cent of the total labour force in rural areas. During the next decade, their numbers rose to 3.7 million (including about 380,000 seasonal workers), but their overall share was reduced to 48.8 per cent. By 1976, the number of workers employed in this sector actually declined for the first time in absolute terms (to about 2.9 million). Even including 600,000 or so seasonally unemployed workers, the total was only just over one-third of all rural labour force (details in Table 7.1).

Moreover, the structure of agricultural employment was significantly affected by the developments of the period. As discussed before, two such trends were manifest in this respect: the fall of wage employment and the consolidation of family labour. While the number of wage and salary earners in agriculture declined by 170,000 (about one in five of such jobs disappeared), the number of unpaid family workers increased by 44,000, or by about 8 per cent. This was indeed the only category of agricultural labour to rise (Table 7.1).

This broad trend, however, conceals another important development in the structure of rural employment. The number of seasonally employed workers rose by as many as 236,000 (a rise of about 62 per

130 Labour transfer and economic development

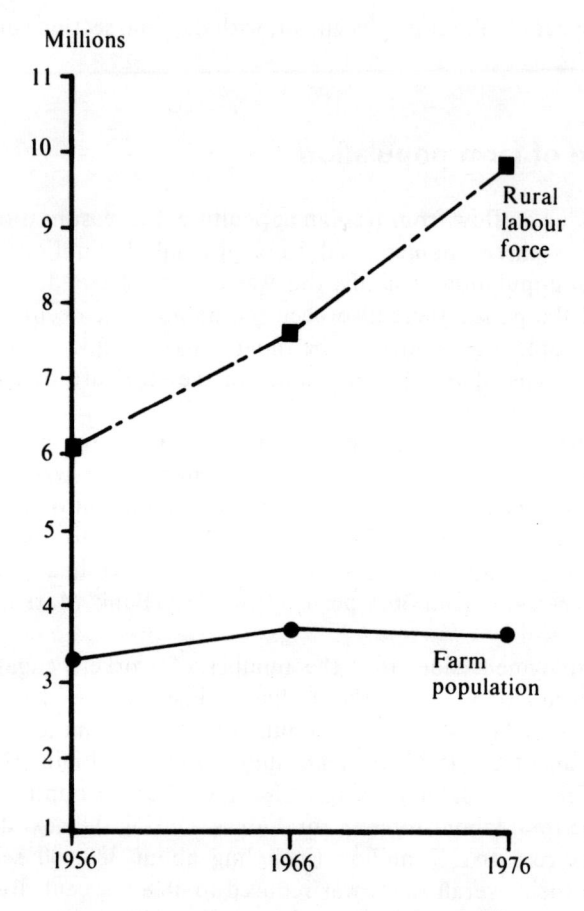

Figure 7.1 Farm population and the rural labour force, 1956-76.

cent). Including these among wage workers (an assumption to be justified on the basis of the piece-rate nature of their employment), it becomes clear that the supply of wage workers in the Iranian countryside rose in aggregate by about 70,000. As indicated before, this expansion in the supply of 'free hands' has to be seen in the context of an all-round contraction in wage employment opportunities.

The once-dominant position of agriculture was also seriously weakened within the rural sector. In 1956, one in two rural adult males (over the age of 10) found employment in this sector. In the course of the subsequent two decades, the proportion fell to less than one in three.

No less interesting was the age pattern underlying this broad trend.

Table 7.1 Changes in the employment status of agricultural workers 10 years of age and over, total country, 1956–76*

Status	Nov. 1956 ('000)	Nov. 1966† ('000)	Nov. 1976 ('000)	Change: 1966–76 ('000)	Change: 1966–76 (%)
Wage and salary earners	912	824	655	−169	−20.0
Non-wage employed	2,369	2,499	2,327	−172	−6.9
(Own-account workers)	(1,786)	(1,902)	(1,704)	(−198)	(−10.4)
(Unpaid family workers)	(541)	(543)	(587)	(+44)	(+8.1)
Total employed‡	3,273§	3,324	2,982	−342	−10.3
Seasonally employed	—	380¶	616	+236	+62.0
Grand total	3,273	3,704	3,598	−106	−2.9

*'Agricultural workers' taken as ISCO major group 6: agriculture, animal husbandry and forestry workers, fishermen, and hunters (rural and urban).
†Adjusted to include 194,000 persons from unsettled population all of whom were assumed to be agricultural workers, and distributed in the table according to the employment status of the settled agricultural workers.
‡Total excludes 'occupations not adequately described'.
§Includes the seasonally employed.
¶Refers to the settled population only.
Sources: Census (1956; 1966:53, 171; 1976:67, 137).

132 Labour transfer and economic development

The decline was most marked in the lower and middle ranges of the age spectrum: the number of agricultural occupations fell by 38 per cent for those between 10 and 19, and by 34 per cent for those between 25 and 34 (Figure 7.2 and Tables C.3 and C.4 in Appendix C). In the case of the very young, despite the sharpest decline there still remained a sizable workforce engaged on the land as unpaid family workers. This trend, which occurred against a background of rising schooling opportunities for the young, stemmed principally from agrarian reorganisations associated with increased peasant proprietorship and, with it, a greater reliance on peasant family labour. Furthermore, the same figure shows that for the rural youths between the ages of 20 and 24, among whom inclination towards agricultural occupations was traditionally weakest, absorption fell to its all-time low. By 1976, fewer than one in five were engaged in this sector. For all others up to the age of 45, the numbers working on the land declined similarly: both in relative and absolute terms.

A notable exception, however, is to be found in the case of those above the age of 45 in general, and those above 65 in particular. In the case of the latter, both numbers and proportions engaged on the land increased against the general trend of employment contraction in agriculture. This reflected a wider trend, namely the mobilisation of 'subsidiary' sources of labour in this sector: as young, active males left for towns, the scope for the participation of the elderly and rural females in the organisation of agricultural activity was markedly broadened.

The overall decline in Iran's farm population reflected two underlying trends: the greater degree of rural diversification away from the traditionally strong agricultural sector, and the growing tide of migration to urban areas. Each of these has already been touched upon, but they must now be studied in more detail.

Rural employment diversification

Although by the end of this period agriculture was still by far the most important single source of economic activity in rural areas, its position was being rapidly eroded by a greater diversification of the rural economy. A variety of non-farm activities ranging from trade, services, and construction to manufacturing and processing, rural crafts, and home industries expanded considerably in this period, attracting part of the agricultural workforce.

The number of new jobs created outside the farm sector increased by about 50 per cent between 1966 and 1976 (Table 7.2). Underlying this trend was a simultaneous expansion in both wage and non-wage

Labour transfer and the rural economy **133**

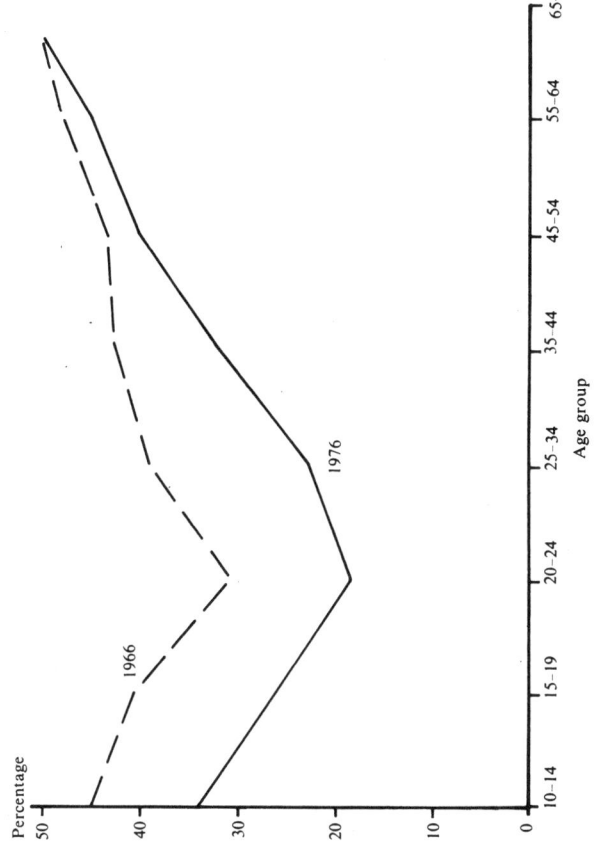

Figure 7.2 The percentage of labour force in each age group engaged in agricultural occupations, 1966–76.

Table 7.2 The employment status of non-agricultural workers in rural areas, 1966–76

Status	Nov. 1966 ('000)	Nov. 1976 ('000)	Change: 1966–76 ('000)	(%)
Wage and salary earners	801	1,231	+430	+53.7
Non-wage employed	506	708	+202	+40.0
Total employed	1,307	1,939	+632	+48.3
Seasonally unemployed	51	21	–30	–58.8

Sources: Census (1966:table 19; 1976:table 21).

opportunities outside agriculture: the former grew by about 54 per cent and the latter by 40 per cent. This process was, however, uneven and contradictory.

On the one hand, the development of some urban industries displaced labour in certain rural crafts and industries. The development of the plastics industry, for instance, which manufactured containers, storage jars, sandals, etc., made redundant a considerable number of the rural pottery workers, metal workers and workers in the traditional slipper-making industry (*giveh*). Similarly, the development of pressed metal and aluminium industries reduced the demand for rural metal craftsmen's utensils (Dhamija, 1976:39).

On the other hand, growing integration into the structure of the national economy and rising urban and rural incomes (particularly in the 1970s) helped the expansion of some old and the creation of other new industries. We have already seen how favourable demand conditions at home and abroad revived the rural carpet- and rug-weaving industry. Given the 'putting-out' nature of this home industry, its expansion took place alongside agricultural activities to the extent that it developed into an important side-line activity for many peasant families.

Similarly, there was a certain relocation of some light labour intensive industries into rural areas. The previously discussed case of the brickmaking industry – flourishing in the oil boom years – epitomises best this much neglected growth of the non-farm sector in Iran.

Moreover, the construction boom and the expansion of the country's infrastructural network, the development of the transportation system, and the growth of the service sector generated new sources of demand for rural labour, absorbing to some extent the mass of labourers leaving agricultural occupations. For others, migration to urban areas was yet another, often more important, alternative.

Migration

Out-migration was by far the most important contributory factor to the consistent decline in Iran's farm population. Every year thousands of villagers left for urban centres, principally in search of a job or a better job, but also for education, marriage, and to join other family members already established in towns. There were, however, significant differences in the nature and form of migration which took place in the two periods that we have been studying.

In the 1960s, the bulk of migrants consisted of poor peasants and landless farm labourers whose economic conditions deteriorated rapidly in the aftermath of the land reform. Increased mechanisation on large lands coupled with intensive use of family labour on small and medium peasant holdings reduced the demand for hired workers in agriculture. Given the sluggish nature of the rural economy at large and the inability of the non-farm sector to absorb those pushed off the land, open unemployment increased visibly in rural areas. This paved the way for large-scale and permanent cityward migration.

In the 1970s, however, the nature of the interaction between agriculture and the rest of the economy was radically altered. With the oil boom, wage-earning opportunities outside this sector improved considerably, as a result of which its income 'effort-price' compared to that of wage-earning in general deteriorated decisively. This induced large sections of the self-sufficient peasantry to seek often temporary employments in the urban sector. Accompanying this development, circular migration was established as a major form of labour transfer in these years.

Unfortunately, it is not possible to differentiate between these two periods of migration at a statistical level. The available data – principally the two national censuses of 1966 and 1976 – from which we have made our calculations of the size and the scope of migration, correspond neither to the beginning nor to the end of either of these two periods. The results, which are summarised in Table 7.3, have, therefore, to be taken as representing the combined effects of migration in both periods.[1]

This table shows that the total (net) rural-to-urban migration in the intercensal period 1966–76 amounted to some 2.5 million people. Though conforming to the results of at least three other independent studies,[2] it is likely that this is an underestimation of the actual extent of migration. The reasons for this lie partly in the semi-slack nature of the period when census surveys were conducted (November), and partly in the growing importance of circular migration in the heyday of the oil boom.[3] The results – involving some quarter of a million people every year – indicate, nonetheless, a considerable transfer of population to urban areas.

136 Labour transfer and economic development

Table 7.3 Estimate of (net) migration and its effects on urban and rural population, 1966–76

	Population in Nov 66*	Expected natural increase 1966–76		Actual increase		Net gain§	
		Average annual rate (%)	Expected cumulative increase	Persons	Average annual rate (%)	Persons	As % of expected increase	As % of actual increase

	Population in Nov 66*	Average annual rate (%)	Expected cumulative increase	Persons	Average annual rate (%)	Persons	As % of expected increase	As % of actual increase
Urban (1966-basis)	9,794,246	2.42‡	2,645,707	5,223,550	4.37	2,577,843	97.4	+49.3
Rural (1966-basis)	15,994,676	2.89†	5,274,114†	2,696,271†	1.57	−2,577,843	−48.9	−95.6
Total country	25,788,923	2.71	7,919,821	2,919,821	2.71			

*Includes estimate for unsettled population, 710,000 of which were distributed among the 1966 rural population.
†Residual figure.
‡Estimate taken from *Population Growth Survey of Iran, Final Report, 1973–76* conducted jointly by the UN and the Statistical Centre of Iran (see SCI, 1978:49). This is an average for the 1973–6 period and corresponds to a rate of natural increase in rural areas of 3.03 per cent. We have treated the urban estimate as more reliable.
§We are assuming (net) international immigration as being insignificant. The figures thus refer to the (survivors) of (net) rural-urban migrants.
Sources: For population, Census (1966:table 1, 1976:table 1) adjusted for urban areas on the 1966-basis as explained in Chapter 8 (n.2). For urban rate of natural increase, SCI (1978). For methodology of calculation, UN (1970:27–35).

Labour transfer and the rural economy 137

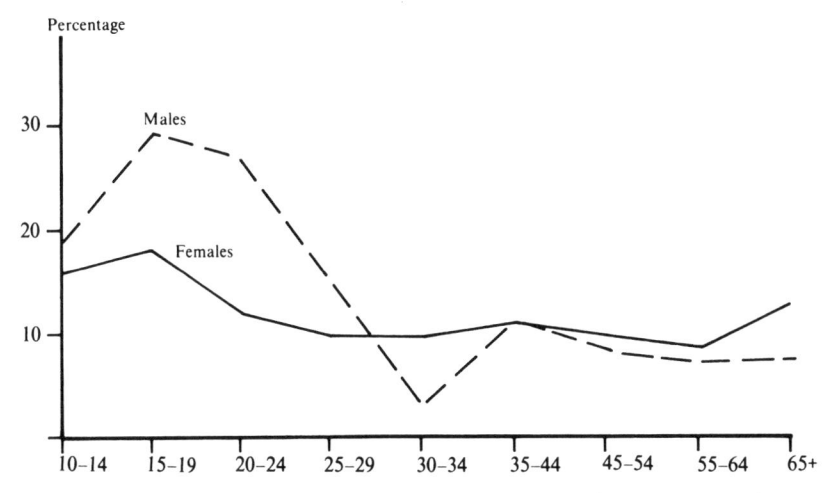

Figure 7.3 Net rural-to-urban population transfer ratios by age and sex, 1966-76.

A closer examination of the data sheds new light on the quantitative significance of migration in the rural context: net migration to urban areas almost equalled the *actual* increase in Iran's village population (about 96 per cent). This meant that, on average, one in two expected additions to the rural population was lost to urban areas. In this sense, therefore, the *expected* rate of growth of rural population was halved through population displacements.

The same calculations also bring out another major feature of migration: the predominance of the young. Although generally in line with evidence from other less developed countries (Connell *et al.*, 1976), this feature appears to have been even more striking in the Iranian context: as many as 70 per cent of men and 60 per cent of women migrants of working age were between 10 and 24 years of age only (see Tables C.5 and C.6 in Appendix C). This tendency is also brought out by calculations of the *rates* of migration in different age groups. These rates, based on net migration per 100 persons of the hypothetical survivors of the 1966 rural population, indicate the probability of departure for the rural population at each age bracket. Figure 7.3 shows clearly that departure rates were highest for both young males and females between the age of 10 and 29. For men, in particular, the probability of exodus peaked in the age range 15-19, indicating that almost one in three young males was likely to leave for the towns (details in Tables C.5 and C.6).

Some authors have ascribed this marked tendency to the nature of the property reforms introduced by the land reform. Basing redistributions on traditional cultivation rights (*haqq-e nasaq*), it is argued, the reforms generally favoured the older generation of peasants by virtue of their established customary rights and superior farming experience. When it came to departures, therefore, it was not surprising that the disaffected rural youths accounted for a disproportionate share of migrants (Research Group in Agricultural Economics, 1970). To this, one may add the rising tide of new educational and employment possibilities in towns, which were becoming increasingly more attractive for the young villagers particularly towards the end of the period.

Labour transfer: dimensions and characteristics

Impressive though population flows generated by migration may be, they have to be distinguished from the flow or transfer of labour. Clearly, not all migrants are economically active, nor does all migration take place for economic reasons. The fact that of the 2.5 million migrants more than 400,000 consisted of children below 10 years of age, as well as the strong presence of females among adult migrants (43 per cent of the total) may indeed be taken as an argument in favour of the importance of family migration, in turn an indication of the possible strength of non-economic factors (Table 7.3 and Tables C.5 and C.6 in Appendix C).

This observation, however, needs to be qualified. Evidence on family migration does not necessarily contradict the predominance of economic motives in population flows: dependants may be following the economically active members of their family in search of a change in their economic conditions. In the context presented above, the fact that over four-fifths of all migrants were of working age seems to sustain this point. Another, perhaps stronger, indication may be seen in the fact that adult males (with generally higher activity rates) accounted for about 57 per cent of all working age migrants. A similar proportion in the overall demographic structure of the country was 49 per cent only.

In order to estimate the rural-to-urban labour flows, two assumptions have been made. Firstly, migrants' activity rates have been taken to be an average of the relevant urban and rural labour force participation rates. Although a simplifying, and possibly also conservative, assumption, this may be justified on the grounds that over a range of socioeconomic parameters, migrants reportedly exhibit a combination of characteristics pertaining to those of both the receiving and departing areas (Lee, 1966). Secondly, to take account of variations over time, migrants' activity rates between 1966 and 1976 have been assumed to conform to the same overall pattern for the country as a whole (chiefly men's declining rates).

Table 7.4 Components of change in the rural labour force (1966-basis) by sex, 1966-76

	Total expected increase* ('000)	(%)	Net out-migration†‡ ('000)	(%)	Actual growth§ ('000)	(%)
Males	+1,222	100	+882	72.2	+340	27.8
Females	+388	100	+110	28.3	+278	71.7
Total	+1,610	100	+992	61.6	+618	38.4

*Derived figures.
†Positive figures signify departures.
‡Estimates.
§Census data.
Source: Census (1976:xxxix, xl). For migration figures, see Appendix A.

The results, summarised in Table 7.4, leave little doubt about the quantitative significance of labour transfer in the rural context.[4] The total amount of labour flow generated by migration in these years amounted to just under 1 million people. On this basis, it appears that as many as 62 per cent of the gross additions to the rural labour force departed for urban areas. For females the ratio was lower (28 per cent), while for males it reached as high as 72 per cent. This discrepancy reflected the sexual composition of working age migrants, which comprised eight times more males than females.

It is hard to ascertain what percentage of the labour force leaving villages came from agriculture. Not all migrants had an occupation before departure, nor were all those with a job restricted to a single activity prior to leaving for towns. Nonetheless, assuming that some half to three-quarters of migrant labourers came from agriculture, it would appear that migration alone drained this sector of some half to three-quarters of a million of its workforce. Add to these the loss of perhaps 250,000-300,000 workers to the rural non-farm sector, and the total number lost from agriculture stands somewhere in the region of three-quarters to one million workers.

The impact on the rural economy

Such scale of both population and labour flows inevitably raises questions about the wider impact of these on the rural economy. Two main areas are examined below: the impact on output, and changes in the pattern of labour use. Let us start by examining the state of agricultural output as a result of labour transfer.

Trends in agricultural output

There is little evidence to suggest that agricultural output declined in the decade after the land reform. Even allowing for disruptions expected in the early years of a major redistribution programme, all indications are that the output of major farming crops was broadly maintained, and sometimes even increased in absolute terms. Most Iranian agronomists seem to agree that on average the output of major crops increased by about 3% per annum until the early 1970s – roughly in line with the rate of population growth (Kaneda, 1973:15-16, among others).

This picture of a stagnant per capita food output has, however, been widely seen as another indication of the 'poor' performance of Iranian agriculture. To some observers, the problem has appeared even more acute considering the adoption of large-scale measures aimed at the reorganisation and modernisation of this sector, growing use of technical inputs, expanding markets, and increasing (though often allegedly insufficient) supply of development funds and credits (see, for instance, Katouzian, 1978:362). Moreover, as shown in Chapter 6, this image, which originated in the 1960s, has been uncritically projected onto the 1970s, when the oil shock is supposed to have pushed agriculture further along its path of 'destruction' and 'degeneration'.

In what follows it is argued that two broad sets of issues might have contributed to a general underrating of the performance of this sector.

Firstly, most studies have ignored the possible impact of spreading peasant proprietorship on output estimates. The elimination of landlord's share, new ownership of land and possible increases in output may encourage peasant households' consumption of own produce. Yet fears of taxation or inhibitions about debt-repayment may lead peasants to systematically under-report their production figures. A rough indication of the extent of this bias in the Iranian context may be seen in the fact that, assuming an improvement of 10 kg in peasant per capita consumption of wheat in 1966/7, the downward bias in the wheat output estimate would be about 3 per cent of total production for that year.[5]

This kind of bias is most accentuated in those studies that have sought the reasons for the 'plight' of Iran's agriculture in the stagnant nature of its *production*, rather than the difficulties of procuring sufficient quantities of *marketed surplus*. This is why this view has, in general, emphasised the political and institutional, rather than economic, factors in its explanation of the government's apparent change of policy in favour of large-scale capitalist farming which came in the late 1960s (Katouzian, 1978:366).

A second, and possibly even more problematic, approach to the study of Iranian agriculture is related to the oil boom years. The last chapter has already shed some light on the diverging interpretations of the agricultural development of the country in this period. While according to one interpretation, 'agriculture shrinks fast', according to another, it grows by 4.6% per annum in real terms; while the former speaks of 'the irreversible destruction of the rural society', the latter draws attention to the expansion of non-farm activities; and finally, while the one sees the human and material resources of 'our society' going 'not "with the wind"...but with the oil', the other puts Iran's rate of growth of agriculture among the highest in the world![6]

This puzzling and apparently paradoxical picture has presented students of Iran's contemporary economic development with a major problem. Some thoughts on this are therefore justified.

We have already shown how a constellation of several factors has led to the emergence of a 'deformed' view of agriculture in the 1970s. Chief among these were Iran's growing dependence on food imports, the embarrassing failure of the state's large-scale agricultural modernisation projects, and last but not least, the overshadowing growth of other sectors, both in the geographical and economic sense.

Of these, the spectacular rise in imports of the main foodstuffs (sometimes by as much as nine- to ten-fold) has, in particular, aroused strong feelings against the loss of Iran's earlier self-sufficiency in food production.[7] Although identifying this trend with the wider performance of agriculture is highly questionable, Iranian economists in general have continued to treat food dependency as *prima facie* evidence in support of the doomed fate of domestic agriculture.[8]

Despite a broad awareness of the dramatic rise in per capita consumption of food in the oil boom years, few of the studies cited have paid adequate attention to its powerful impact on food imports. This phenomenon in turn derived from the dramatic rise in urban incomes and was quite independent of the developments within domestic agriculture. For its part, of course, agriculture struggled through difficult years during which growing disincentives to production culminated in a contraction of the area under cultivation and a fall in the supply of required farming hands. These developments made it difficult for agriculture to maintain its output, but nowhere was it true to say that it was 'washed away with oil', as popularly pictured thus far.

In summary, it appears that the departure of a considerable section of the farm workforce after the land reform did not adversely affect the trend of agricultural production. Output grew at a moderate pace of 3% per annum, although allowing for peasants' increased consumption of own crop, the real improvement could be somewhat higher. It was not until the oil boom years that maintaining the output of some crops ran into difficulties. Even so, this was the *result* and not the *source* of the growing attraction of capital and labour away from agriculture and into other economic sectors.

Changes in the pattern of labour use

Labour transfer was also accompanied by important changes in the pattern of labour use in rural areas.

Firstly, it appears that for those who remained behind and were still engaged in agricultural occupations, work generally assumed a more 'regular' and 'standard' pattern than before. Table 7.5 shows this in relation to the weekly work pattern of agricultural workers. This is based on the number of hours of work reported by these workers in the week preceding enumeration. Although the scope for generalisation is limited by the scanty nature of the data, the results are, nevertheless, interesting. It is obvious that both the number and proportion of those concentrated at the two ends of the weekly time scale declined by between 23 and 37 per cent. This involved people who were either 'overworked' (with a weekly work schedule in excess of 56 hours), or 'underemployed' (working less than 29 hours a week). In contrast, the number and share in total of those working a more regular or 'standard' week of about 43 to 57 hours (6–10 hours daily) increased substantially. By 1976, almost one in every two agricultural workers fell into this category compared with one in three a decade earlier.

Secondly, the departure of young, active males from agriculture drained this sector of one of its primary sources of labour. As a result, other, 'secondary' sources were mobilised, chief among whom were the village elderly and rural females.

Evidence in support of this is presented in Figure 7.4, which shows a contrasting picture in terms of labour force participation rates at the two ends of the age spectrum. As discussed before, the declining trend for the young (below 24 years of age) was at least partially occasioned by increased schooling opportunities, which delayed their entry into the labour force. For the elderly, however, increased responsibilities within the rural division of labour achieved quite the opposite: expanding their roles in production and pushing up their rates of participation in the labour force.

There is further evidence to suggest that for the most part this increase was explained by a growing (re-)integration of this rural group into agricultural occupations. The number of those above the age of 45 who remained engaged in agricultural activities rose by as many as 336,000 (up by 44 per cent) between 1966 and 1976 (see Tables C.3 and C.4 in Appendix C). This is particularly significant given the general trend of

Table 7.5 Weekly hours of work of agricultural workers 10 years of age and over, total country: 1966 and 1976*†

	Nov. 1966 ('000)	(%)	Nov. 1976 ('000)	(%)	Change: 1966–76 ('000)	(%)
Less than 8 hr	92	2.9	34	1.1		
8–14 hr	24	0.8	26	0.9		
15–21 hr	91	2.9	72	2.4		
22–28 hr	91	2.9	96	3.2		
Less than 29 hr	298	9.5	228	7.6	−70	−23.5
29–34 hr	249	7.9	182	6.1		
35–42 hr	371	11.8	392	13.1		
29–42 hr	620	19.7	574	19.1	−46	−7.4
43–49 hr	369	11.8	577	19.3		
50–56 hr	628	20.0	827	27.7		
43–56 hr	997	31.8	1,404	47.0	+407	+40.8
57–63 hr	407	13.0	277	9.3		
64–70 hr	648	20.6	355	11.9		
71 hr or more	168	5.4	145§	4.9		
Over 56 hr	1,223	39.0	777	26.1	−446	−36.5
Total	3,138	100	2,984	100	−154	−4.9
Mean			50.9			
Median			50.9			

*Total number of hours worked in the week preceding enumeration.
†Excludes the seasonally unemployed workers.
‡Refers to the settled population only.
§Includes 5,000 persons who did not report hours of work.
Sources: Computed from Census (1966:table 20; 1976:table 22).

declining farm population in this period.

Similarly, rural females' participation in the labour force was prolonged and its extent across nearly all age groups increased. This was seen in two ways: (1) the rise in their average aggregate activity rate (from 14.2 per cent in 1966 to 16.3 per cent in 1976) (Figure 7.4 and Table C.7)[9], and (2) the rise in estimated total gross years of working life, increasing by almost one year at the age bracket of 10–14.[10]

This development was significant for two reasons. Firstly, as will be shown in the next chapter, this trend ran against the observed trend in towns, where females' activity rates were not only lower but also found to be falling. Secondly, it indicated the more important point about the growing significance of females within the rural division of labour. As with the older generation of males in peasant households, females' direct and indirect responsibilities in the organisation and overseeing of agricultural production increased sharply. This was particularly true at peak harvest times when the absence of their young, active counterparts, mostly engaged on urban construction sites, became most transparent.

This point is borne out by data compiled in Table C.3 (Appendix C). With the exception of those in the age groups 10–14 and 25–34, the number of female agricultural workers rose in absolute terms against a background of falling farm population. This was most pronounced among the higher age brackets (especially those over 45), whose proportions as well as absolute numbers increased.

It would thus appear that in Iran's experience of development, labour transfer was closely allied with changes in the pattern of labour use. On the one hand, a new and more 'standard' pattern of working week began to emerge among the remaining workforce. On the other hand, a process of mobilisation of 'secondary' sources of labour was activated. As a consequence, village women and the older generation of rural men began to assume greater roles in the organisation of agricultural production.

Summary and conclusion

In the two decades from 1960 to 1979, Iran's agrarian economy evolved through a labour surplus phase into one beset by labour shortages. These decades were both characterised by continual labour transfer within and between rural and urban areas. The form, character and mechanisms of this process, however, were markedly different in each of the two subperiods studied.

In the years following extensive reorganisation of the village economy by the land reform, the impetus to labour displacement had a largely institutional character. This is not to discount the role of economic incentives but merely to emphasise that they operated within the new framework of property rights defined by the reforms. It was, therefore, mainly farm labourers and poor peasant families that departed – often for good – for the urban areas. For the new class of well-to-do peasant proprietors who stayed behind, ownership of land, freedom from the centuries-long yoke of the landlord and the newly acquired self-esteem in village society came as a major material and psychological boost. As a result, their efforts on the land increased, the scope for their family's participation in production widened, and the area under cultivation expanded. In this period, output was not a casualty of the labour transfer unleashed by the land reform.

In the subsequent period, labour contraction was brought about by

Labour transfer and the rural economy **145**

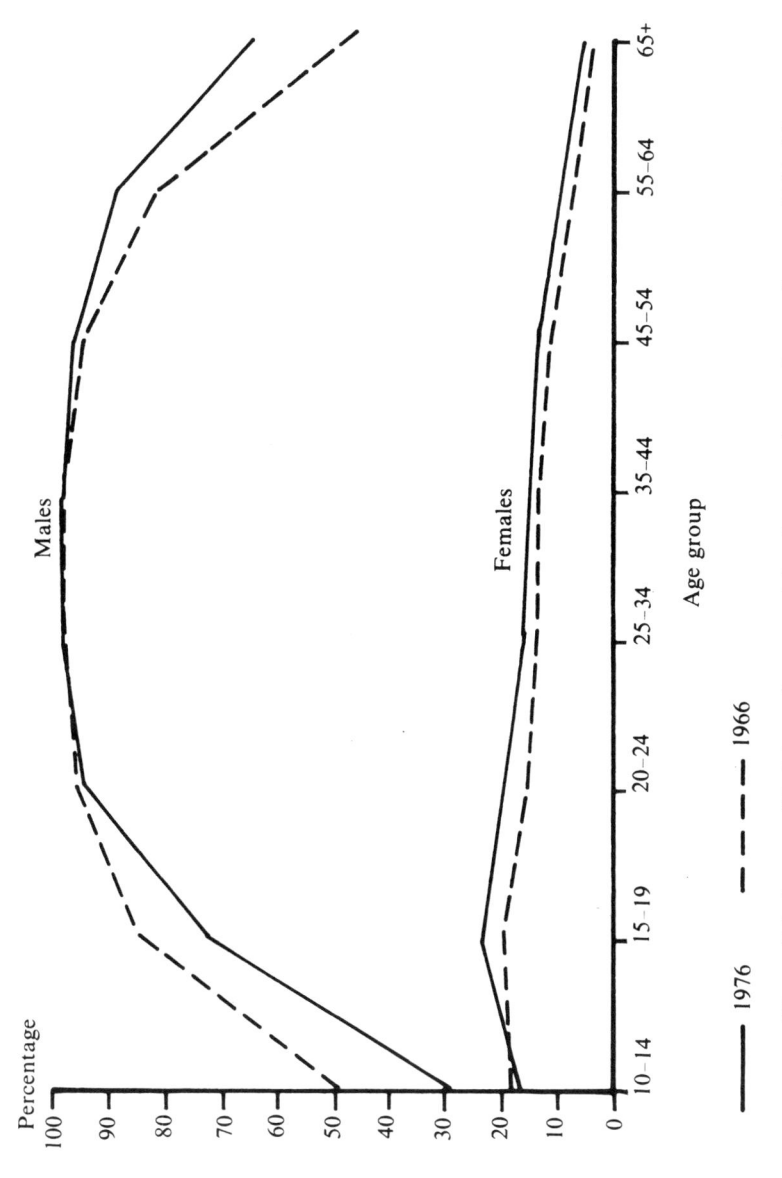

Figure 7.4 Age specific labour force participation rates in rural areas by sex, 1966–76.

changes in the economic incentives governing peasant production. In general new and growing attractions towards cash-earning opportunities in non-skilled jobs outside agriculture induced a large-scale, often temporary, migration of farm workers from self-contained production units to mainly urban areas. This exodus gathered such momentum in so short a period of time that even the rising trend of agricultural wages coupled with the importation of non-skilled immigrant workers from abroad could not alleviate the recurrent labour shortages in the countryside. As a result, the area under cultivation contracted, and with it, sustaining agricultural output proved to be difficult.

Two further observations are worth making regarding the quantitative significance of migration and its characteristics. Calculations presented in this chapter show that the total volume of labour displaced in the period 1966–76 reached about 1 million people. The selective operation of the mechanism was also reflected in the fact that migrants were principally, though not exclusively, men (with a ratio of 8 : 1 in their favour). Moreover, as many as 70 per cent of men and 60 per cent of women migrants were young, that is of working age between 10 and 24. In incremental terms, too, labour transfer was found to drain as many as two-thirds of the expected (net) additions to the rural workforce (three-quarters for men).

It is thus not surprising to see that labour transfer made an important impact on the structure of labour use within the remaining rural workforce. This occurred partly through the reorganisation of the existing pattern of work time, but mainly through the mobilisation of new sources of labour. Over a decade after the implementation of Iran's land reform, the weekly working pattern of the remaining workers was generally more regular. For its part, agriculture was more dependent on 'subsidiary' sources of labour. The role and participation of the elderly had expanded, women had become more integrated into the rural division of labour, and there was still a considerable body of young unpaid family workers, working primarily on owner-cultivated plots.

Notes

1. Alternative data provided by the manpower censuses of the Ministry of Labour and Social Affairs for the intervening years (1968, 1970a and 1972) are neither adequately reliable nor compatible with the results and framework of the two national censuses used here. Further, even with data available, it is doubtful whether it would be possible entirely to separate migration in the two periods as some people would be joining others already established in the towns for reasons related to developments in the earlier period.

2. Barrasi-e Ijmali-e Muhajerat be Manateq-e Shahri (A Summary Study of Migration to Urban Areas), Plan and Budget Organisation, Mimeo, n.d., Tehran, (cited in Kazemi, 1980a:28) gives a total of 2.1 million migrants; *Financial Times*, 25 July 1977, gives a figure of 2.5 million; and Kohli puts a similar estimate at 2.7 million (1977:table 4, p.11).
3. Clearly, these estimates also underrate step-migration through which some villagers move to smaller towns as a preliminary stage in their later move to larger towns and cities.
4. These calculations are set out fully in Appendix A.
5. This is based on the following assumptions: a total peasant population of 12.5 million, average per capita use of wheat (including seed and carry-over requirements) close to 160 kg per annum, and total domestic wheat output of about 4 million tons (based on Madjd, 1983:30).
6. The first viewpoint is formulated in Katouzian (1978:368). For agriculture's growth rate, see Bank Markazi Iran (Annual Report, 1356:15). Data on comparative growth rates for this sector in different countries appear in the World Development Report (1980:table 2, pp. 112–13). It is interesting to note that the same World Bank table indicates negative rates of growth of agriculture in some industrial countries such as Sweden, Belgium, France and Finland, and negligible growth rates in others like the United Kingdom and Italy.
7. See, for instance, H. Afshar, who regrets the reduced share of Iranian agriculture in the overall structure of domestic output and the labour force. This leads her to explore possibilities that will ensure the return of agriculture's 'important position in the Iranian economy' (1981:1106). The wisdom of this argument, which favours keeping substantial proportions of the population on the land in order to feed the rest of the population is questionable.
8. See, for instance, Katouzian who complains: 'We have now reached the position where food is distributed to the rural areas to make up for their consumption deficits!' (1978:367). No distinction is made between deficits arising from lower production and those occasioned by a rise in consumption.
9. Given the erratic nature of women's participation in the labour force (particularly in the rural areas), female activity rates are notoriously inadequate in indicating the true extent of their economic activity. They must, therefore, be used cautiously.
10. Estimate of the total gross years of working life gives an indication of the expected duration of stay in the labour force for the remainder of life at each age group. This is calculated on the basis of the prevailing labour force participation rates. For methodology of calculation, see UN (1971:38), and for results, Table C.8 in Appendix C.

8
Labour transfer from the urban perspective

Introduction

Our discussion of migration and labour transfer in the 1960s and 1970s has so far been confined to the rural context. In this chapter, we turn to the urban areas, with a view to assessing the relative significance of the population and labour flows for the receiving sectors and areas.

Given the enormity of the subject and the limited scope of this chapter, however, the study will be selective and limited only to three aspects of urban development: population, labour supply, and absorption (or employment) in towns. By singling out these three areas for analysis, the aim is to provide estimates of the quantitative impact of migration, and to compare it with other sources of urban growth and change.

Urban population: growth and composition

The years that saw heavy migration from Iran's villages witnessed also a rapid and consistent rise in her urban population. In the decade 1966–76, urban growth averaged about 5% per annum, increasing the total to 15.8 million (from 9.8 million). Rural population, in contrast, grew at a rate of 1.6% per annum only, to reach 17.8 million (from 15.2 million). The process of urbanisation over the two decades after the mid-1950s was even more impressive: the number of towns (defined as areas with a population of 5,000 or more) doubled, while their population increased by as much as 150 per cent. As a result, the urban share in the total population of the country rose constantly: at the time of the first census in 1956, less than one-third of the population were registered as living in

Labour transfer from the urban perspective 149

Table 8.1 Components of change in urban population and population of working age by sex, 1966–76*

	Net natural growth†		Net migration‡		Net overall growth	
	('000)	(%)	('000)	(%)	('000)	(%)
Total population	2,646	50.7	2,578	49.3	5,224	100
Males	1,377	49.8	1,387	50.2	2,764	100
Females	1,269	51.6	1,191	48.4	2,460	100
Population of working age	2,021	49.0	2,099	51.0	4,120	100
Males	986	45.0	1,205	55.0	2,191	100
Females	1,035	53.7	894	46.3	1,929	100

*1966-basis; see Chapter 8 (n.2).
†Treated as residual.
‡Estimate.
Sources: Computed from Census (1966:table 1; 1976:table 1); Table 7.3; and Tables C.5 and C.6 in Appendix C for migration figures.

towns; by 1976 when the third census was conducted, this proportion was fast approaching half (47 per cent). In some provinces, indeed, this share had already reached as high as 60–80 per cent of the total.[1]

Leaving aside the reclassification of urban areas, which undoubtedly inflates the above picture of urban growth and expansion,[2] there are two other main ways in which such growth comes about: through natural increase and through rural-to-urban migration.

According to a UN-sponsored survey of population growth, the annual rate of natural increase in Iranian towns was 2.42 per cent between 1973 and 1976. A similar rate for the rural areas was estimated to be 3.49 per cent. The discrepancy between these two rates was attributed to both higher birth and death rates in the rural areas: the urban birth rate of 32.5 per thousand was 33 per cent lower than the rural rate, while the urban death rate of 83 per thousand was 40 per cent lower than the corresponding rural rate (SCI, 1978:48–52).

Our calculations of migration in the last chapter (Table 7.3) combine the results of this survey with those of the relevant national censuses in 1966 and 1976. This enables us to make a relative assessment of the effect of net rural-to-urban migration on the population of urban areas.

As may be seen in Table 8.1, the scale of changes brought about by rural-to-urban population transfers matched that of natural growth in the urban population.[3] Amounting to more than 2.5 million people, net migration in this period contributed to almost half of the gross (or actual) population increase in towns. This meant that, on average, one in two net additions to the latter was likely to be a rural immigrant. In this way,

150 Labour transfer and economic development

Table 8.2 Components of change in urban population 10 years of age and over by age group and sex, 1966–76*

Age group	Males			Females		
	A	B	C	A	B	C
10–14	+286	+87	77	+215	+103	68
15–19	+347	+146	70	+207	+182	53
20–24	+215	+140	61	+102	+233	31
25–34	+100	+204	33	+113	+182	38
35–44	+117	+104	47	+109	+102	52
45–54	+79	+211	27	+72	+164	30
55+	+62	+93	40	+75	+70	52
Total†	+1,205	+986	55	+894	+1,035	46

*1966-basis.
†Totals may not add up due to rounding.
A = net rural urban migrants ('000).
B = net natural growth ('000).
C = migrants as a percentage of the total increase.
Source: Constructed from material in Appendices A and B.

migration *doubled* the growth momentum of urban population, and was an essential component of the rapid urbanisation process which swept the country in the 1960s and the 1970s.

As expected, for some age groups the impact was even more significant. Table 8.2 shows that young migrant boys and girls between 10 and 19 years of age, for instance, accounted for between 53 and 77 per cent of the net additions to urban population in their age groups. For boys, this tendency was even more marked: the ratio never fell below 61 per cent in any of the three age groups between 10 and 24. This characteristic confirms yet again – this time from the perspective of the receiving areas – the predominance of the young among migrants, which we encountered in Chapter 7.

This feature, coupled with the sheer scale of transfers involved, manifested itself in the changing age composition of the urban population. Partly as a result of the levelling-off of the earlier decade's baby boom, but mainly because of the predominance of the young incoming migrants, the demographic composition of the towns' population showed signs of change in favour of the working age groups. This is evident again from Table 8.1, which shows that over 51 per cent of the expansion of the latter was due to migration (55 per cent for males). As a result, the share of working age groups in the population of urban areas increased from 69 per cent in 1966 to 72.5 per cent in 1976.

The urban labour supply

The expansion of the urban labour supply lagged behind the growth of the urban population: the former grew by 48.3 per cent compared to 53.3 per cent for the latter. As the study of the structure of Iran's urban labour supply in Appendix B demonstrates, the principal reason for this was a declining trend in the urban labour force participation rates: in 1966, out of every 1,000 urban inhabitants, 283 had been in the labour force; by 1976, despite natural increase, incoming migration, and a shift in the age composition towards the working age brackets, this ratio had fallen to 273.

This trend was true of both urban males and females. In the case of men, the pattern is in accord with observed international trends. The decline was concentrated in the lower age groups due principally to expanding educational opportunities, which delayed their entry into the labour force. In the case of women, however, given the unusual scale and pattern of the decline, an extended discussion follows below.

A second notable feature about the urban labour supplies appears in relation to the structure of additions to the urban workforce: despite a larger impact of migration in lower age groups, the biggest expansions in labour supply took place in higher age brackets. The reasons for this again have to do with the varied economic activity rates of different age groups, as well as their evolution over time.

Given higher activity rates among the middle and upper/middle age groups (particularly for men), the same size population increase in their case generates a greater quantity of additional labour supply than a similar rise for lower age groups. A second contributory factor was a decline in the urban youths' activity rates. As a consequence of this, the number of urban young (10-14 years of age) in the labour force fell by 42,000 for boys and 21,000 for girls (Table 8.3). Let us now examine the components of growth for urban labour supply: namely, natural growth and migration.

Natural growth and migration

The centrality of migration as a vehicle of labour transfer in the Iranian context becomes clear once again from an examination of its contribution to the formation of urban labour supplies. Our calculations, summarised in Table 8.4, show that labour inflows generated by migration accounted for almost 1 million out of a total expansion in the urban workforce of 1.3 million. This is no doubt a remarkable figure as what it means is that on average, *three out of four* net additions to the

152 Labour transfer and economic development

Table 8.3 Changes in Iran's urban labour supply by age groups and sex, 1966–76*

Age group	Net additions ('000) Males	Females
10–14	–42	–21
15–19	+126	+17
20–24	+260	+69
25–34	+284	+67
35–44	+217	+8
45–54	+262	+2
55+	+92	–5
Total†	+1,200	+138

*1966-basis; 10 years of age and over.
†Does not add up due to rounding.
Source: Adapted from Appendix B (Table B.4).

Table 8.4 Components of change in urban labour supply, 1966–76*

	Net natural growth† ('000)	(%)	Net migration‡ ('000)	(%)	Net overall growth ('000)	(%)
Labour force	346	25.9	992	74.1	1,338	100
Males	318	26.5	882	73.5	1,200	100
Females	28	20.2	110	79.8	138	100

*1966-basis; 10 years of age and over.
†Residual figure.
‡Estimate.
Source: Adapted from Appendices A and B.

urban workforce consisted of rural immigrants. For females, whose numerical presence in the urban labour force was generally much more limited, the ratio reached as high as *four-fifths*. Thus, by effectively *quadrupling* the pace of growth of the urban labour force, migration was undoubtedly the most important factor in the generation of urban labour supplies in the period studied in the previous four chapters.

Women and the labour force

The contribution of the rural-to-urban labour transfers appears to have been even more significant with an examination of the extent of women's integration into the structure of Iran's urban labour force. Paradoxically, in the years following their much-avowed 'emancipation', women's participation in the urban workforce – already one of the lowest in the world – seems to have declined further. This widely neglected trend runs counter both to the official projections of their wide-ranging participation in the country's economic development, as well as the critics' expectations that women's labour would be tapped as a cheap source following the social reforms of the early 1960s.[4]

A number of factors have unduly inflated the image of Iranian women as an ever more active partner to the country's development process after the early 1960s. Firstly, some changes in their legal and social status, which, even though modest in scope and restrained in character, opened up important new areas to women. Such was the case of greater protection against divorce, new rights of custody over children, and the like, which might arguably have increased their independence *vis-à-vis* the family, and raised prospects for them to take a more active profile in paid activities outside the home.[5]

Secondly, women's education, though still lamentably disparate compared to men's, made significant strides in this period. The rate of literacy for females (over the age of 7) doubled every decade between 1956 and 1976, going up from 8 to 35 per cent. In the urban areas, this proportion now embraced over half of all women (55 per cent) against 22.4 per cent only two decades earlier (*Salnameh-e Amari-e Keshvar*, 1361:112; Census, 1976:18). In villages, given a much lower base, the diffusion of reading and writing skills was even more impressive: almost quadrupling every decade, women's literacy rate climbed to 16.5 per cent from a negligible low of 1.2 per cent in the same period. A similar pattern was observed in relation to the number of women in higher education.[6] Such growth rates, perhaps some of the highest in the world, have undoubtedly strengthened images of increased social and economic participation for Iranian women.

Thirdly, although still lagging far behind men in employment, the number and proportion of women in various industries and occupations rose gradually. The share of women in the technical and professional occupations, for instance, rose from one in five of the total in 1956 to one in four in 1966, and one in three by 1976.[7] Similarly, in most major sectors of economic activity, women's share of employment was gradually increasing. For the country as a whole, this ratio rose from less than 10 per cent in 1956 to nearly 14 per cent by 1976 (Table C.9 in Appendix C).

Despite the above trends and the common perceptions built around them, I argue that there was indeed no real breakthrough in women's *economic* integration in Iran in the period under consideration. On the contrary, a close re-examination of the relevant data reveals that females'

154 Labour transfer and economic development

contribution to the generation of urban labour supplies was at best stagnant, if not actually declining, in several important respects.

The most general indication of this came in the fact that the total (net) increase in the urban female workforce amounted to no more than 138,000 between 1966 and 1976 (Table 8.3). Although in growth terms, this matched the figure for men (43 per cent against 49 per cent), the real significance of females' labour generation was limited for two reasons: (1) this rate concealed a very small base; (2) on an average incremental basis, only one in ten of the new additions to the urban workforce was likely to be a female. As a result, women's share in the total urban labour force remained static at around 11 per cent.

More specifically, my findings draw from a close study of the structure of Iran's urban labour supply, which is detailed in Appendix B. Several interesting features appear. These are summarised below:

1. The increase in the urban female workforce was almost exclusively concentrated in the lower/middle age groups. The phenomenal growth rates of 156 and 105 per cent for those in the 20–24 and 25–34 age groups respectively meant that *of every 100 persons newly added to the urban female workforce, an overriding 98.5 were between 25 and 34 years of age.* Thus by 1976, as much as 54 per cent of the total female labour force fell into these categories (compared to 42 per cent for men in the same year, and 34 per cent for women a decade earlier).
2. Despite natural growth and incoming migration, the supply of young, economically active females in towns (10–14 years of age) contracted in absolute terms. As with young males, education was the most likely single cause of this.
3. Perhaps most importantly, *the number of females over the age of 35 lost all credible significance in Iran's urban labour supply.* This is partly evident from a generally stagnant total figure for women above this age, and partly from the changing age structure of (net) entries into the urban female workforce. Nearly 80 per cent of such entries occurred below the age of 24 (compared with 65 per cent for men). Thus, while the average age of entry for men was on the rise, quite the opposite was true for women.

    It appears that, unlike the advanced industrial countries where the real breakthrough in women's economic integration comes with an appreciable entry of married females into the workforce, in Iran marriage and participation in the labour force continued to be competing social phenomena. Although a study of the exact reasons for this raises an important agenda for future scholarly research into the women's question in Iran, it is hard to ignore the persistence of family traditions and the continued subordinate position of women as being as least partially responsible for this.

4. Underlying the above trends, there was also a decline in women's economic activity rates, which occurred across all age groups except those between 25 and 34. By 1976, this had gone down to 8.9 from 9.9 per cent a decade earlier. Reflecting this trend, my calculations show that there was a significant fall in Iranian women's total gross years of working life (expected length of stay in the labour force). By 1976, urban females at the age of 10 expected to spend on average only 5.1 years of the rest of their lives (up to the age of 74) in the labour force. This figure had gone down by one year over a decade earlier – already very low by world standards. In comparative terms, this implied a decline five times more drastic than for men, widening further the existing labour force participation gaps. In 1966, urban men expected to spend 7.7 times longer than women in the labour force; by 1976, this ratio had risen to almost 9 times.
5. Had it not been for the impact made by migration, the expansion of urban women's labour supply would have been even more limited. Appendix A shows that of every 100 new adult female migrants, on average 12 were expected to enter the labour force. By contrast, the figure for non-migrant females was as low as 2.7.

The above findings are significant not only for their apparent contradiction of the popular conceptions persisting to date, but also for two further reasons.

Firstly, it appears that this trend was a reversal of the trend for a previous intercensal period (1956–66). Urban females' aggregate activity rate rose slightly from 9.3 per cent in 1956 to 9.9 per cent in 1966. Moreover, the *rate* of expansion in women's labour supply in this period surpassed that of men's by about three times (Bartsch, 1970b, for a detailed study of the period 1956–66). The sluggish performance in the later decade (1966–76) is even more puzzling considering the general buoyancy of demand for labour, rising real wages, and improved employment opportunities during the years that embraced the oil boom.

Secondly, this trend also contradicts our observation about females in rural areas, whose participation in the workforce witnessed unchecked growth for virtually all age groups. The previous chapter showed how this was intensified by the exodus of young, active males. By 1976, women's labour force participation rate (LFPR) in villages was nearly twice that in towns. For the young village girls (10–14 years), in particular, the gap was widest (nearly four times). This reflected in part the continued short-run economic importance of rural children, and in part the growing importance of expanding educational possibilities in towns.

To sum up this section, therefore, a study of Iran's urban labour supply

Table 8.5 Comparative indicators of change in industrial employment and wage employment (1956-76)

	Average increase in manufacturing employment for every 100 additions to:		Average increase in the number of wage employees for every 100 additions to:	
	1956-66	1966-76	1956-66	1966-76
Total employment	40	22.2	50	79
Total labour force	27	19.1	45	70.3
Total population (over 10 years)	11.4	6.2	18.2	22.8

Source: Hakimian (1981:table 2).

suggests a much more limited degree of integration for women in the structure of the urban workforce than assumed to date. The major implication of this finding, albeit at a preliminary and speculative stage, is that labour generated through transfers as discussed in the last few chapters made an even more disproportionate contribution to the process of labour supply generation in towns than might have been conceived thus far.

Labour absorption

The main thrust of labour absorption for migrants and non-migrants came in general wage employment, and not in the modern manufacturing sector, as one might expect. There are two indications to this effect.

The first is a general one, pertaining to the pattern of employment generation in the country as a whole. Estimates in Table 8.5 contrast the wider trend of wage employment with the expansion of manufacturing jobs. It can be seen that out of every 100 extra persons employed between 1966 and 1976, nearly 80 were general wage workers, whereas a comparable figure for industry amounted to 22 only. Moreover, the tempo of expansion was accelerating for the former and decelerating for the latter: the incremental proportion of population finding wage employment rose from 50 per cent in 1956-66 to 79 per cent in 1966-76; by contrast, the proportion for industrial employment was almost halved (from 40 per cent down to 22 per cent). Similar considerations against changes in the labour force and the working age population (in the same table) confirm this contrasting pattern.

The second point reflects the geographical division of employment

Labour transfer from the urban perspective 157

Table 8.6 Changes in the structure of employment by broad economic sectors, total country, 1956–76

	1956–66 ('000)	1956–66 (%)	1966–76 ('000)	1966–76 (%)
Primary sector	+54	4.3	−388	−22.2
Secondary sector	+698	56.1	+1,126	+64.6
(Manufacturing)	(+482)	(38.7)	(+374)	(21.4)
(Construction)	(+174)	(14.0)	(+679)	(38.8)
Tertiary sector	+492	39.6	+1,010	+57.8
(Services)	(+278)	(14.3)	(+586)	(33.5)
Total	+1,244	100.0	+1,748	100.0

Source: Adapted from Hakimian (1981:table 1), based on census data.

creation. This is seen in Table 8.6 which gives an overview of changes in the structure of employment by broad economic sectors.

On the one hand, the important trend of falling primary sector activities, encountered in the previous chapter, was unmistakably a rural phenomenon. With as much as 90–92 per cent of all agricultural employment concentrated in villages, the loss of about 400,000 primary sector jobs between 1966 and 1976 was a significant loss of employment to these areas. On the other hand, the constantly growing absorptive capacity of the secondary and tertiary sectors was predominantly (though not exclusively) urban in character. Over 2.1 million new jobs were created in these two sectors in the same period, but about 90 per cent of all net job creation took place in the urban areas. In other words, for every job lost in the primary sector nearly five were created in the secondary and tertiary sectors, of which between three and four were located in towns.

This predominantly 'wage-pull' nature of expanding urban employment is even more clearly evident from another perspective: amounting to 1.1 million, the newly created wage- and salary-paid jobs accounted for roughly three-quarters of all net job expansion in towns (Table 8.7). By 1976, the greatest bulk of Iran's employees (nearly two-thirds of the total for the country) were, in fact, concentrated in urban areas.

The main impetus to this came from the sudden and massive explosion in the urban construction and public service sectors, which were the direct beneficiaries of the oil boom. Characteristically, employment in the construction sector increased by 112 per cent, absorbing some 300,000 extra jobs. The greatest majority of those employed in this sector were rural wage-workers with over 40 per cent of them less than 29 years of age. With about 90 per cent of all construction employees concentrated in the private sector, there is no doubt that this sector was not only

158 Labour transfer and economic development

Table 8.7 Changes in urban employment, 1966–76

	Nov. 1966	Nov. 1976	Change: 1966–76	
	('000)	('000)	('000)	(%)
Wage and salary earners	1,810	2,950	+1,140	+63
(Public sector)	(574)	(1,405)	(+831)	(+145)
(Private sector)	(1,236)	(1,545)	(+309)	(+25)
Non-waged employed	800	1,163	+363	+45
(Unpaid family workers)	(49)	(86)	(+37)	(+75)
(Own-account workers)	(624)	(915)	(+291)	(+47)
Total employment	2,610	4,113	+1,503	+58

Sources: Computed from Census (1966:54; 1976:68).

in the forefront of job creation in the private sector but also an important venue for the absorption of incoming young migrants.

Similarly, the increase in the state's oil revenues provided the main impetus to the expansion of public sector employment. With another 800,000 people added to the state's payroll in urban areas in the span of just ten years, the state accounted for as much as three-quarters of all new urban wage jobs and well over half of all employment creation in towns.

Yet contrasting this was the limited capacity of the industrial sector. The case of 'large' urban industries (defined as those employing ten and more persons) is particularly noteworthy. These accounted for a modest fraction of the urban industrial establishments (less than 3 per cent) and only about 17–20 per cent of the total manufacturing workforce in the country (Hakimian, 1980). In incremental terms, our calculations show that only one in five of the new industrial jobs were accounted for by these industries: *out of every 100 extra jobs created in this decade, as few as 4.5 went to large urban manufacturing establishments*. A similar incremental ratio for the labour force was 3.8, and for the population of working age as low as 1.2 (Hakimian, 1981:9).

On a crude assumption that migrants were assimilated into urban jobs in a similar fashion to the non-migrant urban population (an assumption most likely to underplay their actual absorption into 'informal' activities and the construction sector), the following gives a broad macro pattern of the way migrants were likely to be drawn into urban sectors: some three-quarters of a million migrant workers found wage employment; one in five were drawn into the construction sector; and about one in seven were absorbed by the large industrial establishments. In reality, however, given the highly capital intensive nature of the technology used as well as the greater skill requirements within these industries, it is most likely that their absorption capacity was far more limited and that of the construction sector substantially higher.

Summary and conclusion

This chapter reconfirms, this time in the urban context, the quantitative significance of migration and labour transfer during the 1960s and 1970s. The discussion in Chapter 7 had already shed light on this issue in its rural context. What is undoubtedly of added significance is that in the urban areas, too, labour transfer played an important role in generating and allocating labour use. Between 1966 and 1976, nearly *half* of all urban population growth and as much as *three-quarters* of all additions to the urban labour supplies could be attributed to migration. Given the declining labour force participation of the urban population and the limited degree of urban women's integration into the labour force, there is little doubt that the single most important message emerging out of this discussion is that: *migration was the principal mechanism of labour generation in the towns in this period.*

There was another important respect in which labour transfer made a disproportionate contribution to the process of urban growth and expansion: amounting to as much as two-thirds of all (net) job creation in towns, it fulfilled also a strategic function in catering for the labour requirements of those sectors which were most affected by rapid growth and transformation.

Notes

1. These were the following four *Ostans* (provinces): Central, Isfahan, Yazd and Khuzistan. There was, at the same time, a process of urban concentration: in 1976, there were four cities with a population of over half a million compared to only one in 1966. Moreover, the population of the capital (Tehran) alone amounted to 11 per cent of the total for the country and as much as 30 per cent of the urban population. As one observer put it: 'Iran's urban growth since 1956 is clearly a "big" city phenomenon and largely attributable to changes in the metropolitan Tehran' (Kohli, 1977:8).
2. The number of localities classified as urban changed in each intercensal period, hence altering aggregate 'urban' population. While a few towns lost population and, therefore, their 'urban' status, a great many others, which were formerly classified as rural, reached 'urban' size via a rise in their population. The (net) number of areas thus affected was 112 in this intercensal

160 Labour transfer and economic development

period, with a total population of no less than 840,000. To eliminate any possibility of 'statistical' illusion, these areas are systematically excluded from my estimates. 'Urban areas' defined in this way, therefore, have a common basis related to 1966. For more details, see Hakimian (1987:appendix B).
3. This estimate seems to be in line with a similar observation in Goldscheider (1983:186).
4. This projection is widely shared in writings on the subject. See among others the quotation by OIPFG on page 100. Similarly, Sedghi and Ashraf speak of 'the increasing trend of women's economic activity in the urban areas' (1976:205). Afkhami (1985) echoes the same optimism, when asserting that the total number of women in the labour force in 1979 reached 2 million. Apart from a discrepancy of some half a million with the results of the latest comprehensive national census in 1976, she overlooks also the more important fact that of this figure only 1.2 million were employed; as many as 1 million were concentrated in the rural areas; and as much as one-half of the latter consisted of unpaid family workers.
5. These changes were highlighted in the Family Protection Acts of 1967 and 1975, which were generally concerned with laws of marriage, divorce and family relations. The 1975 Act, for instance, increased the age of marriage for girls to 18 from 15. For a summary of other provisions introduced, see Sedghi and Ashraf (1976:203-4) and Sanasarian (1982:93-9).
6. According to Sedghi and Ashraf, between 1961/2 and 1971/2, the average annual growth rate for female students at the different educational levels was: 13 per cent for primary schools, 30 per cent for high schools, 88 per cent for technical and vocational schools, 76 per cent for teacher training schools, and 65 per cent for institutions of higher education (1976:207). Clearly, these figures have to be balanced against the lower absolute bases which they conceal.
7. Census figures. The number of women in these occupations increased from 52,179 in 1966 to 187,756 in 1976 - that is, a growth of 260 per cent. This figure is most probably inflated by a large increase in the number of women teachers in this period. Similarly, the number of women in clerical jobs increased from 13,723 to 63,340, but 98 per cent of these were secretarial and office jobs in the towns. In general, the main impetus to women's employment came from the public sector, which comprised mainly clerical and teaching jobs. See Table C.10 in Appendix C.

9
Conclusion

The first point which emerges from this book is the relative importance of labour transfer in economic development. As I have tried to demonstrate, this issue has been an important dividing line in major schools of economic thought since Adam Smith. Although for different reasons and from different perspectives, Smith, Marx and postwar labour surplus theorists all attached great significance to labour transfer in the process of economic growth and capital accumulation. Malthus and Ricardo, in contrast, were primarily concerned with the 'overproduction' of population, not its transfer. This perspective is also shared by the present dominant mode of thinking in development theory.

In all the three periods selected for study in this book, labour transfer appears to have been an integral part of the wider development process, which affected the country. In the first case, discussed in Chapter 3, the migration of Persian workers to Russia was estimated to have amounted to about half a million people between 1880 and 1914. On the Russian side, this fulfilled a major function in catering for the labour requirements of the fast growing industrial centres in the south; while in Iran, the same process accommodated the embryos of a new wage-labouring class. Moreover, from Persia's perspective, this had the added significance of opening up new inlets for the importation of ideas and social and political awareness, at a time when both countries were undergoing important socioeconomic transformations.

If this was true of the early twentieth century, it was even truer of the two decades from 1960 to 1979. My calculations of the combined effect of the land reform and the oil boom periods put the total population displaced between the rural and urban areas during the period 1966–76 at 2.5 million: of these approximately 1 million were economically active

(Chapter 7). The bulk of the labour transferred consisted of men (with a sexual composition of 8 : 1 in their favour), and the young (70 per cent of men and 60 per cent of women migrants over the age of 10 were between 10 and 24 years only). Moreover, labour transfer was estimated to have drained the countryside of some *two-thirds* of expected net additions to its workforce (three-quarters for men). Yet more significantly, this process accounted for as much as 75 per cent of the net generation of labour supply in towns. In the light of the declining labour force participation rates of the urban population in general, and women's relatively decreasing integration into the workforce in particular, there is little doubt that this particular mechanism was the most important in generating labour supplies in the urban areas of Iran.

Secondly, this book confirms the importance of structural change in the process of labour transfer. Among those who have stressed the importance of labour displacement in economic development, Adam Smith and Marx have been most outstanding for their recognition of the dynamic context in which a re-allocation of the society's labour time takes place. Early development theorists of the postwar era, in contrast, operated broadly within a *ceteris paribus* framework in which few variables of substance were envisaged to change. A mirror image of this is also found in the present discussions of migration *control*, in whch marginal variations in a few economic variables (such as a cut in urban wages or an improvement in rural incomes) are expected to make a critical impact on the pace, direction and flow of labour from rural to urban areas. Yet my findings clearly demonstrate that labour transfer and structural change are two inseparable processes. This is brought out in every one of the three case studies, in which major developments were found either to precede or accompany labour transfer: in two such cases (the land reform and the oil boom years), these originated in transformations within the domestic economy; in another (migration to Russia), in the international context in which Iran was situated.

Thirdly, it is also clear that Marx's view is a limiting rather than a general case. Emphasising expropriation and labour extrusion, this view has been traditionally counterposed to the economists' interpretation of migration, in which 'free' choice and the individual's motivation have been stressed. Yet the discussions in the preceding chapters have brought out just this varied nature of migration mechanisms even in a single country. Two implications arise from this. On the one hand, the apparent polarity of 'structural' factors and 'motivational' issues behind migration turns out to be overemphasised. If individuals appear to base their migration decisions on considerations of material incentives, the reasons for this are often connected to the deeper structural changes which condition their motivations; and if, from an opposite angle, they seem to be driven by changing socioeconomic structures, this indicates that their motivation to stay behind must have been eroded, diminished, or even destroyed. A successful analysis will supplement, not substitute, these two. On the other hand, when viewed over time, both these mechanisms are situated within a whole array of historical possibilities governing labour transfer. What unites them all is their common roots in structural change and socioeconomic transformation. Our studies of the Iranian experience clearly substantiate these points.

In at least two of them, economic incentives and material inducements were found to have a major significance in determining the direction, scale and form of labour transfer. In the historical chapter, this was shown to come from regional growth and a new industrial drive in Russia's southern states; in the oil boom chapter, from the expansion of the domestic non-farm activities in general, and the urban construction sector, in particular. In the land reform period, by contrast, it was institutional change and the consequent restructuring of land tenure relations that acted as the main propellant of labour transfer from the countryside. In all three cases, however, labour transfer appeared as a derivative of the deeper undercurrents of economic development and structural dislocation and was not separated from it.

Fourthly, there seems to be a certain degree of affinity between the mechanism of migration on the one hand, and its form and composition, on the other. When induced by new motivations, this tends to assume a largely temporary or semi-permanent form, comprising a wider range of social groupings and individuals (peasants, workers, artisans, etc.). But when brought about by institutional change, it tends to be mostly permanent in form and more selective in scope (agricultural labourers and the bottom layer of the peasantry). The implications of this point are very clear in the case of the two comparable periods of the land reform (1960s) and the oil boom (1970s) in Iran.

In the early years following extensive reorganisations of the village economy by agrarian reform, the departure of a considerable number of farm labourers and poor peasant families was coupled with the rise and strengthening of a new class of well-to-do peasant farmers. For these, ownership of land, freedom from the centuries-long yoke of the landlord, and the newly acquired self-esteem in village society came as a major material and psychological boost. As a result, not only was agricultural output sustained, but their effort on the land increased, the scope of their family participation widened, and the area under cultivation expanded. This situation contrasted sharply with labour transfer in the oil boom years, which was brought about mainly by growing disincentives to peasant production. With the departure of some of the self-sufficient peasantry operating small farms for short-term cash earning opportunities in towns, the area under cultivation contracted and agricultural output showed signs of declining.

Fifthly, it appears that at the same time as mobilising labour out of agriculture, labour transfer also fulfils an important role in restructuring the pattern of labour use within this sector. This is brought about partly by restructuring the existing division of labour and regularising the working pattern of the remaining workforce, but also, and perhaps more importantly, by mobilising new sources of labour. Again, the study of the combined effects of the land reform and the oil boom in this book have made it clear that by the mid-1970s Iranian agriculture was more dependent on 'subsidiary' sources of labour than ever before. The role and participation of the elderly in the countryside had expanded, women had become more integrated into the rural division of labour, and despite a considerable outflow of the youths, there still persisted a sizable body of young, unpaid family workers who worked on owner-cultivated plots.

As for the implications of the book for the study of Iran specifically, my aim has been partly to excavate and reinterpret a number of old problems, and partly to raise new issues and set directions for future research. The analysis of the land reform falls into the first of these two categories. In Chapters 4 and 5, I sought to go beyond the distributional effects and the motivational causes of the programme by focusing on the impact of agrarian change on rural labour. But while there appeared to be no great surprises in the findings (that the land reform did actively encourage labour transfer), I questioned this being its intended objective, as well as documenting in detail the specific mechanisms through which labour was released from the countryside.

In contrast, the analysis of the other two cases directly challenged prevailing perceptions. Ever since Iran's Constitutional Revolution some ninety years ago, the causes of the mass migration of Persian workers to southern Russian provinces have been commonly attributed to poverty and political oppression in Iran at the turn of the century. My detailed documentation of this phenomenon, however, has shown this interpretation to be inadequate and failing to explain such salient features of the migration as its dynamics, form and geographical concentration. An alternative explanation was instead formulated to bring to light the nature of Russian industrialisation in general, and the subsumption of Iran's border regions into her economic orbit, in particular.

A similar 'immiserisation' view of the developments of the oil boom years was also shown to be without analytical and empirical foundations. According to this view, the coming of the boom dealt a fatal blow to Iran's already ailing rural economy in general, and her agriculture in particular. The wealth and accumulation of these years, it has been widely suggested, precipitated rural poverty and decay which in turn degenerated into mass migration from the rural areas. On a closer examination, however, I have shown that the alleged mass flight was for the most part temporary and circular migration largely in response to better cash earning opportunities outside agriculture. Moreover, if labour flow was hastened in these years, this was not *caused by* agricultural decline, but was in fact a constant *source* of difficulty to this sector. In both this and the historical case study, the findings in this book throw new light on some neglected or misjudged aspects of Iran's economic history and call for a rethinking of the prevailing perceptions.

Some implications also arise for future research. The limited degree of Iranian women's integration into the urban workforce is one such prime example. As it has been argued, this goes against many common and official expectations and interpretations of the social reforms introduced in the early 1960s. A close scrutiny of the reasons for this apparent paradox could constitute an important area of research for the emerging feminist literature on Iran. Similarly, on the situation of rural women, my discussion has outlined but the barest framework in which the outflow of male labour increased females' economic and social responsibilities. There seems to be enormous scope in pursuing these and other related issues for a fuller understanding of the position of women in society and economy on the eve of the Revolution. The tumultuous upheavals in the country since February 1979 have affected the situation of few social groups as radically and as dramatically as that of women. As a result, the study of the women's question in Iran has reached a critical stage. It is hoped that some of the issues raised in this book will receive critical attention in the forthcoming literature before any major generalisations are made at this preliminary and speculative stage.

A second possible area for closer scrutiny relates to the expansion of rural industries in the 1970s. Until recently, similar studies of the Industrial Revolution in Britain had been divided along the lines of demographic change and socioeconomic transformation. With the rise of the 'proto-industrialisation' debates – linking the pattern of industrial structure with fertility trends – there seems to be a greater recognition of the need to integrate the two approaches. It is possible that a similar study of the proto-industries (rural crafts, cottage industries, etc.) in the Iranian context will not only enhance our limited understanding of this important period of the country's recent economic history, but it will also shed light on the wider industrialisation debates elsewhere.

Finally, it is to the implications of the book for the present state of development thinking that I wish to turn in the closing pages. As with many debates in economics, the discussions of labour transfer in the past 200 years have evolved through various contradictory phases. But as with the free trade debates, it appears that the prevailing economic climate has had an important bearing on the direction of interest in the subject: in periods of expansion in general (and buoyancy of the demand for labour), it has moved to the forefront; at times of recession and decline, it has been pushed back by concerns about unemployment and excess population growth.

In its present cycle, development theory is undergoing a phase in which a reassertion of the Malthusian population problematic has reversed much interest in the subject of labour transfer. Marx is now reproached for having considered in a positive light the villagers' ability and desire to leave 'the idiocy of rural life'; postwar interest in labour transfer is considered to have been ill-conceived; and even Adam Smith is looked down upon for a certain degree of 'urban bias' in his portrayal of agriculture as a reservoir of labour and as a source of savings for towns. Instead, focus seems to have shifted decisively towards finding ways of controlling the labour flow by limiting population growth and/or promoting 'rural development'. Substantive interests in the industrialisation of the Third World seem to have been scaled down or heavily modified in the mainstream development literature.

There is no doubt that this turn-about is rooted in the inadequacies and the misjudgements of the development debates and policies in the 1950s and 1960s. Population growth is now widely admitted to have been underestimated at the time. Similarly, widespread urban unemployment seems to have been a logical outcome of those policies which paid insufficient attention to the wider impacts of technical change and/or industrial transformation. Yet, in its legitimate concern with the unpalatable effects of labour transfer during these two decades, development theory seems to have taken a step in the wrong direction.

By emphasising overpopulation, it has taken the myopic perspective of controlling 'numbers' rather than addressing itself to the more fundamental issue of the society's productive capacity within which such numbers acquire meaning and significance. There is no *a priori* basis for treating population as a *source* of development problems. In fact, much evidence points in the opposite direction. As eloquently summed up by Kuznets:

> More population means more creators and producers, both of goods along established production patterns and of new knowledge and inventions. Why shouldn't the large number achieve what the small numbers accomplished in the modern past – raise total output to provide not only for the current population increase but also for a rapidly rising supply per capita. . .?
> (1974:3)

It is this challenge, establishing the circumstances under which population growth can be a stimulant to economic growth and social and economic advance, that development theory in its current mood has chosen to ignore.

Moreover, by arguing the case for 'rural development', it has also turned the old agriculture versus industry debate on its head. The problem with this position is that it ignores the need for an integrated approach to development. It also leaves unresolved serious questions about the viability and the desirability of a strategy which involves preserving large sections of the population on the land. To judge by history (if this can be regarded as a valid criterion), the case for the 'land-led' path to development is yet to be proven. Tying large sections of the population to the land will necessarily confine them to limited resources and capacity for growth. If productivity and living standards are to be discontinuously increased – always the mark of the major industrial revolutions – promoting industrialisation, both in the sense of the old manufacturing industries of the past and the new tertiary sectors of the future (not to mention the industrialisation of agriculture itself), will continue to point the direction forward for any development strategy. As long as that is so, labour transfer too will remain one of the few and most central issues of development theory.

Appendix A: Estimating labour flows to urban areas, 1966-76

A prior knowledge of migrants' labour force participation rates (LFPRs) is necessary for an estimation of the labour flows generated by migration. Given a lack of such data, this appendix aims to estimate these and to use them to evaluate the size and composition of the labour flow attributable to migration.

My estimates here rest on two sets of considerations. Firstly, on the observation that 'the characteristics of migrants tend to be intermediate between the characteristics of the population at origin and the population at destination' (Lee, 1966:57). I have thus taken migrants' LFPRs to be an average of the corresponding rural and urban rates. Secondly, to allow for changes over time, I have selected average rates between 1966 and 1976. The results, 73.2 per cent for men and 12.3 per cent for women migrants (over 10 years of age), are thus derived from averaging the corresponding LFPRs in the urban and rural areas between these two dates. Although the results are grossly oversimplified, they are nevertheless in line with the findings of at least one other study, based on unpublished results of a Ministry of Labour survey in 1964/5 (Barstch, 1970b:38). Finally, these estimates are derived and applied at an aggregate level only, treating age-specific estimates to be unreliable (UN, 1968:51).

Based on these rates, the total number of migrants in the urban workforce is estimated to be just under 1 million, with a composition of 8 : 1 males to females (Table A.1). This accounted for 25 per cent of the total urban labour force in 1976, which contrasted with a similar share of only 17 per cent in the total urban population. Moreover, the same table shows that of every 100 male migrants (over 10 years of age), who survived to 1976, 73 were likely to join the labour force, compared to 61 only among the non-migrants. The rates were far lower for women:

Estimating labour flow 169

Table A.1 Estimates of the economic activity rates of urban population (1966-basis) by immigrant status and sex, 1966–76

	Males			Females		
Immigrant status	Population*	LFPR	Number active	Population*	LFPR	Number active
	('000)	(%)	('000)	('000)	(%)	('000)
Urban population	4,524†	61.2‡	2,767†	4,244†	8.2‡	347†
Survivors of (net) rural immigrants 1966–76	1,205§	73.2§	882‡	894§	12.3§	110‡
Total urban population	5,729	63.7	3,649	5,138	8.9	457

*Ten years of age and over.
†Residual figure.
‡Derived figure.
§Estimate.
Sources: For total and economically active population, Census (1976:table 16) adjusted for 1966-basis urban areas. For migrant population, Tables C.5 and C.6. For activity rates, Tables C.7 and B.2.

Table A.2 Estimates of incremental economic activity rates of urban population (1966-basis) by immigrant status and sex, 1966–76

	Males			Females		
Immigrant status	Increase in population*	Marginal LFPR	Increase in number	Increase in population*	Marginal LFPR	Increase in number
	('000)	(%)	('000)	('000)	(%)	('000)
Urban population	986†	32.2‡	318†	1,035†	2.7‡	28†
Survivors of (net) rural immigrants 1966–76	1,205§	73.2§	882‡	894§	12.3§	110‡
Total urban population	2,191	54.8	1,200	1,929	7.1	138

*Ten years of age and over.
†Residual figure.
‡Derived figure.
§Estimate.
Sources: As for Table A.1, plus Census (1966:table 12).

12 per cent for migrants, and only 8 per cent for non-migrants. In incremental terms, the differentials were even wider: 73.2 per cent and 32.2 per cent for migrant and non-migrant men; 12.3 per cent and 2.7 per cent for migrant and non-migrant women respectively (see Table A.2).

Appendix B: Urban supplies of labour 1966–76

Two sets of factors influence the size of the urban workforce: (1) the size of the total population and its demographic composition, and (2) the labour force participation rates (LFPRs) of the population of working age. This point may be better seen from the following identity:

$$Lf \equiv Lw.(Lf/Lw)$$

Where Lf is the labour force, Lw the population of working age, and Lf/Lw the proportion of the latter which are economically active (LFPR). Data on these appear in Tables B.1 and B.2 respectively and are used to make estimates about the size, structure and growth of the urban labour force. The results appear in Tables B.3–B.6.

Table B.1, which shows changes in the broad composition of population, suggests a change in favour of those in working age groups. This in turn indicates the tailing-off of an earlier decade's baby boom. Table B.2 shows declining aggregate LFPRs, for both urban men and women. For the former, this trend is well in line with international observations (Durand, 1975), but in the case of the latter, the decline is more curious given the already very low bases over which such a drop in activity rates seems to have come about.

The findings are interesting in a number of ways. Table B.3 shows that despite a higher rate of growth for the supply of male labour (49 per cent compared to 43.3 per cent for females), the sexual composition of the labour force remained stable and primarily made up of men: about 11 per cent of the total only consisted of women. In incremental terms, this meant that *only one in ten net additions to the labour force was likely to be a woman.*

172 Appendix B

Table B.1 Size and broad age structure of the urban population (1966-basis), 1966–76

Age group	Nov. 1966		Nov. 1976		Net change 1966–76	
	('000)	(%)	('000)	(%)	('000)	(%)
0–9	3,048	31.1	4,151	27.6	+1,103	+36.2
10 and over	6,746	68.9	10,867	72.4	+4,121	+61.1
Total	9,794	100.0	15,018	100.0	+5,224	+53.3
(Males)	(5,097)	(52.0)	(7,861)	(52.3)	(+2,764)	(+54.2)
(Females)	(4,697)	(48.0)	(7,157)	(47.7)	(+2,460)	(+52.4)

Sources: Computed from Census (1966:table 1) and Census (1976:table 1) adjusted for 1966-basis urban areas.

Table B.2 Sex and age specific labour force participation rates in urban areas (1966-basis), 1966–76*

Age group	Males		Females		Both sexes	
	1966	1976	1966	1976	1966	1976
10–14	17.2	7.0	8.9	3.5	13.3	5.4
15–19	48.6	37.1	9.8	7.3	29.9	23.3
20–24	85.9	80.0	12.1	16.2	50.7	49.3
25–34	95.7	95.0	10.2	14.2	54.4	55.8
35–44	96.2	97.4	10.6	8.6	57.6	56.1
45–54	91.6	91.0	11.0	6.5	53.6	52.1
55–64	74.3	73.7	8.9	5.3	42.0	41.6
65+	45.5	44.0	5.7	3.6	26.6	23.7
All ages	69.2	63.7	9.9	8.9	41.0	37.8

*Refers to population 10 years of age and over.
Sources: Computed from Census (1966:table 12) and Census (1976:table 16) adjusted for 1966-basis urban areas.

The supply of young labour, both males and females between the ages of 10 and 14, declined in absolute terms (Table B.4). This is most probably due to rising educational opportunities.

The supply of male labour grew for all other age groups (including the elderly), and despite the fastest growth rates in the ranges 20–24 and 45–54 (74.7 and 84.5 per cent respectively), the overall age structure of the urban male workforce remained generally stable.

The pattern and structure of growth for female labour was markedly different, however. Firstly, urban female labour expanded almost

Table B.3 Size of and changes in urban labour supply (1966-basis), 1966–76

Sex	Nov. 1966		Nov. 1976		Net change	
	('000)	(%)	('000)	(%)	('000)	(%)
Males	2,449	88.5	3,649	88.9	+1,200	+49.0
Females	319	11.5	457	11.1	+138	+43.3
Total	2,768	100.0	4,106	100.0	+1,338	+48.3

Source: Computed from Census (1976:xxxiv).

exclusively because of concentrated growth at the lower/middle age groups: 156 and 105 per cent in the case of those in the ranges 20–24 and 25–34 respectively. Thus, by 1976 as much as 54 per cent of all female labour fell in these categories (compared with 34 per cent a decade earlier). Secondly, and perhaps characteristically indicating the strength of family traditions and women's social position in Iran, the amount of female labour above the age of 35 lost all credible importance. This is seen in the fact that there were some very modest additions to the 35–54 age group, while earlier retirement brought down, in absolute terms, the number of those above 55.

These results are also supported by an analysis of the (net) entries and separations from the labour force. According to Table B.5, the age structure of (net) entries into the urban workforce appears to have been much younger in case of females than for males. Nearly 80 per cent of all net entries for the former occurred below the age of 24, against 65 per cent for the latter. Furthermore, the average age of entry for men was on the rise. The prime reason for this was delayed entry into the labour force in turn occasioned by longer and more widespread possibilities of schooling.

Unsurprisingly, these characteristics of female labour are also reflected in their expected length of working life. Total gross years of working life (expected duration of stay in the labour force for the remainder of life at each age group) were shortened both for men and women but more markedly so for the latter (Table B.6).

By 1976, men at the age of 10 expected to spend 46.3 years of the rest of their lives up to the age of 74 in the labour force. This compared with a slightly higher expectation of 47.9 years a decade earlier. For women, in accordance with the general observations so far, the decline was more drastic: going down to a low of 5.1 years only (from 6.1), it had in fact fallen five times faster than for men.

174 Appendix B

Table B.4 Structure of urban labour supply (1966-basis) by age and sex, 1966–76

Age group	Females Nov. 1966 ('000)	(%)	Females Nov. 1976 ('000)	(%)	Net change ('000)	(%)†	Males Nov. 1966 ('000)	(%)	Males Nov. 1976 ('000)	(%)	Net change ('000)	(%)†
10–14	54	16.9	33	7.1	−21	−39.4	115	4.7	73	2.0	−42	−36.5
15–19	45	14.0	62	13.5	+17	+38.0	239	9.8	364	10.0	+126	+52.7
20–24	44	13.9	114	24.9	+69	+156.1	348	14.2	607	16.6	+260	+74.7
25–34	64	20.1	131	28.7	+67	+104.9	643	26.3	927	25.4	+284	+44.2
35–44	51	15.9	59	13.0	+8	+16.7	555	22.6	772	21.2	+217	+39.2
45–54	33	10.4	35	7.7	+2	+5.9	310	12.6	572	15.7	+262	+84.5
55–64	19	5.8	14	3.1	−5	−24.7	159	6.5	222	6.1	+64	+40.2
65+	9	2.9	9	2.0	−0.2	−2.3	82	3.3	110	3.0	+28	+34.2
All ages*	319	100.0	457	100.0	+138	+43.3	2,449	100.0	3,648	100.0	1,200	+49.0

*Totals do not add up due to rounding.
†Precise rather than rounded figures used for estimation here.
Sources: Computed from Census (1966:table 12; 1976:table 16).

Urban supplies of labour 175

Table B.5 Net entries and net separations from urban labour force (1966-basis) by sex and age groups, 1966–76

Age in Nov. 1966	Nov. 1976	Females Number active in 1966	Females Number active in 1976	Females Change, 1966–76 Net entries	Females Change, 1966–76 Net separations	Males Number active in 1966	Males Number active in 1976	Males Change, 1966–76 Net entries	Males Change, 1966–76 Net separations
0–4	10–14	—	32,627	32,627	—	—	72,815	72,815	—
5–9	15–19	—	61,776	61,776	—	61,776	364,235	364,235	—
10–14	20–24	53,859	113,710	59,851	—	114,677	607,420	492,743	—
15–19	25–29	44,760	81,843	37,083	—	238,596	506,928	268,332	—
20–24	30–34	44,404	49,459	5,055	—	347,617	420,364	72,747	—
25–34	35–44	64,068	59,429	—	4,639	643,103	772,210	129,107	—
35–44	45–54	50,901	35,101	—	15,800	554,770	571,695	16,925	—
45–54	55–64	33,168	14,023	—	19,145	309,952	222,182	—	87,770
55+	65+	27,903	9,161	—	18,742	240,583	110,159	—	130,424
Total		319,063	457,129	196,392	58,326	2,449,298	3,648,008	1,416,904	218,194

Sources: Computed from Census (1966:table 12; 1976:table 16). For methodology of calculation, see UN (1971:35–8).

Table B.6 Total gross years of working life by age groups and sex in the urban areas (1966-basis), 1966–76

| | Males | | Females | |
Age groups*	1966	1976	1966	1976
10–14	47.91	46.35	6.18	5.17
15–19	47.05	46.0	5.73	4.99
20–24	44.62	44.15	5.24	4.63
25–34	40.33	40.15	4.64	3.82
35–44	30.76	30.65	3.62	2.4
45–54	21.14	20.91	2.56	1.54
55–64	11.98	11.81	1.46	0.89
65–74	4.55	4.44	0.57	0.36

*Male and female working age assumed to be in the age range 10–74.
Source: Calculations based on Table B.2. For methodology see UN (1971:38).

Appendix C:
Statistical data

Appendix C

Table C.1 Index of average wholesale prices of selected agricultural products, and wages of unskilled construction workers, 1962–77 (1973=100)

Year	Index of agricultural prices							Index of construction wages	
	Wheat	Sugarbeet	Barley	Rice Champa	Rice Sadrie	Cotton Local	Cotton Carcass	Money wages	Real wages*
1962	99.2	—	66.2	92.4	76.1	67.3	58.4	41.0	58.6
1963	93.6	—	64.8	66.3	65.7	65.6	59.8	41.8	59.2
1964	100.4	—	79.9	69.6	62.4	64.2	60.1	44.2	60.0
1965	105.2	—	82.6	87.4	68.9	64.8	57.8	44.7	60.4
1966	93.2	—	63.8	85.8	72.6	63.5	56.7	46.2	61.9
1967	75.5	—	71.4	86.6	79.6	63.2	63.0	49.0	65.2
1968	69.7	—	70.1	97.7	82.3	70.7	67.2	57.2	75.0
1969	77.5	82.6	63.8	77.4	77.6	64.9	54.3	68.4	86.5
1970	97.0	82.7	89.3	76.7	78.2	63.5	56.3	71.6	89.2
1971	106.1	85.8	113.1	100.5	86.2	73.5	68.0	73.0	86.2
1972	89.8	89.0	78.5	103.1	93.0	84.1	77.0	85.6	95.2
1973	100.0	100.0	100.0	100.0	100.0	100.0	100.0	100.0	100.0
1974	158.9	139.5	152.6	170.0	148.4	121.0	113.4	132.0	114.4
1975	169.2	190.9	—	—	—	—	—	198.0	156.0
1976	134.8	212.1	—	—	—	—	—	269.2	182.0
1977	159.1	226.4	—	—	—	—	—	359.2	194.7

*Deflated by the consumer price index.

Sources: For wheat, Aresvik (1976:258); Madjid (1983:53); and Shafaeddin (1980:table A.7). For sugar beet, Madjid (1983:40). For barley, Aresvik (1976:235), and *Bayan-e-Amari* (1355:85–112). For cotton and rice, *Bayan-e Amari* (1355:85–112), and Aresvik (1976:258). For construction wages and the consumer price index, Bank Markazi Iran (various issues).

Statistical data 179

Table C.2 Consumer price index, real and nominal monthly budget expenditure of rural households, 1963-77 (1973=100)

Year	Monthly budget expenditure Current prices (Rials)	Index	Consumer price index	Monthly budget expenditure Constant prices* (Rials)	Index
1963	4,092	68.4	70.6	5,796	96.8
1964	3,479	58.1	73.8	4,714	78.8
1965	3,770	63.0	74.0	5,095	85.1
1966	3,988	66.6	74.6	5,346	89.3
1967	4,387	73.3	75.2	5,834	97.5
1968	4,005	66.9	76.3	5,249	87.7
1969	3,958	66.1	79.1	5,004	83.6
1970	4,187	69.8	80.3	5,203	86.9
1971	4,985	83.3	84.7	5,885	98.3
1972	4,940	82.5	89.9	5,495	91.8
1973	5,985	**100.0**	**100.0**	5,985	**100.0**
1974	11,044	184.5	115.4	9,570	159.9
1975	12,835	214.4	126.9	10,114	169.0
1976	12,678	211.8	147.9	8,572	143.2
1977	17,267	288.5	184.9	9,339	156.0
Average annual rate of growth:					
1963-73		3.9	3.5		0.0
1973-7		30.3	16.6		11.8

*Deflated by the consumer price index in urban areas, as this is the only index provided by the Central Bank.
Sources: For rural monthly budget expenditure, Azimi (1982:186) adapted for 1973=100. For consumer price index as in Table C.1.

Table C.3 Total labour force, number and percentage of agricultural workers in each age group by sex, total country, 1966 and 1976

Age group	Females 1966 A ('000)	B ('000)	B/A (%)	1976 A ('000)	B ('000)	B/A (%)	Change in B 1966-76 (%)	Males 1966 A ('000)	B ('000)	B/A (%)	1976 A ('000)	B ('000)	B/A (%)	Change in B 1966-76 (%)
10-14	202	40	19.8	220	35	15.9	-12.5	571	307	53.8	415	181	43.6	-41.2
15-19	166	35	21.1	280	42	15.0	+20.0	721	325	45.1	970	287	29.6	-11.7
20-24	126	22	17.5	260	27	10.4	+22.7	720	239	33.2	1,159	235	20.3	-1.7
25-34	206	43	20.1	300	38	12.7	-11.6	1,617	674	41.7	1,791	439	24.5	-34.9
35-44	153	33	21.6	193	39	20.2	+18.2	1,468	662	45.1	1,687	567	33.6	-14.3
45-54	83	17	20.5	128	30	23.4	+76.5	798	368	46.1	1,397	584	41.8	+58.9
55-64	43	8	15.1	44	10	22.7	+25.0	448	230	51.4	574	271	47.2	+17.8
65+	21	3	14.3	25	6	24.0	+100.0	241	132	54.8	353	193	54.7	+46.2
Total	1,000	201	20.1	1,449	227	15.7	+12.9	6,584	2,937	44.6	8,347	2,757	33.0	-6.1

A = Economically active population.
B = Agricultural workers.
Sources: Computed from Census (1966:tables 12 and 16; 1976:tables 16 and 18).

Table C.4 Percentage of economically active population in each age group in agricultural occupations and percentage changes in their numbers, both sexes, total country, 1966 and 1976

Age group	1966 B/A (%)	1976 B/A (%)	Change in B 1966–76 (%)
10–14	44.9	34.0	–37.8
15–19	40.6	26.3	–8.6
20–24	30.9	18.5	0
25–34	39.3	22.8	–33.5
35–44	42.9	32.2	–12.8
45–54	43.7	40.3	+59.5
55–64	48.5	45.5	+18.1
65+	51.5	52.6	+47.4
Total	41.4	30.5	– 4.9

A = Economically active population.
B = Agricultural workers.
Source: Table C.3.

182 Appendix C

Table C.5 Estimates of (net) rural-to-urban migration and migration rates by age groups (males), 1966–76

Age groups in 1966	1976	Urban population (1966-basis) 1966 (A)	1976 (B)	Total population 1966 (C)	1976 (D)	Estimated net rural–urban migration 1966–76* (E)	Survivors of 1966 rural population 1976 (F) = (D − B + E)	Net migration rates† (%) (G) = (E/F)
0–4	10–14	792,947	1,038,346	2,379,598	2,258,635	+285,707	1,505,996	19.0
5–9	15–19	766,450	982,657	2,192,294	1,818,539	+346,876	1,182,758	29.3
10–14	20–24	665,407	759,547	1,637,888	1,340,858	+214,811	796,122	27.0
15–19	25–29	490,523	542,314	1,087,051	1,010,195	+86,472	554,353	15.6
20–24	30–34	404,810	433,230	811,310	842,453	+12,881	422,104	3.0
25–34	35–44	672,179	792,557	1,712,089	1,720,541	+117,060	1,045,044	11.2
35–44	45–54	572,218	628,218	1,545,812	1,482,699	+79,362	933,843	8.5
45–54	55–64	338,407	301,558	874,132	698,107	+31,296	427,845	7.3
55+	65+	393,713	250,927	1,115,627	624,387	+30,576	404,036	7.6
Total (10 years and over)		5,096,654	5,729,353	13,355,801	11,796,414	+1,205,041	7,272,102	16.6

*Net migration or net apparent rural-to-urban transfer refers to the difference between the hypothetical survivors of 1966 urban population and 1976 urban population actually enumerated. This has been calculated by applying total country survival ratios to the 1966 urban population, and, therefore, excludes those who migrated between 1966 and 1976 but who died before 1976: (E) = [A × (D/C)] − B].

†These rates give the probability of migration for survivors of the 1966 rural population at each age group, i.e. chances of residence in urban areas in 1976 among those 1966 rural inhabitants who were still alive by 1976. Alternatively: (F) = [E/((C-A)) × (D/C) + E].

Sources: Based on Census (1966, 1976). For methodology of estimation, UN (1970: 27–35, 40–2).

Table C.6 Estimates of (net) rural-to-urban migration and migration rates by age groups (females), 1966–76

Age groups in 1966	Age groups in 1976	Urban population (1966-basis) 1966 (A)	Urban population (1966-basis) 1976 (B)	Total population 1966 (C)	Total population 1976 (D)	Estimated net rural–urban migration 1966–76* (E)	Survivors of 1966 rural population 1976 (F) = (D − B + E)	Net migration rates† (%) (G) = (E/F)
0–4	10–14	758,025	921,828	2,191,397	2,044,483	+214,622	1,337,277	16.0
5–9	15–19	730,385	846,899	2,035,069	1,781,726	+207,439	1,142,266	18.2
10–14	20–24	603,912	702,572	1,460,589	1,451,357	+102,477	851,262	12.0
15–19	25–29	457,845	522,617	1,096,730	1,101,390	+62,827	641,600	9.8
20–24	30–34	368,083	398,612	912,906	864,544	+50,028	515,960	9.7
25–34	35–44	627,184	690,147	1,699,258	1,574,763	+108,913	993,529	11.0
35–44	45–54	478,545	537,190	1,272,012	1,235,815	+72,263	770,888	9.4
45–54	55–64	301,235	265,646	754,240	589,924	+30,037	354,315	8.5
55+	65+	372,378	252,520	1,010,718	562,083	+45,432	354,995	12.8
Total (10 years and over)		4,697,593	5,138,031	12,432,921	11,206,085	+894,038	6,962,092	12.8

Notes and sources as in Table C.5.

Table C.7 Age and sex specific labour force participation rates* in rural areas, 1966† and 1976

Age group	Males 1966 (%)	Males 1976 (%)	Females 1966 (%)	Females 1976 (%)	Both sexes 1966 (%)	Both sexes 1976 (%)
10–14	49.2	28.1	18.1	16.7	34.6	22.6
15–19	84.7	72.5	19.8	23.4	51.1	46.6
20–24	96.0	94.9	15.6	19.5	49.9	52.2
25–34	98.2	98.5	13.8	16.1	55.3	53.7
35–44	98.2	98.5	13.5	15.1	60.1	57.8
45–54	95.3	96.6	11.7	13.2	57.0	59.9
55–64	81.7	88.8	7.5	9.1	46.4	53.0
65+	47.5	64.8	3.9	5.2	27.3	37.8
All ages	82.6	77.4	14.2	16.3	49.2	46.9

*Refers to population 10 years of age and over.
†Refers to the settled population only for 1966.
Sources: Computed from Census (1966:table 12; 1976:table 16).

Statistical data 185

Table C.8 Gross and total gross years of working life by sex in rural areas, 1966 and 1976

Age group	Age group interval	Age specific activity rates (%) Males 1966	Males 1976	Females 1966	Females 1976	Gross years of working life within each age group Males 1966	Males 1976	Females 1966	Females 1976	Total gross years of working life Males 1966	Males 1976	Females 1966	Females 1976
10–14	5	49.2	28.1	18.1	16.7	2.46	1.4	0.90	0.83	53.6	54.5	7.71	8.85
15–19	5	84.7	72.5	19.8	23.4	4.23	3.62	0.99	1.17	51.12	53.1	6.81	8.0
20–24	5	96.0	94.9	15.6	19.5	4.8	4.74	0.78	0.97	46.89	49.46	5.82	6.85
25–34	10	98.2	98.5	13.8	16.1	9.82	9.85	1.38	1.61	42.09	44.72	5.04	5.87
35–44	10	98.2	98.5	13.5	15.1	9.82	9.85	1.35	1.51	32.27	34.87	3.66	4.26
45–54	10	95.3	96.6	11.7	13.2	9.53	9.66	1.17	1.32	22.45	25.02	2.31	2.75
55–64	10	81.7	88.8	7.5	9.1	8.17	8.88	0.75	0.91	12.92	15.36	1.14	1.43
65–74	10	47.5	64.8	3.9	5.2	4.75	6.48	0.39	0.52	4.75	6.48	0.39	0.52

Notes and sources as for Table B.6.

Table C.9 Women as a percentage of total employment in broad economic sectors, 1956–76

	1956	1966	1976
Agriculture	4.3	6.2	7.6
Manufacturing/mining	33.1	40.5	36.5
Construction	0.4	0.4	0.7
Public utilities	2.6	1.3	3.1
Transport and communication	0.6	1.1	2.0
Commerce*	1.0	1.6	2.8
Services	21.4	12.1	18.9
Total	9.7	13.3	13.8

*Includes insurance, real estate, etc.
Sources: Census (1956:table 26; 1966:table 24;1976:table 26).

Table C.10 Urban women by employment status, 1966–76

	Nov. 1966 ('000)	Nov. 1976 ('000)	Change 1966–76 ('000)	Change 1966–76 (%)
Total employment	307	460	+153	+49.8
Wage and salary earners	237	361	+124	+52.3
(Public sector)	(54)	(224)	(+170)	(+315)
(Private sector)	(183)	(137)	(–46)	(–25.1)
Non-wage employed	70	99	+29	+41.4
(Unpaid family workers)	(17)	(51)	+34	(+200)

Sources: Computed from Census (1966:table 19; 1976:table 26).

Bibliography

Abdullaev, Z. Z. (1963) *Promyshlennost i zarozhdenie rabochego klassa Irana v kontse XIX- nachale XX vv*. Baku.

Abercrombie, K. C. (1972) 'Agricultural mechanisation and employment in Latin America', *International Labour Review*, vol. 106, no. 1.

Abrahamian, E. (1980) 'Structural causes of the Iranian Revolution', *Merip Reports*, no. 87, May.

Abrahamian, E. (1982), *Iran Between Two Revolutions*. Princeton, NJ: Princeton University Press.

Adamiyat, F. (1984) *Fekr-e Democracy Ijtima'iy dar Nahzat-e Mashruteh-e Iran* (The idea of democracy in Iran's constitutional movement). Tehran: Payam.

Adamiyat, F. and H. Nateq (1977) *Afkar-e Ijtima'iy va Siyasi va Iqtisadi dar Asar-e Muntasher-nashudeh-e Duran-e Qajar* (The social, political and economic thought in unpublished works of the Qajar period). Tehran: Agah.

Adelman, I. and E. Thorbecke (eds) (1966) *The Theory and Design of Economic Development*. Baltimore: Johns Hopkins University Press.

Afkhami, M. (1985) 'Iran: a future in the past – the "prerevolutionary" women's movement', in Morgan (1985).

Afshar, H. (1981) 'An assessment of agricultural development policies in Iran', *World Development*, vol. 9, nos 11/12.

Afshar, H. (ed.) (1985) *Iran: A Revolution in Turmoil*. London: Macmillan.

Agarwal, B. (1981) 'Agricultural mechanisation and labour use: a disaggregated approach', *International Labour Review*, vol. 120, no. 1.

Agarwala, A. N. and S. P. Singh (eds) (1958) *The Economics of Underdevelopment*. Bombay: Oxford University Press.

Agarwala, A. N. and S. P. Singh (eds) (1969) *Accelerating Investment in Developing Economies*. Bombay: Oxford University Press.

Agricultural Census (1960) Ministry of Interior, Department of Public Statistics, Office of Agricultural Statistics, vol. 15, National summary, Mehr 1339. Tehran.

Agricultural Census (1974), *Natayej-e Amargiri-e Keshavarzi, Marhaleh-e Dovum-e Sarshomari-e Keshavarzi* (Second stage results). Tehran: Plan and Budget Organisation, The Statistical Centre of Iran, Esfand 1355.

Bibliography

Ajami, I. (1973) 'Land reform and modernisation of the farming structure in Iran', *Oxford Agrarian Studies*, vol. 2, no. 2.
Ajami, I. (1977), *Sheshdangi*. Tehran: Toos, 1356.
Amin, S. (ed.) (1974) *Modern Migrations in Western Africa*. London: Oxford University Press.
Amuzegar, J. (1977) *Iran: An Economic Profile*. Washington DC: Middle East Institute.
Antoun, R. T. and I. F. Harik (eds) (1972) *Rural Politics and Social Change in the Middle East*. Indiana University, International Development Research Centre, Studies in Development, no. 5. Bloomington: Indiana University Press.
Aresvik, O. (1976) *The Agricultural Development of Iran*. New York: Praeger.
Arfa, General H. (1964) *Under Five Shahs*. London: John Murray.
Arrighi, G. (1970) 'Labour supplies in historical perspective: a study of the proletarianisation of the African peasantry in Rhodesia', *The Journal of Development Studies*, vol. 6, no. 3.
Ashraf, A. and A. Banuazizi (1980) 'Policies and strategies of land reform in Iran', in Inayatullah (1980).
Ashraf, A. and M. Safaei (1977) *The Role of Rural Organisations in Rural Development: The Case of Iran*. Tehran: Plan and Budget Organisation of Iran.
Ashton, T. S. (1961) *An Economic History of England: The 18th Century*. London: Methuen.
Azimi, H. (1982) 'Towzi-e Zamin va Dar-Amad dar Astaneh-e Eslahat-e Arzi' (The distribution of land and income on the eve of the land reform), in *Masa'el-e Arzi va Dehghani* (Land and peasant issues). Tehran: Agah, 1361.
Bakhash, S. (1978) *Iran: Monarchy, Bureaucracy and Reform under the Qajars, 1858–1896*. London: Ithaca.
Balfour, J. M. (1922) *Recent Happenings in Persia*. London: Blackwood.
Banaji, J. (1980) 'Summary of selected parts of Kautsky's "The Agrarian Question" ', in Wolpe (1980).
Bank Markazi Iran (The Central Bank of Iran) *Annual Report and Balance Sheet*. Tehran, various issues.
Barbier, P. (1984) 'Inverse relationship between farm size and land productivity: a product of science or imagination?' *Economic and Political Weekly*, vol. 19, nos 52/53.
Barnum, H. N. and R. H. Sabot (1976) *Migration, Education and Urban Surplus Labour – The Case of Tanzania*, Development Centre Studies, Employment Series no. 13. Paris: OECD.
Barnum, H. N. (1977) 'Education, employment probabilities and rural–urban migration in Tanzania', *Oxford Bulletin of Economics and Statistics*, vol. 39, no. 2.
Barton, E. (ed.) (1977) *Arid Land and Irrigation in Developing Countries*. Oxford: Pergamon.
Bartsch, W. H. (1970a) *The Problems of Employment Creation in Iran*. Employment Research Papers. Geneva: ILO.
Bartsch, W. H. (1970b) 'Labour supply and employment creation in Iran, 1956–1966', PhD thesis, University of London.
Bartsch, W. H. (1971) 'Unemployment in less developed countries: a case study of a poor district of Tehran', *International Development Review*, no. 1.
Bayan-e Amari-e Tahavvolat-e Eqtesadi va Ejtemai-e Iran dar Dowran-e por-Eftekhtar-e Dudman-e Pahlavi (1355) (Social and economic statistics of Iran

during fifty proud years of Pahlavi dynasty). Tehran: Plan and Budget Organisation of Iran, The Statistical Centre of Iran, serial no. 627.
Belova, N. K. (1956) 'Ob otkhodnichestve iz severozapadnogo Irana, v Kontse XIX- nachale XX veka', *Voprosy istorii*, vol. 10.
Berry, A. and R. H. Sabot (1978) 'Labour market performance in developing countries: a survey', *World Development*, vol. 6, nos 11/12.
Berry, R. A. and W. R. Cline (1979) *Agrarian Structure and Productivity in Developing Countries*. Baltimore: Johns Hopkins University Press.
Bhalla, S. S. (1979) 'Farm size, productivity, and technical change in Indian agriculture', appendix A in Berry and Cline (1979).
Bharier, J. (1971) *Economic Development in Iran*. London: Oxford University Press.
Bienefeld, M. (1975) 'Measuring unemployment and the informal sector', *IDS Bulletin*, vol. 7, no. 3.
Bienefeld, M. and M. Godfrey (1978) 'Surplus labour and underdevelopment', Institute of Development Studies, Discussion Paper, no. 138, Brighton, England.
Bilsborrow, R. E., A. S. Oberai and G. Standing (1984), *Migration Surveys in Low Income Countries: Guidelines for Survey and Questionnaire Design*. London: Croom Helm.
Bouvat, L. (1913) 'Le commerce et l'agriculture dans la Perse du Nord, d'après, MM. H.-L. Rabino et F. Lafont', *Revue du Monde Musulman*, vol. 23, June.
Bowen-Jones, H. (1968) 'Agriculture', ch. 18 in Fisher (1968).
Breman, J. (1978) 'Seasonal migration and cooperative capitalism: the crushing of cane and of labour by the sugar factories of Bardoli, South Gujarat', *Journal of Peasant Studies*, vol. 6, nos 1/2.
Brenner, R. (1976) 'Agrarian class structure and economic development in pre-industrial Europe', *Past and Present*, no. 70, February.
Brenner, R. (1977) 'The origins of capitalist development: a critique of neo-Smithian Marxism', *New Left Review*, no. 104, July/August.
Brigg, P. (1973) 'Some economic interpretations of case studies of urban migration in developing countries', IBRD Staff Working Paper, no. 151, March.
Bruton, H. J. (1973) 'Economic development and labour use: a review', *World Development*, vol. 1, no. 12.
Byres, T. J. (1981) 'The new technology, class formation and class action in the Indian countryside', *Journal of Peasant Studies*, vol. 8, no. 4.
Cairncross, A. and M. Puri (eds) (1975) *The Strategy of International Development*. London: Macmillan.
Census (1956) *National and Provincial Statistics of the First Census of Iran, November 1956*, Tehran: Ministry of Interior, Public Statistics Department, 1961.
Census (1966) *The National Census of Population and Housing, November 1966*, vol. 168 (1968). Tehran: Plan and Budget Organisation, The Statistical Centre of Iran.
Census (1976) *The National Census of Population and Housing, November 1976*, vol. 186 (1981). Tehran: Plan and Budget Organisation, The Statistical Centre of Iran.
Chambers, C. (1953) 'Enclosure and the labour supply in the industrial revolution', *Economic History Review*, vol. 5, no. 3.
Chaqueri, C. (1979) *La social-démocratie en Iran: articles et documents* (Social

democracy in Iran). Vol. 1, *Histoire du mouvement ouvrier en Iran*. Florence: Mazdak.

Chaqueri, (ed.) *Historical Documents: The Workers', Social-Democratic, and Communist Movement in Iran*, 7 vols (Persian text). Florence: Mazdak.

Chaudhuri, P. (1979) *The Indian Economy*. London: Crosby Lockwood Staples.

Cliffe, L. (1977) 'Rural class formation in East Africa', *Journal of Peasant Studies*, vol. 4, no. 2.

Cliffe, L. (1978) 'Labour migration and peasant differentiation: Zambian experiences', *Journal of Peasant Studies*, vol. 5, no. 3.

Cole, W. E. and R. D. Sanders (1985) 'Internal migration and urban employment in the Third World', *American Economic Review*, vol. 75, no. 3.

Collier, P. and D. Lall (1986) *Labour and Poverty in Kenya, 1900–1980*. Oxford: Clarendon Press.

Connell, J. (1974) 'Economic change in an Iranian village', *The Middle East Journal*, vol. 28, no.3.

Connell, J., B. Dasgupta, R. Laishley and M. Lipton (1976) *Migration from Rural Areas: The Evidence from Village Studies*. New Delhi: Oxford University Press.

Cook, M. A. (ed.) (1970) *Studies in the Economic History of the Middle East*. London: Oxford University Press.

Craig, D. (1978) 'The impact of land reform on an Iranian village', *The Middle East Journal*, vol. 32, no. 2.

Curzon, G. N. (1892) *Persia and the Persian Question*, 2 vols, 2nd impression 1966. London: Frank Cass.

Dana, F. R. (1979) *Amperialism va Forou-pashi-e Keshavarzi* (Imperialism and the disintegration of agriculture). Tehran.

Danesh, Mirza Reza Khan (Arfa'ad-Dawlah) (1966) *Iran-e Diruz* (Yesterday's Iran). Tehran: Ministry of Culture and Arts.

Dehbod, A. (1960) 'Landownership and use in Iran', *Cento Symposium on Rural Development, Tehran*.

Dehqani-Tafti, H. B. (1981) *The Hard Awakening*. London: Triangle Books.

Delaney, F. (1964) 'Labour law and practice in Iran', US Department of Labor, Bureau of Labor Statistics, report no. 276, May 1964.

Delphy, C. (1984) *Close to Home*. London: Hutchinson.

Denman, D. R. (1973) *The King's Vista*. Berkhamsted, England: Geographical Publishers.

Dhamija, J. (1976) '*Non-farm Activities in Rural Areas and Towns: The Lessons and Experiences of Iran*', Studies in Employment and Rural Development, no. 31. Washington: IBRD. July.

Dixit, A. (1973) 'Models of dual economies', in Mirrlees and Stern (1973).

Dobb, M. (1946) *Studies in the Development of Capitalism*. London: Routledge.

Dobb, M. (1973) *Theories of Value and Distribution Since Adam Smith*. Cambridge: Cambridge University Press.

Durand, J. D. (1975) *The Labour Force in Economic Development. A Comparison of International Census Data, 1946–66*. Princeton, NJ: Princeton University Press.

Edmund, C. J. (1924) 'An autumn tour in Daylam', *Journal of Central and Asian Society*, vol. 11, part 4.

Ehlers, E. (1977) 'Social and economic consequences of large-scale irrigation development – the Dez irrigation project, Iran', in Barton (1977).

Eicher, C. K. and L. W. Witt (eds) (1964) *Agriculture in Economic Development*.

New York: McGraw-Hill.
Elkan, W. (1959) 'Migrant labour in Africa: an economist's approach', *American Economic Review*, vol. 49, no. 2.
Ellis, F. (1988) *Peasant Economics: Farm Households and Agrarian Development*. Cambridge: Cambridge University Press.
Ellis, H. S. (ed.) (1951) *Economic Development for Latin America*, London: Macmillan.
Entner, M. L. (1965) *Russo-Persian Commercial Relations, 1828-1914*, Social Sciences Monograph, no. 28. Gainsville: University of Florida.
Ettela'at (Tehran), (Persian newspaper), various issues.
Falkus, M. E. (1972) *The Industrialisation of Russia, 1700-1914*. London: Macmillan.
FAO, *Trade Year Book*. Rome: Food and Agricultural Organisation, various issues.
Fei, John C. H. and G. Ranis (1964) *Development of the Labour Surplus Economy*. Homewood, Ill: Irwin.
Financial Times (London), various issues.
Findlay, R. (1982) 'On W. Arthur Lewis's contributions to economics', ch. 1 in Gersovitz, Diaz-Alejandro, Ranis and Rosenzweig (1982).
Fisher, W. B. (ed.) (1968) *The Cambridge Economic History of Iran*. vol. 1, *The Land of Iran*. Cambridge: Cambridge University Press.
Floor, W. M. (1980a), 'The revolutionary character of the Iranian Ulama: wishful thinking or reality?' *International Journal of Middle East Studies*, vol. 12.
Floor, W. M. (1980b) 'Traditional handicrafts and modern industry in Iran, 1800-1914', paper presented to International Conference on the Economic History of the Middle East, 1800-1914, Haifa, 14-18 December.
Frank C.R., Jr (1968) 'Urban unemployment and economic growth in Africa'. Yale Economic Growth Centre, paper no. 120, New Haven. Also in abridged form in Jolly, de Kadt, Singer and Wilson (1973).
Galjart, B. (1974) 'Class and "following" in rural Brazil', *America Latina*, vol. 7.
George, S. (1977) *How the Other Half Dies*, Harmondsworth: Penguin.
Gersovitz, M. (ed.) (1983) *Selected Economic Writings of W. Arthur Lewis*. New York: New York University Press.
Gersovitz, M., C. F. Diaz-Alejandro, G. Ranis and M. R. Rosenzweig (eds) (1982) *The Theory and Experience of Economic Development: Essays in Honor of Sir W. Arthur Lewis*. London: George Allen & Unwin.
Ghatak, S. and K. Ingersent (1984) *Agriculture and Economic Development*. Hemel Hempstead: Harvester Wheatsheaf.
Gilbar, G. (1976) 'Demographic developments in late Qajar Persia, 1870-1906', *Asian and African Studies* (Jerusalem), vol. 11, no. 2.
Godfrey, E. M. (1967) 'Measuring the removable surplus of agricultural labour in low-income economies', *The Journal of Economic Studies*, vol. 2, no. 1.
Godfrey, E. M. (1973), 'Economic variables and rural-urban migration: some thoughts on the Todaro hypothesis', *Journal of Development Studies*, vol. 10, no. 1.
Godfrey, E. M. (1979) 'Rural-urban migration in a "Lewis-model" context', *Manchester School*, vol. 47, no. 3.
Godfrey, E. M. (1986) *Global Unemployment: The New Challenge to Economic Theory*. Hemel Hempstead: Harvester Wheatsheaf.
Goldscheider, C. (1983) *Urban Migrants in Developing Nations*. Boulder, Colorado: Westview.

192 Bibliography

Goodell, G. E. (1986) *The Elementary Structures of Political Life: Rural Development in Pahlavi Iran.* Oxford: Oxford University Press.

Gordon, E. (1981) 'An analysis of the impact of labour migration on the lives of women in Lesotho', *Journal of Development Studies*, vol. 17, no. 3.

Gordon, Sir Thomas Edward (1896) Persia Revisited. London: Edward Arnold.

Graham, R. (1978) *Iran, The Illusion of Power* (rev. edn). London: Croom Helm.

Greenwood, M. J. (1969) 'The determinants of labour migration in Egypt', *Journal of Regional Science*, vol. 9, no. 2.

Greenwood, M. J. (1971) 'An analysis of the determinants of internal labour mobility in India', *Annals of Regional Science*, vol. 5.

Griffin, K. (1974) *The Political Economy of Agrarian Change.* London: Macmillan.

Hakimi, A. H., H. Nehrir and K. Eghbal (1969), 'Farm mechanisation in Iran', University of Reading, Department of Agriculture, Study no. 8.

Hakimian, H. (1980) 'Iran: dependency and industrialisation', *IDS Bulletin*, vol. 12, no. 1.

Hakimian, H. (1981) 'The evolution of employment and the formation of the working class in Iran', paper presented to the IDS Workshop on Iran, May 1981.

Hakimian, H. (1985) 'Wage labour and migration: Persian workers in southern Russia: 1880–1914', *International Journal of Middle East Studies*, vol. 17, no. 4.

Hakimian, H. (1987) 'Structural change and labour transfer in Iran's economic development, 1900–79', PhD thesis. Institute of Development Studies, University of Sussex.

Hakimian, H. (1988) 'Industrialisation and the standard of living of the working class in Iran: 1960–79', *Development and Change*, vol. 19, no. 1.

Halliday, F. (1979) *Iran: Dictatorship and Development.* Harmondsworth: Penguin.

Hansen, B. (1973) 'An economic model of Ottoman Egypt or the economics of collective tax responsibility', Berkeley: University of California.

Harris, J. R. and M. P. Todaro (1970) 'Migration, unemployment, and development: a two sector analysis', *American Economic Review*, vol. 60, no. 1.

Hart, K. (1973) 'Informal income opportunities and urban employment in Ghana', *Journal of Modern African Studies*, vol. 11, no. 1.

Hartman, H. (1979) 'The unhappy marriage of Marxism and feminism: towards a more progressive union', *Capital and Class*, no. 8, summer. Reprinted in Sargent (1981).

Heydari, A. and P. K. Das (1977) 'Rural industries and rural non-farm activities development in Iran', UNIDO, Expert Group Meeting on Industrialisation in Relation to Integrated Rural Development, ID/WG.257/19, Vienna.

Hilton, R. (ed.) (1976) *The Transition from Feudalism to Capitalism.* London: New Left Books.

Hirschman, A. O. (1958) *The Strategy of Economic Development.* New Haven: Yale University Press. An abridged version in Agarwala and Singh (1969).

Hobsbawm, E. J. (1977) *The Age of Revolution.* London: Abacus Books.

Hollander, S. (1973) *The Economics of Adam Smith.* London: Heinemann.

Hooglund, E. J. (1973) 'The *khowshneshin* population of Iran', *Iranian Studies*, vol. 6, no. 4.

Hooglund, E. J. (1975) 'The effects of the land reform programme on rural Iran, 1962–72', PhD thesis, Johns Hopkins University.

Hooglund, E. J. (1982) *Land and Revolution in Iran*. Austin: University of Texas Press.
ILO (1969) '*Rural Employment Problems in the United Arab Republic*', Employment Research Papers. Geneva: ILO.
ILO (1970) *Towards Full Employment. A Programme for Colombia*. Geneva: ILO. Also in abridged form in Jolly, de Kadt, Singer and Wilson (1973).
ILO (1972) *Employment, Incomes and Equality: a Strategy for Increasing Productive Employment in Kenya*. Geneva: ILO.
ILO (1973) *Employment and Incomes Policy for Iran*. Geneva: ILO.
Inayatullah (ed.) (1980) *Land Reform: Some Asian Experiences*, Policies and Implementation of Land Reform Series, vol. 4. Kuala Lumpur: Asia and Pacific Administration Centre.
Industrial Statistics, Iran – Ministry of Industry and Mines. General Department of Statistics and Research, Tehran, various years.
Issawi, C. (1970) 'The Tabriz–Trabzon trade, 1830–1900: rise and decline of a trade route', *International Journal of Middle East Studies*, vol. 1.
Issawi, C. (ed.) (1971) *The Economic History of Iran: 1800–1914*, Chicago: Chicago University Press.
Ivanov, M. S. (1978) *Enqelab-e Mashrutiyat-e Iran* (The constitutional revolution of Iran). Tehran: Ketab-Haye Jibi.
Jacqz, J. W. (1976) *Iran: Past, Present, and Future*. New York: Aspen Institute for Humanistic Studies.
de Janvry, A. (1981) *The Agrarian Question and Reformism in Latin America*. Baltimore: Johns Hopkins University Press.
Jolly, R. (1973) 'Economic development and labour use: a comment', *World development*, vol. 1, no. 12.
Jolly, R., E. de Kadt, H. Singer and F. Wilson (eds) (1973) *Third World Employment, Problems and Strategy*. Harmondsworth: Penguin.
Jorgenson Dale W. (1966) 'Testing alternative theories of the development of a dual economy', in Adelman and Thorbecke (1966).
Kaldor, N. (1956) 'Alternative theories of distribution', *Review of Economic Studies*, vols 23/4, no. 2.
Kando Kav (London) (Persian periodical): no. 6, Autumn 1977; no. 8, Autumn 1978.
Kaneda, H. (1973) *Agriculture*, Employment and Incomes Policies for Iran, Mission Working Paper no. 3. Geneva: ILO.
Kao, C. H. C., K. R. Anschel and C. K. Eicher (1964) 'Disguised unemployment in agriculture: a survey', in Eicher and Witt (1964).
Kasravi, A. (1967) *Tarikh-e Mashruteh-e Iran*. Tehran: Amir Kabir.
Katouzian, H. (1978) 'Oil versus agriculture, a case of dual resource depletion in Iran', *Journal of Peasant Studies*, vol. 5, no. 3.
Katouzian, H. (1981a) *The Political Economy of Modern Iran, 1926–79*. London: Macmillan.
Katouzian, H. (1981b) *The Agrarian Question in Iran*, World Employment Programme, Rural Employment Policy Research Programme, Working Paper no. 47. Geneva: ILO.
Kazemi, F. (1980a) *Poverty and Revolution in Iran*. New York: New York University Press.
Kazemi, F. (1980b) 'Urban migrants and the revolution', *Iranian Studies*, vol. 13 nos 1–4.
Kazemi, F. and E. Abrahamian (1978) 'The nonrevolutionary peasantry of

Bibliography

modern Iran', *Iranian Studies*, vol. 11.
Keddie, R. N. (1960) 'Historical obstacles to agrarian change in Iran', *Claremont Asian Studies*, vol. 8, September.
Keddie, R. N. (1972) 'Stratification, social control, and capitalism in Iranian villages: before and after land reform', in Antoun and Harik (1972).
Keyhan (Tehran) (Persian newspaper), various issues.
Khosravi, Kh. (1969) 'Abyari va Jameh-ye Rustaei dar Iran' (Irrigation and village society in Iran), *Ulum-e Ijtemaie*, Tehran: Bahman, 1348.
Khosravi, Kh. (1979) *Jameh-e Dehghani dar Iran* (Village society in Iran). Tehran: Payam.
Kitching, G. (1982) *Development and Underdevelopment in Historical Perspective*. London: Methuen.
Kohli, K. L. (1977) *Current Trends and Patterns of Urbanisation in Iran, 1956–76*. Analytical and Technical Population Studies Series, Report no. 1, November. Tehran: Plan and Budget Organisation of Iran, The Statistical Centre of Iran.
Kristjanson, B. H. (1960) 'The agrarian-based development of Iran', *Land Economics*, vol. 36, no. 1.
Kuznets, S. (1966) *Modern Economic Growth*, New Haven: Yale University Press.
Kuznets, S. (1971) *Economic Growth of Nations*. Cambridge, Mass: Harvard University Press.
Kuznets, S. (1974) *Population, Capital and Growth*. London: Heinemann.
Lambton, A. K. S. (1953) *Landlord and Peasant in Persia*. London: Oxford University Press.
Lambton, A. K. S. (1969) *The Persian Land Reform: 1961–1966*. London: Oxford University Press.
Landes, D. S. (1969) *The Unbound Prometheus*. Cambridge: Cambridge University Press.
Lane, D. (1975) *The Roots of Russian Communism*. London: Martin Robertson.
Lazonick, W. (1974) 'Karl Marx and enclosures in England', *Review of Radical and Political Economics*, vol. 6, no. 2.
Lee, E. S. (1966) 'A theory of migration', *Demography* (Chicago), vol. 3, no. 1.
Leeson, P. (1979) 'The Lewis model and development theory', *Manchester School*, vol. 47, no. 3.
Legassick, M. and H. Wolpe (1976) 'The Bantustans and capital accumulation in South Africa', *Review of African Political Economy*, no. 7, Sept./Dec.
Leibenstein, H. (1957a) *Economic Backwardness and Economic Growth*. New York: John Wiley. (Science edition, 1963.)
Leibenstein, H. (1957b) 'Disguised unemployment and underemployment in agriculture', *Monthly Bulletin of Agricultural Economics and Statistics* (FAO), July/Aug.
Levy, M. and W. Wadycki (1972) 'Lifetime versus one-year migration in Venezuela', *Journal of Regional Science*, vol. 12, no. 3.
Lewis, W. A. (1954) 'Economic development with unlimited supplies of labour', *Manchester School*, vol. 22, May. Reprinted in Agarwala and Singh (1958) and Gersovitz (1983).
Lewis, W. A. (1958) 'Unlimited labour: further notes', *Manchester School*, vol. 26, no. 1. Also in Gersovitz (1983).
Lewis, W. A. (1972) 'Reflections on unlimited labour', in di Marco (1972); also in Gersovitz (1983).

Lewis, W. A. (1984) 'Development economics in the 1950s', in Meier and Seers (1984).
Leys, C. (1973) 'Interpreting African underdevelopment: reflections on the ILO report on employment, incomes, and equality in Kenya', *African Affairs*, vol. 72, no. 289.
Lowe, A (1954) 'The classical theory of economic growth', *Social Research*, vol. 21, no. 2.
Lipton, M. (1977) *Why Poor People Stay Poor: A Study of Urban Bias in World Development*. London: Temple Smith.
Lucas, R. E. (1985) 'Migration amongst the Batswana', *The Economic Journal*, vol. 95, no. 378.
Maclachlan, K. S. (1968) 'The land reform in Iran', ch. 2 in Fisher (1968).
Madjd, M. G. (1983) 'Land reform and agricultural policy in Iran, 1962–78', *Cornell/International Agricultural Economic Study*, Department of Agricultural Economics, no. 16, April.
Madjd, M. G. (1987) 'Land reform policies in Iran', *American Journal of Agricultural Economics*, vol. 69, no. 4.
Mahdavy, H. (1965) 'The coming crisis in Iran', *Foreign Affairs*, vol. 44, no. 1.
Mahdavy, H. (1970) 'The patterns and problems of economic development in Rentier states: the case of Iran', in Cook (1970).
Mahdavy, H. (1982) 'Tahavollat-e Si Saleh-e Yek Deh dar Dasht-e Ghazvin' (The thirty year developments of a village in Ghazvin Plain), in *Masa'el-e Arzi va Dehghani* (Land and peasant issues). Tehran: Agah, 1361.
Malthus, T. R. (1798) *An Essay on the Principle of Population as it Affects the Future Improvement of Society* (1966 edition). New York: Macmillan.
Maraghe-i, Haj Zain al-'Abedin (1974), *Siyahatnameh-e Ibrahim Baig* (The travel memoirs of Ibrahim Baig). Tehran.
di Marco, L. E. (ed.) (1972) *International Economics and Development*. New York: Academic Press.
Marx, K. (1867) *Capital*, vol. 1 (1954 edition). London: Lawrence & Wishart.
Marx, K. (1959), *Capital*, vol. 3. London: Lawrence & Wishart.
Marx, K. (1969) *Theories of Surplus Value*, part 2. London: Lawrence & Wishart.
Marx, K. (1972) *Theories of Surplus Value*, part 3. London: Lawrence & Wishart.
Marx, K. (1973) *Grundrisse*. Harmondsworth: Penguin.
Marx, K. and F. Engels (1969) *Selected Works*, vol. 2. London: Lawrence & Wishart.
Marx, K. and F. Engels (1971) *Ireland and The Irish Question*. Moscow: Progress Publishers.
Marzi, M. (n.d.), 'Barrasy-e Moghadamaty-e Sherkathay-e Kesht-o-San'at-e Mojud dar Howzeh-e Abkhour-e Sad-e Dez' (A preliminary investigation into the existing agribusiness companies downstream of the Dez dam), Ministry of Finance and Economic Affairs, Tehran, Mimeo.
Meek, R. L. (ed.) (1971) *Marx and Engels on the Population Bomb*. Berkeley, Calif.: Rampart Press.
Meier, G. M. (1976) *Leading Issues in Economic Development* (3rd edn). Oxford: Oxford University Press.
Meier, G. M. and D. Seers (1984) (eds) *Pioneers in Development*. Oxford: Oxford University Press.
Meillassoux, C. (1981) *Maidens, Meals and Money*. Cambridge: Cambridge

University Press.
Mennoune, M. (1981) 'Origins of the Algerian proletariat', *Merip Reports*, no. 94 February.
Mingay, G. (1963) *English Landed Societies in the Eighteenth Century*. London: Routledge & Kegan Paul.
Ministry of Labour and Social Affairs (1968) *A Study on Manpower of Iran* (2nd edn). Tehran: General Department of Statistics.
Ministry of Labour and Social Affairs (1970a) *Natayej-e Amargiri-e Niruy-e Ensani* (Results of the manpower survey). Tehran, 1975.
Ministry of Labour and Social Affairs (1970b) *Gozaresh-e Bazar-e Kar dar Sal-e 1348* (A report on the labour market in 1348 (1969)). Tehran, 1970.
Ministry of Labour and Social Affairs (1972) *Natayej-e Amargiri-e Niruy-e Ensani* (Results of the manpower survey). Tehran, 1974.
Minorsky, V. (1905) 'Dvizhenie persidskikh rabochikh na promysly v Zakavkaze', *Sbornik konsulskikh doneseniy* (Consular reports of the Ministry of Foreign Affairs), 3, St Petersburg.
Mir-Hosseini, Z. (1987) 'Some aspects of changing economy in rural Iran: the case of Kalardasht, a district in the Caspian provinces', *International Journal of Middle East Studies*, vol. 19, no. 4.
Mirrlees, J. A. and N. H. Stern (eds) (1973) *Models of Economic Growth*. London: Macmillan.
Misawa, T. (1971) 'Agrarian reform, employment and rural incomes in Japan', in Sternberg (1971).
Moghadam, F. E. (1985) 'An evaluation of the productive performance of agribusinesses: an Iranian case study', *Economic Development and Cultural Change*, vol. 33, no. 4.
Molho, I. (1986) 'Theories of migration: a review', *Scottish Journal of Political Economy*, vol. 33, no. 4.
Momeni, B. (1980) *Mas'aleh-e Arzi va Jang-e Tabaghati dar Iran* (The agrarian question and class struggle in Iran). Tehran: Payvand.
Morgan, R. (ed.) (1985) *Sisterhood is Global: The International Women's Movement Anthology*. Harmondsworth: Penguin.
Moridi, S. (1979) 'Land reform and the development of capitalism in rural Iran', PhD thesis, University of Keele.
Myint, H. (1980) *The Economics of Developing Countries* (5th edn). London: Hutchinson.
Napoleoni, C. (1975) *Smith Ricardo Marx*. Oxford: Basil Blackwell.
Nashat, G. (ed.) (1983) *Women and Revolution in Iran*. Boulder, Colorado: Westview.
Nazem al-Islam Kermani (1953) 'Telegram from Baku', in his *Tarikh-e Bidari*, 3 vols in one edition. Tehran.
Nazem al-Islam Kermani (1960) *Tarikh-e Bidari-ye Iranian* (The history of the awakening of the Iranians) 3 vols. Tehran.
Nowshirvani, F. (1976) *Agricultural Mechanisation in Iran*, World Employment Programme, Research Technology and Employment Programme, Working Paper, WEP 2-22/WP28. Geneva: ILO.
Nowshirvani, F. (1980) 'The beginnings of commercial agriculture in Iran', in Udovitch (1980).
Nurkse, R. (1953) *Problems of Capital Formation in Underdeveloped Countries*. Oxford: Basil Blackwell.
Oberai, A. S. (1981) 'State policies and internal migration in Asia', *International*

Labour Review, vol. 120, no. 2.
OIPFG (The Organisation of Iranian People's Fedaii Guerrillas) Iranian Rural Research Series:
  (No. 1) *Land Reform and its Direct Effects in Iran*, English text translated and published by the Iran Committee, London, January 1976.
  (No. 2) 'A study of farm corporations' (Persian text). Iran, 1973.
  (No. 3) *Barrasy-e Sakht-e eqtesady-e Rustahay-e Fars* (A study of the economic formation of the rural areas in Fars province). Iran, 1974.
  (No. 4) *Barrasy-e Sakht-e eqtesady-e Rustahay-e Kirman* (A study of the economic formation of the rural areas in Kirman province). Iran, 1974.
Okazaki, S. (1968) 'The development of large-scale farming in Iran, The case of the province of Gorgan', The Institute of Economic and Asian Affairs, Occasional Papers, no. 3, Tokyo.
Orsolle, E. (1885) *La Caucase et la Perse*. Paris.
PAP (United Kingdom Parliamentary Accounts and Papers):
  (1878) H. L. Churchill, Consular Report, 'Gilan', vol. 74.
  (1892) Consul-General J. Maclean, *Report on the Trade of Khurasan and Seistan for the Year 1890-91*, vol. 83.
  (1895) vol. 99, (1897), vol. 92; (1906), vol. 127 [all on Tabriz and Azerbaijan].
  (1903) Consular Report, *Caucasus Tea Industry*, vol. 76.
  (1906) vol. 128 [Consular Report, 'Baku'].
Pavlovitch, M. (1910) 'La situation agraire en Perse à la veille de la révolution', *Revue du Monde Musulman*, vol. 12, December.
Peek, P. (1980) 'Agrarian change and labour migration in the Sierra of Ecuador', *International Labour Review*, vol. 119, no. 5.
Peek, P. and G. Standing (1979) 'Rural-urban migration and government policies in low-income countries', *International Labour Review*, vol. 118, no. 6.
Perry, J. P. (1975) 'Forced migration in Iran during the seventeenth and eighteenth centuries', *Iranian Studies*, vol. 8, autumn.
Pesaran, M. H. (1985) 'Economic development and revolutionary upheavals in Iran', in Afshar (1985).
Platt, K. B. (1970) 'Land reform in Iran', *Spring Review*. Washington DC: US Agency for International Development.
Quijano, A. (1980) 'The marginal pole of the economy and the marginalised labour force', in Wolpe (1980).
Rabbani, M. (1971) 'A cost-benefit analysis of the Dez multi-purpose project', *Tahqiqat-e Eqtesadi*, vol. 8, nos 23/4.
Rachidzadeh, E. (1978) 'Le secteur rural et le développement économique: le cas de l'Iran', thesis, University of Geneva, Institut Universitaire des Hautes Etudes Internationales, no. 309.
Ray Brown, M. (1983) 'The adjustment of migrants to Tehran, Iran', in Goldscheider (1983).
Razavi, H. and F. Vakil (1984) *The Political Environment of Economic Planning in Iran, 1971-83: From Monarchy to Islamic Republic*, Boulder, Colorado: Westview.
Research Group in Agricultural Economics (1970) 'The age of rural labour force and land reform', *Tahqiqat-e Eqtesadi*, vol. 7, no. 18.
Reynolds, Lloyd G. (1969) 'Economic development with surplus labour – some complications', *Oxford Economic Papers*, vol. 21, no. 1.
Reza-Zadeh Malek, R. (1973) *Haidar Khan-e 'Amu Oghli*. Tehran: Donya.

Rhoda, R. (1983) 'Rural development and urban migration: can we keep them down on the farm?' *International Migration Review*, vol. 17, no. 1.

Ricardo, D. (1821) *The Principles of Political Economy and Taxation*, (1973 edn). London: Dent, Everyman's Library.

Richards, H. (1975) 'Land reform and agribusiness in Iran', *Merip Reports*, no. 43, December.

Roberts, B. (1978) 'Agrarian organisation and urban development', in Wirth and Jones (1978).

Robinson, W. C. (1969) 'Types of disguised rural unemployment and some policy implications', *Oxford Economic Papers*, vol. 21, no. 3.

Rosenstein-Rodan, R. N. (1951) 'Notes on the theory of the "Big Push" ', in Ellis (1951).

Rubin, I. I. (1979) *A History of Economic Thought*, edited by D. Filtzer. London: Ink Links.

Sahota, G. S. (1968) 'An economic analysis of internal migration in Brazil', *Journal of Political Economy*, vol. 76, no. 2.

Salmanzadeh, C. (1980) *Agricultural Change and Rural Society in Southern Iran*. Wisbech, England: Middle East and North African Studies Press.

Salnameh-e Amari-e Keshvar (The statistical yearbook of Iran). Tehran: Plan and Budget Organisation, The Statistical Centre of Iran, various issues.

Sanasarian, E. (1982) *The Women's Rights Movement in Iran*. New York: Praeger.

Sargent, L. (ed.) (1981) *The Unhappy Marriage of Marxism and Feminism*. London: Pluto.

Saville, J. (1969) 'Primitive accumulation and early industrialisation in Britain', in *The Socialist Register*. London: Merlin.

Schultz, T. (1964) *Transforming Traditional Agriculture*. New Haven: Yale University Press.

Schultz, T. (1967) 'Significance of India's 1918-19 losses of agricultural labour: a reply', *Economic Journal*, vol. 77, no. 305.

Schultz, T. P. (1971) 'Rural-urban migration in Columbia', *Review of Economics and Statistics*, vol. 53, no. 2.

SCI (1978) *Population Growth Survey of Iran, Final Report: 1973-76*, serial no. 777. Tehran: Plan Budget Organisation of Iran, Statistical Centre of Iran, June.

Seccombe, W. (1983) 'Marxism and Demography', *New Left Review*, no. 137, Jan./Feb.

Sedghi, M. and A. Ashraf (1976) 'Dynamics of women's condition in Iran', in Jacqz (1976).

Sen, A. K. (1960) *Choice of Techniques*. Oxford: Basil Blackwell.

Sen, A. K. (1967) 'Surplus labour in India: a critique of Schultz's statistical test', *Economic Journal*, vol. 77, no. 305. Also 'A rejoinder', *ibid*.

Sen, A. K. (1975) *Employment, Technology, and Development*. Oxford: Clarendon Press.

Seyf, A. (1982) 'Some aspects of economic development in Iran, 1800-1906', PhD thesis, University of Reading.

Shafaeddin Banadaki, S. M. (1980) 'A critique of development policies based on oil revenues in recent years in Iran', PhD thesis, Department of Economics, Oxford University.

Shrestha, N. R. (1987) 'Institutional policies and migration behavior: a selective review', *World Development*, vol. 15, no. 3.

Singer, H. W. (1975) 'Recent trends in economic thought on underdeveloped countries', in Cairncross and Puri (1975).

Sinha, J. N. (1973) 'Agrarian reforms and employment in densely populated agrarian economies: a dissenting view', *International Labour Review*, vol. 108, no. 5.

Smith, A. (1776) *The Wealth of Nations* (1974 edition), edited by A. Skinner. Harmondsworth: Penguin.

Sodagar, M. (n.d.) *Roshd-e Ravabet-e Sarmay-e Dari dar Iran* (The development of capitalist relations in Iran). Tehran.

Soltanie, G. R. (1974) 'The effects of farm mechanisation on labour utilisation and its social impact', *Indian Journal of Agricultural Economics*, vol. 29, no. 1.

Speare A. Jr (1976) 'A cost benefit model of rural to urban migration in Taiwan', *Population Studies*, vol. 25, no. 1.

Spengler, J. J. (1959) 'Adam Smith's theory of economic growth', *The Southern Economic Journal*, part I in vol. 25, no. 4: part II in vol. 26, no. 1.

Standing, G. (1981a) *Labour Force Participation and Development* (2nd edn). Geneva: ILO.

Standing, G. (1981b) 'Migration and modes of exploitation: social origins of immobility and mobility', *Journal of Peasant Studies*, vol. 8, no. 2.

Standing, G. (1982) *Circulation and proletarianisation*, World Employment Programme Research, Population and Labour Policies Programme, Working Paper no. 119. Geneva: ILO.

Standing, G. (1985) *Labour Circulation and the Labour Process*. London: Croom Helm.

Sternberg, J. (ed.) (1971) 'Agrarian reform and employment', Geneva: ILO.

Stewart, F. (1973) 'Economic development and labour use: a comment', *World development*, vol. 1, no. 12.

Sunkel, O. (1977) 'The development of development thinking', *IDS Bulletin*, vol. 8, no. 3.

Sutcliffe, R. B. (1971) *Industry and Underdevelopment*. London: Addison-Wesley.

Sykes, P. (1930) *A History of Persia*, 2 vols (vol. 2, 3rd edn, 1963). London: Macmillan.

Tahqiqat-e Eqtesadi (Quarterly journal of economic research), Institute for Economic Research, Faculty of Economics, University of Tehran, various issues.

Todaro, M. P. (1969) 'A model of labour migration and urban unemployment in less developed countries', *American Economic Review*, vol. 59, no. 1.

Todaro, M. P. (1976) 'Migration and economic development: a review of theory, evidence, methodology and research priorities', IDS Occasional Paper, no. 18, Nairobi.

Todaro, M. P. (1985) *Economic Development in the Third World*. London: Longman.

Tria, T. (1911) 'La Caucase et la révolution persane', *Revue du Monde Musulman*, vol. 13, February.

Turnham, D. (1970) *The Employment Problem in Less Developed Countries*, Paris: OECD. Also in abridged form in Jolly, de Kadt, Singer and Wilson (1973).

Udovitch, A. L. (ed.) (1980) *The Islamic Middle East, Studies in Economic and Social History, 700-1900*, Princeton, NJ: Darwin Press.

Bibliography

UN (1951) '*Measures for the economic development of under-developed countries*', Department of Economic Affairs, E/1986. New York: UN, May.
UN (1967) *Principles and Recommendations for the 1970 Population Censuses* (ST/STAT/SER.M/44). New York: UN.
UN (1968) *Methods of Analysing Census Data on Economic Activities of the Population*, Department of Economic and Social Affairs, Population Studies, no. 43 (ST/SOA/SER.A/43). New York: UN.
UN (1970) *Methods of Measuring Internal Migration*, Manuals on Methods of Estimating Population, VI, Department of Economic and Social Affairs, Population Studies, no. 47, (ST./SOA/SER.A/47). New York: UN.
UN (1971) *Methods of Projecting the Economically Active Population*, Manuals on Methods of Estimating Population, V, Department of Economic and Social Affairs, Population Studies, no. 46 (ST/SOA/SER.A/46). New York: UN.
US Agricultural Attaché, 'Iran: grain and feed report', Foreign Agricultural Service, American Embassy, Tehran, various reports: IR6004, 17 February 1976; IR6031, 20 December 1976; IR8002, 26 January 1978; IR8011, 15 May 1978.
Vahidi, M. (1968) *Water and Irrigation in Iran*. Tehran: Plan and Budget Organisation of Iran, Bureau of Information and Reports.
Viner, J. (1976) 'The concept of "disguised unemployment" ', in Meier (1976).
Warriner, D. (1948) *Land and Poverty in the Middle East*. London: Royal Institute of International Affairs.
Warriner, D. (1970) 'Employment and income aspects of recent agrarian reforms in the Middle East', *International Labour Review*, vol. 101, no. 6.
Webster Johnson, V. (1960) 'Agriculture in the economic development of Iran', *Land Economics*, vol. 36, no. 4.
Weeks, J. (1971) 'The political economy of labour transfer', *Science and Society*, vol. 35, no. 4.
Whigham, H. J. (1903) *The Persian Problem*, London.
Wilson, A. T. (1925) 'The opium trade through Persian spectacles', *The Asiatic Review*, vol. 21, April.
Wirth, J. D. and R. L. Jones (eds) (1978) *Manchester and São Paulo, Problems of Rapid Urban Growth*. Stanford: Stanford University Press.
Wolpe, H. (ed.) (1980) *The Articulation of Modes of Production*. London: Routledge & Kegan Paul.
World Bank (1975) *Land Reform*, Sector Policy Papers. Washington DC, May.
World Development Report (1980) *The World Bank*. New York: Oxford University Press.
Worrell, K. (1980) 'The dual economy since Lewis: a survey', *Social and Economic Studies*, vol. 29, no. 4.
Yap, L. Y. L. (1977) 'The attraction of cities, a review of the migration literature', *Journal of Development Economics*, vol, 4, no. 3.

Index

Abbott, K. E., 45
Abdullaev, Z. Z., 51, 54, 61, 63, 65-6
Abercrombie, K. C., 94
Abrahamian, E., 66, 75, 82
Adamiyat, F., 57, 65
Afkhami, M., 160
Africa, 3, 27, 37-8, 120
Afshar, H., 125-6, 147
Agarwal, B., 94
agrarian change, 3, 169
  reform, 38, 40, 80, 101, 168
agribusiness companies, 37, 74, 96-8, 109, 120
agricultural census, 69, 130
  output, 121-3, 140-2
  prices, 112-15, 126
  wages, 4, 17, 25-6, 115-16, 119-23, 126-7
  workers, 71, 84-6, 87, 91, 163
Agricultural Development Bank of Iran, 97
agriculture, commercialisation of, 38, 56, 99
  diminishing returns in, 14
  large-scale farming, 38, 56, 69, 74-5, 77, 92-9, 140
  and oil boom, 108-10, 112-16, 119-23
  relative decline, 1, 3-5, 16, 18, 109-11, 129, 140-1, 157
Ajami, I., 72-3, 75, 91, 127
Alexandropol, 54
Amin, S., 35, 38
Amu Oghli, 63
Amuzegar, J., 74
Anschel, K. R., 25
Ardebil, 54, 62
Aresvik, O., 78, 113

Arfa, General H., 47-8
Arfa'd-Dawlah, 49, 66
Argentina, 38
Armenia, 63
Arrighi, G., 37, 125
Arsanjani, H., 106
Ashkabad, 47, 55
Ashraf, A., 68, 73-5, 82, 99, 160
Ashton, T. S., 32
Asia, 3
Astarabad, 49-50, 58
Azerbaijan, 45, 50, 54, 57, 61-2, 95, 98
Azimi, H., 82, 122-3

Bakhash, S., 56, 58, 66
Baku, 47-8, 51, 54, 59, 60, 63-4
  the committee, 63
  labour unrest, 63
  oil industry, 54, 60, 64
Balfour, J. M., 46
Banaji, J., 90
Bank Markazi, 111-13, 124, 129, 147
Bantustans, 40
Banuazizi, A., 68, 73-5, 82, 99
Barbier, P., 105
Barnum, H. N., 35
Barton, E., 193
Bartsch, W. H., 92, 155, 168
Belgium, 47
Belova, N. K., 48-9, 51, 54-5, 60-1, 63-6
Bengal, 8
Berry, A., 35, 105
Bhalla, S. S., 105
Bharier, J., 101, 106
Bienefeld, M., 22, 43
Bolsheviks, 64

201

Index

Botswana, 35
Bouvat, L., 46
Bowen-Jones, H., 105
Brazil, 35, 38-9
Brenner, R., 44
Brigg, P., 35
Britain, 3, 5, 165
Bruton, H. J., 29, 30
Byres, T. J., 37

cash crops, 37, 56, 115, 120-1, 127
Chambers, C., 32
Chaqueri, C., 55-6, 63-5
Caucasus, 48, 59, 60-4
  the economic boom in, 60
Cereals Organisation, 112, 126
Chaudhuri, P., 104
cholera, 54
Cliffe, L., 37-8
Cline, W. R., 105
Cole, W. E., 35
Collier, P., 34
Colombia, 35, 38-9
Communist Party of Iran, the, 64
Connell, J., 137
Constantinople, 65
Constitutional Revolution, the, 45, 60, 63-4, 164
construction sector, the, 111-12, 157-9, 163
Cook, M. A., 198
Craig, D., 86, 87
Curzon, D. N., 60-1

Dana, F. R., 100, 125
Danesh, Mizra Reza Khan, 47, 49, 54, 66
Das, P. K., 119
Dehbod, A., 68
Dehqani-Tafti, H. B., 124
Delphy, C., 32
Denman, D. R., 82, 106
Dez Irrigation Project, 69, 96, 121
Dhamija, J., 134
Dixit, A., 27
Dobb, M., 43, 104, 106
Dominican Republic, 38
Durand, J. D., 170

Ecuador, 40
Edmund, C. J., 46
'effort-intensity' of income, 110-16, 125, 135
Eghbal K., 192
Egypt, 35, 38, 42, 104
Ehlers, E., 97
Elizavetpol, 48-9, 51, 54
Elkan, W., 38

Ellis, F., 105
enclosures, 9, 17, 19, 32, 37-8
Engels, 15, 17-18, 42
England, 1-2, 11, 14-15, 17, 32, 37, 56
Entner, M. L., 48-9, 59, 61
Enzeli, 64
Erivan, 45, 48, 60
Ettela'at, 124, 127
expropriation, 17, 67, 86, 162
Europe, 5, 9-10, 20, 41, 56, 61

Falkus, M. E., 60
Family Protection Acts, 160
famine, 15, 24, 58, 65
FAO, 108
farm corporations, 74, 98-9, 106, 109, 121-3
Fars, 58, 91, 95, 98, 106
Fei, John C. H., 22-3, 25-8, 32, 35, 43
Fei-Ranis model, 22-3, 25, 27-8, 35
female work, 40, 132
feudal reaction, 56
Financial Times, 96, 147
Findlay R., 2
Finland, 147
First World War, the, 49, 61, 64
Floor, W. M., 57
food
  imports, 125, 141
  per capita consumption, 125, 141
  prices, 26, 39, 112-15
  subsidies, 113
  surplus, 10-12, 31, 33
  trade policy, 39, 112-13
Fourth Development Plan, the, 101, 111, 113
France, 3, 5, 56, 147
Frank, C. R., Jr., 28

Galjart, B., 38
gender relations, 33, 36
George, S., 37
Ghana, 35
Ghatak, S., 43
Ghazvin, 105
Gilan, 46, 61, 69, 99
Gilbar, G., 59, 65-6
Giroft, 96, 99
Godfrey, E. M., 22, 25, 29, 35
Goldscheider, C., 160
Gorgan, 69, 94
Goodell, G. E., 105
Gordon, E., 40
Gordon, Sir Thomas Edward, 51, 59, 66
Graham, R., 124
Green Revolution, the, 37
Greenwood, M. J., 35

Griffin, K., 37
gross years of working life, 143, 147, 155, 173, 185
Grundrisse, the, 15, 42

Hakimi, A. H., 95
Hakimian, H., 106, 112, 125, 158, 160
Halliday, F., 82
Hamadan, 54, 58
Hansen, B., 38
Harris, J. R., 30
Harrod–Domar model, 20
Hart, K., 43
Hartman, H., 32
Hemmat, 63
Heydari, A., 119
Hilton, R., 44
Hirschman, A. O., 42
Hobsbawm, E. J., 38
Hollander, S., 9–11
Hooglund, E. J., 73, 75, 84, 85, 88, 95, 99, 104–5, 123
Hoveida, A. A., 124

IBRD, 96
Idalat, 64
Ijtima'yun 'Amiyun, 63
ILO, 28, 43, 92, 104
imperialism, 100–1
import substitution, 43
India, 40, 43, 55, 104–5
Industrial Revolution, the, 165
inflation, 101, 111–12
informal sector, 29, 35, 43, 158
Ingersent, K., 43
Ireland, 15
Isfahan, 58, 87, 89, 105, 126, 159
Issawi, C., 51, 54, 56–7, 61–3, 65–6
Italy, 147
Ivanov, M. S., 58, 63, 65

de Janvry, A., 39
Japan, 27, 71
Jolly, R., 30
Jorgenson Dale W., 25

Kaldor, N., 42
Kando Kav, 82, 95, 126–7
Kaneda, H., 126, 140
Kao, C. H. C., 25
Kars, 54
Kasravi, A., 50, 57
Katouzian, H., 116, 125–6, 140, 147
Kautski, K., 90
Kazemi, F., 66, 116, 125, 147
Keddie, R. N., 56–7, 85
Kennedy, J. F., 79

Kermani, Mirza Agha Khan, 55
Kermanshahan, 98
Keyhan, 124, 127
Keynes, J. M., 11
Khalkhal, 54
Khosravi, Kh., 105, 115, 120, 126
Khowshneshins, 85–6, 104
Khurasan, 51, 55, 57, 61–2
Khuzistan, 83, 96–7, 120, 159
Kirman, 68, 87–8, 96, 105–6
Kitching, G., 44
Kohli, K. L., 147, 159
Kristjanson, B. H., 106
Kurdistan, 62, 69, 96
Kuznets, S., 5, 166
labour
 absorption, 96, 156–9
 average product of, 21–2
 domestic, 32
 extrusion, 3, 32, 37–8, 41, 162
 family, 38, 89–90, 92, 110, 115, 129, 132, 135, 160
 marginal product of, 20–1, 22–3, 43
 mobility, 12, 101, 106, 126
 natural and market price, 13
 productivity, 8, 10, 12, 15, 26, 32
 removable, 2–3, 20, 23, 30–1, 33–4
 reserve army, 7, 18–19, 28–9
 scale of transfer, 138–9
 shortage, 29, 60–1, 80, 101–2, 109, 119–23, 144
 supply, 8, 13, 15, 17, 19, 26–7, 33, 60, 79, 84–9, 100, 111, 119–21, 130, 141, 151–2, 161, 170–6
 unions, 63–4
 unlimited supplies of, 4, 21, 27, 31, 34, 40, 43
 unrest, 63–4
 use, 142–4, 164
Lall, D., 34
Lambton, A. K. S., 56, 66, 68, 72, 82–3, 85, 87–8, 104–6
land concentration, 56, 79
land reform
 causes of, 79–81
 evasion, 72, 86–7
 Law, 71–3, 81, 85–6, 88, 106
Landes, D. S., 32
Lane, D., 60
Latin America, 3
Lazonick, W., 32
Lee, E. S., 138, 168
Leeson, P., 23, 26
Legassick, M., 40
Leibenstein, H., 42
Levy, M., 35
Lewis, W. A., 2, 21–36, 43–4

Lewis model, 21-2, 25, 35
Leys, C., 43
Lipton, M., 39, 43
Lowe, A., 11
Lucas, R. E., 35

Maclachlan, K. S., 56
Madjd, M. G., 74, 116, 117-23, 125, 126, 147
Mahdavy, H., 82, 105-6, 125, 127
Majlis, 65
Malthus, R. M., 1, 7, 11-16, 19, 161, 166
Maraghe-i, Haj Zain al-'Abedin, 49, 55, 62
di Marco, L. E., 198
market surplus, 78, 140
Marx, K., 2-3, 5, 7, 11, 15-20, 24, 28-9, 32-3, 37, 41-3, 123, 161-2, 166
Marzi, M., 97
Mashad, 49, 50, 58, 63
Mazandaran, 61-2, 69
mechanisation, 11, 24, 38, 92-5, 97-9, 105, 115, 120, 123, 135
Meek, R. L., 12-13, 42
Meillassoux, C., 39
Mennoune, M., 37
Mexico, 38
Mgeladze, V. D., 64
Middle East, the, 39, 41
migrants' labour force participation rates, 168-70
migration, causes of, 34-5, 55-62, 162-3
 circular, 39-40, 135
 features of, 50, 137-8, 150
 forced, 46
 illegal immigration, 48
 rates, 137-8
 remittance, 59
 rural-to-urban, 22, 29-31, 89, 100, 108, 110, 125, 135-8, 149
 the scale of, 46, 135-8, 161, 163
 the social and political significance, 62-4
 and structural change, 36-7, 162-3
 temporary, 4, 39-40, 45-6, 49, 51, 59, 62, 135, 163, 165
Mingay, H., 32
Ministry of Labour and Social Affairs, 102, 146, 168
Minorsky, V., 50, 59
Mir-Hosseini, Z., 115, 117, 125
Misawa, T., 71
Mitchell Cotts, 120
Moghadam, F. E., 105
Momeni, B., 68, 73, 8, 100, 106
Moridi, S., 85, 96-7, 106
Mughan, 57
Myint, H., 24, 42

Muzzafar ad-Din Shah, 57

Nazem al-Islam Kermani, 47, 65
Nateq, H., 57, 65
Nigeria, 39
Nobel Prize, 2
non-farm sector, 89, 116-19, 163
Nowshirvani, F., 66, 93-4, 97, 106
Nurske, R., 20, 24, 27, 42

Oberai, A. S., 31
October Revolution, the, 63-4
OIPFG, 82, 87, 95, 100-1, 105-6, 160
Okazaki, S., 69, 94
Orsolle, E., 47, 51, 59
Ottoman Empire, the, 55
owner-cultivators, 69, 77, 124, 164

Pavlovitch, M., 56, 66
peasants
 common rights, 56, 71
 family holdings, 77-9, 89-92
 nasaq-rights, 68, 91, 103, 138
 standard of living, 27, 55-7, 64
Peek, P., 38, 41
Perry, J. P., 65
Peru, 38
Pesaran, M. H., 106
Platt, K. B., 82
poll tax, 38
Poor Laws, 11-13
population
 forms of surplus population, 15
 growth, 149, 166
 'iron law' of, 12-13
 theory of, 12, 15, 33-4, 43
poverty, 13, 40, 46, 57-8, 88, 107-8, 110, 123, 125, 164
primitive accumulation, 16, 18, 28, 37
proletarianisation, 3, 17, 32, 89
Punjab, 94
push factors, 46, 55, 107, 125

Qanat, 68, 88-9
Qarache-dagh, 62
Qaran, the, 59
Qom, 105, 126
Quijano, A., 43

Rabbani, M., 97
Rachidzadeh, E., 97-8
Ranis, G., 22-3, 25-8, 32, 35, 43
Rasht, 49, 50, 63
rate of profit, 11, 14
Razavi, H., 124
rent, 14, 73
Reynolds, Lloyd G., 23, 27, 35, 28

Index 205

Reza-Zadeh Malek, R., 55, 57, 58
Rhoda, R., 31
Ricardo, D., 1, 7, 11, 13–15, 16, 161
Richards, H., 96–7, 106, 120
Roberts, B., 139
Robinson, W. C., 24–5
Rosenstein-Rodan, R. N., 42
Rubin, I. I., 10
rural
  consumption expenditure, 116–19
  co-operatives, 74
  crafts, 17, 109, 116–19, 132–4
  diversification, 132–4
  savings, 21, 31
Russia, 3–5, 47–57, 161–3
  first national census, 47
  industrialisation, 59–61, 164

Sabot, R. H., 35
Safaei, M., 74
Sahota, G. S., 35
Salmanzadeh, C., 69, 83, 96, 98, 104, 126
Salmas, 45
Salnameh-e Amari-e Keshvar, 98, 127, 153
Sanasarian, E., 160
Sanders, R. D., 35
Sao Paulo, 39
Sattar Khan, 64
Saville, J., 32
Schultz, T., 35, 42
Schumpeter, J., 11
Seccombe, W., 32–3, 44
Sedghi, M., 160
Sen, A. K. S., 23, 43
Seyf, A., 45, 58, 62
Shah, the (Mohamad RezaPahlavi), 4, 57, 109, 124
sharecropping, 68–9, 75, 116, 121
Shiraz, 58, 86, 105
Shrestha, N. R., 31
Singer, H. W., 11, 20
Sinha, J. N., 94
Sistan, 51
small farmers, 25–7, 89–92
Smith, A., 1–2, 7–12, 14–16, 24, 29, 32–3, 37, 43, 161–2, 166
Sobotsinskii, 49
socialism, 63
Sodagar, M., 82, 100
Soltanie, G. R., 95
Soltanzadeh, A., 55, 64
Speare, A. Jr., 35
Speenhamland System, 37
Spengler, J. J., 9
Stabilisation Programme, 101
Standing, G., 38–40
Stewart, F., 30

Suez Canal, 62
Sunkel, O., 20
Sutcliffe, R. B., 6
Sweden, 147
Sykes, P., 51

Tabataba-i, 56–7
Tabriz, 45, 49, 50, 58, 62–3
Tabriz–Trebizond route, 62
Tahqiqat-e Eqtesadi, 105
Taiwan, 35
Tanzania, 35
Tasooj, 105
technical change, 9, 11, 57, 165
Tehran, 59, 62–3, 120, 125, 159
Thailand, 40
Tiflis, 45, 47–9, 51, 54
Todaro, M. P., 29–31, 35–7
trade deficit, 101
Transcaspian, railway, 54, 62
  labour markets, 61
Transcaucasia, 45, 51–5, 60
Tria, T., 64
Turkestan, 55
Turkey, 62
Turnham, D., 28
'turning point', 21–3, 28

Udovitch, A. L., 200
underemployment, 2, 31–3, 42, 142
unemployment, 2–3, 11, 20, 23, 28–31, 97–9, 101–2, 135, 165
  disguised, 20–5, 43
  seasonal, 24
United Kingdom, 147
urban bias, 29, 43, 165
urban concentration, 159
urbanisation, 148–50
Urumiah, 50, 62
USA, 5, 60
US Agricultural Attache, 113, 120, 125–6
USSR, 6

Vahidi, M., 105
Vakil, F., 124
Venezuela, 35
Viner, J., 25

Wadycki, W., 35
wage labour, 4, 16, 27, 32, 38, 54, 72, 89, 90–2, 100, 129, 157, 161
wages, 8, 18–19, 21–3, 25–7, 34, 54, 59–60, 100, 102, 109, 111–12, 115, 162
Wakefield, G., 43
Warriner, D., 42, 71, 82, 88, 104–5
water rights, 88–9
Webster Johnson, V., 106

206 Index

Weeks, J., 27–8
Whigham, H. J., 59
'White Revolution', the, 82
Wilson, A. T., 46
Witte, S., 59
Wolpe, H., 40
women, 25, 36, 40, 48, 62, 81, 101, 127, 138, 142–4, 147, 161, 164
  and the urban labour force, 151–6, 160, 165, 168–70, 170–6

workers' conditions, 54–5
  movement, 55, 63–4
World Bank, 74, 147
Worrell, K., 23, 43

Yap, L. Y. L., 35
Yazd, 126, 159

Zambia, 37